COMMON LISP

An Interactive Approach

PRINCIPLES OF COMPUTER SCIENCE SERIES

Series Editors

Alfred V. Aho, Bellcore, Morristown, New Jersey
Jeffrey D. Ullman, Stanford University, Stanford, California

COMMON LISP

An Interactive Approach

STUART C. SHAPIRO
State University of New York at Buffalo

COMPUTER SCIENCE PRESS

An Imprint of W. H. Freeman and Company • New York
The Book Publishing Arm of Scientific American

Library of Congress Cataloging-in-Publication Data

Shapiro, Stuart Charles
    Common LISP: an interactive approach / by Stuart C. Shapiro.
        p. cm.
    Includes index.
    ISBN 0-7167-8218-9
    1. LISP (Computer program) I. Title. II. Title: LISP.
QA76.73.L23S53 1991
005. 13'3—dc20   91-12377
                                                                      CIP

Printed in the United States of America

Computer Science Press

An imprint of W. H. Freeman and Company
The book publishing arm of Scientific American
41 Madison Avenue, New York, NY 10010
20 Beaumont Street, Oxford OX1 2NQ, England

    2 3 4 5 6 7 8 9 0 RRD 9 9 8 7 6 5 4 3 2

To Caren

CONTENTS

PREFACE

The purpose of this book is to teach the COMMON LISP programming language. The book is intended to be a self-paced study guide, requiring additional information from an instructor, manual, consultant, or friend only to fill in the details of the local operating system and a few implementation-dependent features. This book is a COMMON LISP version of *LISP: An Interactive Approach*, published by Computer Science Press in 1986. The major motivation for creating the new version was the widespread adoption of COMMON LISP as the standard LISP dialect. In the earlier edition, I presented LISP in a dialect-independent way and discussed the different approaches of the major dialects. In this edition, however, I am strictly following the COMMON LISP standard set out in Guy L. Steele, Jr.'s *COMMON LISP: The Language*, Second Edition (Bedford, MA: Digital Press, 1990). (Steele's book is often referred to as CLtL-2, and I will do so hereafter.) The LISP version of this book has been used as the text of the LISP portion of data structures, programming languages, and artificial intelligence courses and as a self-study guide for students, faculty members, and others learning LISP independently. Draft versions of this book have also been used in COMMON LISP courses, artificial intelligence courses, and for self-study.

Teaching LISP

LISP is the language of choice for work in artificial intelligence and in symbolic algebra. It is also important in the study of programming languages, because, since its inception over thirty years ago, it has had full recursion, the conditional expression, the equivalence of program and data structure, its own evaluator available to the programmer, and extensibility—the syntactic indistinguishability of programmer-defined functions and "built-in" operators. It is also the paradigm of "functional," or "applicative," programming. Because of the varied interests in LISP, I have tried to present it in a general and neutral setting, rather than specifically in the context of any of the special fields in which it is used.

Above all, LISP is an *interactive* language. A LISP program is not built up from imperative statements, but from *forms*, each of which has a *value*. The LISP programmer sits in front of a terminal, interacting with the LISP listener. During such a session, a program gets written, read, tested, modified, and saved for future use. Most LISP implementations provide more than just a programming language, they provide an entire environment including tracing, inspectors, debuggers, and other programmer aids, almost all written in LISP itself.

I learned LISP by experimenting with it, typing S-expressions and seeing what happened. That is the learning style I encourage in this book. Teaching LISP by having the student sit down at a terminal and experiment right from the start influences the order of topics. For peace of mind, the first thing a novice needs to know about being in a new environment is how to get out. Therefore, Chapter 1 is concerned solely with getting into LISP and getting back out. LISP input is not tied to line boundaries, and extra spaces are ignored. Students need to experience this flexibility early so they do not feel they are under more constraints than they really are. A novice makes mistakes (and so do we all). Therefore, it is important to show the debugger and error messages early. Since typing errors will occur, backspace and delete keys are important, and the student should experience the entire character set. The general approach is to prepare the student for the unexpected. Since new concepts must be built on existing conceptual structures, numeric examples are used before symbolic examples.

Since the best language for defining LISP is LISP itself, many LISP functions are introduced by having the student define them first. This means that some functions I have been tempted to discuss early have been put off until the student has enough background to define them.

I have written the exercises so that it is reasonable to expect the student to do all of them. Therefore the only long projects are those that are distributed throughout the text as exercises that have the student modify and extend functions that are saved on files.

Because I suspect that many students will have had experience with some imperative programming language, I teach pure LISP before the imperative constructs. This forces the student away from the "Pascal with parentheses" style that I saw so much in the past. By the time I introduce imperative LISP in Part III, the student should be used to the functional style of pure LISP and should be able to develop a good, balanced programming style.

A COMMON LISP Approach

Rather than just translating the earlier version of this book into COMMON LISP, I have incorporated a thorough COMMON LISP approach. Although COMMON LISP is still obviously a dialect of LISP, the quantitative additions of functions and features have made a qualitative difference. Besides the obvious, well-known, and pervasive change from dynamic scoping to lexical scoping, I think that the most important developments have been: the introduction of packages, the change in focus from S-expressions to forms, and the development of a mature typing system. These are all given prominent attention in this book.

The existence of packages (multiple name spaces for symbols) in COMMON LISP is very important for allowing several people to cooperate in producing a large system. Most COMMON LISP texts, however, seem to be direct translations of their LISP predecessors and relegate the discussion of packages to a section of advanced topics at the end of the book, if they discuss packages at all. Those authors seem to feel that the novice LISPer will be programming alone, not as a member of a team, and therefore doesn't need to worry about packages. This is false because as soon as one sits down to a terminal with a loaded COMMON LISP one is part of a team; the other team members are the people who implemented the COMMON LISP environment being used. Before users even start defining new functions, there are at least four packages in the environment they must use: the **user** package, the **lisp** package, the **keyword** package, and at least one package for implementation-specific functions. The fact that there are so many predefined functions means that unless users are willing to be greatly constrained in their choice of function names, they need to define their functions in their own packages. However, packages can be very confusing for LISPers who have not learned about them in an organized way. I have seen experienced, Ph.D.-level LISPers hack away, adding qualifications to symbol names in their code, with no understanding of the organized structure of the package system. The reasons that packages are even more confusing in LISP than in other, compiler-oriented languages, such as Ada, is that in LISP one may introduce symbols on-line, and one typically stays in one LISP environment for hours, losing track of what symbols have been introduced. A symbol naming conflict may be introduced in the course of debugging that will not occur when the fully developed files are loaded into a fresh environment in the proper order. To teach the student about packages in an organized way, I introduce them early in Chapter 7, which follows the initial discussion of symbols in Chapter 6. I then use packages consistently and frequently throughout the rest of the book and have the students do every set of exercises in a different package. If the students do every exercise they will have created at least seven different files, each in its own package with some files making use of others. I often ask the students to write their own versions of predefined COMMON LISP functions, and I always have them do this in a different package and shadow the predefined function first.

Package Systems, S-expressions, and Forms

The development of the package system is related to the change of focus from S-expressions to forms. The index of CLtL-2 contains no entry for S-expressions or symbolic expressions, but the entry for forms contains 14 subentries and points to a total of 39 different pages. S-expressions are syntactic units, sequences of characters that form the written version of LISP programs and data structures. We used to say that the LISP language consisted of S-expressions, the major action of LISP was the evaluation of S-expressions, and the **read-eval-print** loop consisted of reading an S-expression, evaluating it, and then printing the value as an S-expression. A form, on the other hand, is a COMMON LISP object that can be evaluated, and the major action of COMMON LISP is the evaluation of such forms, or objects. The COMMON LISP `read-eval-print` loop really has five steps: reading an S-expression, creating the object the S-expression denotes, evaluating the object, choosing a printed representation of the value, and printing that representation. One reason this distinction is important is that there are so many different printed representations of the same COMMON LISP object. Consider the symbol `mypackage::frank`, and consider the situation where that symbol has been exported from the `mypackage` package and imported into the `user` package. How many different ways do we have to type that symbol to the COMMON LISP listener if we are in the `user` package? The package qualifier may be typed as `mypackage`, `MYPACKAGE`, or it may be omitted. In fact, each character of `mypackage` may be typed independently in lowercase or uppercase, or in uppercase preceded by an escape character, giving $3^9 = 19,683$ ways to type the package name (ignoring all the ways of using escape brackets), plus one way to omit it. Since the symbol has been exported, if we type the package name, we may type the package name/symbol name connector either as :: or as :, giving $19,683 \times 2 = 39,366$ ways to type the qualifier, plus one way to leave it out. Each character of `frank` may also be typed in uppercase or lowercase or in uppercase preceded by an escape character, giving $3^5 = 243$ ways of typing the symbol name (ignoring the various ways of using escape brackets), for a total of $39,367 \times 243 = 9,566,181$ ways of typing the printed representation of one symbol (ignoring escape brackets). I have heard inadequately taught LISPers claiming that such expressions were different symbols and talking about the "symbol with the pipes" as if the escape brackets were part of the symbol's name. In this book, I distinguish the S-expression from the form—the printed representation from the object—in Chapter 1 and continue making the distinction consistently and explicitly through the entire book.

COMMON LISP Types

The change in focus from S-expressions to forms is bound up with the development of a mature typing system, since COMMON LISP has typed objects rather than typed expressions. Previous LISPs had only two prominent data types: lists and atoms. Numbers and strings existed but weren't considered all that significant for LISP programming. Literal atoms were distinguished in several ways but didn't form their own data type. On the other hand, COMMON LISP has an extensive set of types, each with a predicate to recognize objects of that type and a collection of operations defined for it, all organized into a type hierarchy. This book does not discuss all the COMMON LISP types, but those covered include: numbers (integers, floating-point numbers, and ratios), characters, strings, symbols, packages, lists, conses, functions, hash tables, and single dimensional arrays. COMMON LISP is an object-oriented language similar to the way that CLU is object-oriented, as opposed to the modern meaning of that phrase in object-oriented programming. (CLOS, which is discussed in Part IV of this book, is object-oriented in that way.) COMMON LISP is object-oriented in the sense that: variables have objects as their values, and two variables can be bound to the same object; composite objects have objects as their parts; objects, rather than expressions, have values and types.

To see the significance of COMMON LISP's typing of objects, compare an untyped language such as Fortran with a strongly typed language such as Pascal with COMMON LISP. In Fortran, one may store a value of one type into a variable, and then pass that variable by reference to a procedure that operates on it as if it were another type. In Pascal, the compiler would catch this as an error because the variable would be declared as one type, whereas the formal parameter would be declared as another type. In COMMON LISP, this would be caught as an error during execution because the operator would complain that the object it was given to operate on was of the wrong type.

COMMON LISP has a macro **check-type** that can be used to make sure the objects passed to a function are of the correct type. One may choose never to use **check-type**, but one then runs the risk of a built-in function, called many levels deep in user-defined functions, complaining that some object is of the wrong type. It then can be very hard to find which function actually made the mistake. I introduce **check-type** in Chapter 16 as a special case of **assert**, which is introduced in Chapter 15 as a way of making sure that actual arguments of recursive functions satisfy the criteria that ensure that the recursive function will terminate. Once introduced, **check-type** is used consistently throughout the rest of the book.

New Features in This Book

Other changes made in this version of the book because of the change
to COMMON LISP include:

- The documentation string is a required part of a function definition.

- `first` and `rest` are used instead of `car` and `cdr`.

- `eql` is the standard equality function instead of `eq` because all
  the COMMON LISP functions that take a `:test` keyword use `eql`
  as their default test.

- `setf` is used instead of `setq`.

Besides the change to COMMON LISP, I have made other revisions
in this version of the book:

- Part I is extensively reorganized and includes a clear explanation
  of the differences between symbols, symbol names, and printed
  representations of symbols.

- There is a two-chapter introduction to CLOS, the COMMON LISP
  Object System in Part IV. Although all of the features of CLOS
  are not covered, I have presented enough to get the student
  started in object-oriented COMMON LISP programming. Learning
  the rest of CLOS should not be too difficult.

- Many example interactions illustrate the material in the text, so
  that students will know what to expect when they experiment on
  their own.

- Each exercise is labeled as either review, instruction, drill, utility,
  or part of one of the extended programming projects, so that an
  intelligent choice can be made when only selected exercises are to
  be done.

- Solutions to about one-third of the programming exercises are
  included in Appendix A.

- An instructor's manual that contains solutions to all the programming exercises is available from the publisher.

- Appendix B is a COMMON LISP reference manual. This includes all COMMON LISP functions, macros, and special forms introduced in the text. They are shown at a level understandable to a student who finishes this text. Quite a few of the functions, macros, and special forms listed in Appendix B have additional features and options. For those, the reader is referred to CLtL-2.

Acknowledgments

I appreciate the comments and suggestions made on drafts of this book by Susan Anderson-Freed, Kulbir Arora, James Hightower, Robin Hill, Jack Hodges, Bharat Jayaraman, Gerald Maguire, Will Mathys, Gregory Rawlins, Guy Steele, and Jeffrey Ullman. Any remaining problems are my own fault. I am grateful to: João Martins and Ernesto Morgado for many discussions of abstract data types, which form the basis for the organization of Appendix B; Ruth E. Davis for providing me with her LaTeX style file; the folks at Computer Science Press/ W. H. Freeman and Company, including Bill Gruener, Nola Hague, Tina Hastings, Diana Siemens, and Carol Loomis for their help and encouragement; and, above all, to my wife Caren, for her constant support and understanding.

TO THE READER

The purpose of this book is to help you learn the COMMON LISP dialect of the programming language LISP (LISt Processing language) by experimenting with it via an interactive computer terminal. The recommended method is to read a chapter or two, sit down at a terminal and try the examples and exercises of those chapters, leave the terminal and go on to the next chapters, and so on.

It would be best for you to complete every exercise, but for your guidance, they are coded *(r)*, *(i)*, *(d)*, *(u)*, *(p1)*, or *(p2)*, meaning,

(r) A *review* of the material in the text. The purpose of such an exercise is for you to see for yourself that COMMON LISP behaves as described in the text.

(i) An *instructional* exercise. It provides information not otherwise mentioned in the text. These are the most important exercises to do.

(d) A *drill* exercise. It provides additional practice with COMMON LISP.

(u) A *utility* exercise. It asks you to prepare or to modify programs you will be expected to use in later work. These are also extremely important to do, because later exercises will depend on them.

(p1) A *project 1* exercise. These exercises are distributed throughout
the book, and, by doing all of them, you will write a small rule-
based system, and use that to implement a miniversion of the
program Eliza, that carries on conversations with humans. Unless
you are going to skip this project entirely, do all its exercises.

(p2) A *project 2* exercise. These exercises are distributed throughout
the book, and by doing all of them, you will write an interactive
desk calculator program. Unless you are going to skip this project
entirely, do all its exercises.

Answers to about one-third of the programming exercises appear in
Appendix A. Appendix B contains a COMMON LISP manual. Since
this manual is intended to help you even after you have finished this
book, some of the material in it will not be understandable until you
are well into the book. If you find the manual too advanced for you,
use the index to find where the material was discussed in the text. Appendix B.2 lists implementation-dependent material which you should
fill out during the course of your study for easy reference later on.

Unlike other programming languages, LISP does not operate on a
series of imperative statements—"do this, then do this, and so on,"
but rather on expressions, called symbolic expressions or S-expressions,
which LISP evaluates. More accurately, a session with COMMON LISP
involves an interaction with a LISP *listener,* during which the following
five steps are repeated until you decide to stop.

1. You type an S-expression to the LISP listener.

2. The LISP listener interprets your S-expression as the *printed representation* of a COMMON LISP *object.*

3. That object is *evaluated.* Its value is also a COMMON LISP object.

4. The LISP listener chooses a printed representation for the value
   object.

5. That printed representation is printed for you to read.

COMMON LISP is *object-oriented* in the sense that objects, rather than
expressions, are evaluated, and unlike many other programming languages, objects, rather than expressions, have *types.* COMMON LISP is
not object-oriented in the sense of *object-oriented programming,* but it

does have an object-oriented programming facility, which is the subject of Part IV of this book.

The evaluation of some objects cause new functions to be defined which can be used later in the programming session. This is how complicated programs are written in LISP. Programs, in the form of sequences of S-expressions, can be saved in files for later use. You will learn how to do this in the course of working through this book.

The basic instructional style of this book is for you to learn by experimenting. Don't worry about making mistakes. That's part of learning. If one of your inputs causes an error, try to figure out what it was, do it again correctly, and then continue.

Part I

THE BASICS

CHAPTER 1

GETTING STARTED

Your goal for this chapter is to learn how to access your system's COMMON LISP and how to exit from it. Although this may not seem like much, it is obviously very important. It is also very dependent on the particular system you are using, so you will have to get much of the information from a manual, a teacher, a consultant, or a friend.

The first problem is to *log onto* your computer system. This might involve simply turning on your microcomputer or it might require typing in some accounting information.

If you are using a LISP machine or have "booted" a microcomputer with a COMMON LISP disk, you may already be talking to COMMON LISP. Otherwise, you will have to access it. This might require just typing `lisp`, `cl`, some abbreviation of the implementation of COMMON LISP that you are using, or it might require first retrieving the COMMON LISP system.

Once you have started your COMMON LISP, you are ready to interact with it. We say that you are about to interact with the *top-level* LISP *listener,* or simply the *top level* of LISP.

Most COMMON LISP listeners will tell you they are waiting for input by printing a *prompt.* This can be a greater-than symbol, a question mark, an arrow, a colon, or something else. You are now supposed to type something to LISP called a *symbolic expression*, or *S-expression*.

3

We will get into great detail about what an S-expression is, but for now, let's use small numerals, like 3.

When you type an S-expression to LISP (remember to end each entry by pressing the CARRIAGE RETURN key), LISP will perform the following sequence of actions:

1. It will *read* your S-expression.

2. It will interpret your S-expression as the *printed representation* of a *form*—a LISP *object* intended to be evaluated.

3. It will *evaluate* the form as some other (or perhaps as the same) *value object*.

4. It will choose a printed representation for the value object.

5. It will *print* the printed representation it has chosen.

Because of this sequence, LISP listeners are also called *read-eval-print* loops (combining steps 1 and 2 into the read step, and steps 4 and 5 into the print step).

After printing each value, the LISP listener will again print a prompt (or not, if it's one of those COMMON LISPs that don't use prompts) and will wait for your next S-expression. That's all there is to using LISP: you type the printed representation of a form; LISP evaluates it and types back a printed representation of the value of the form.

For our first example, the S-expression we will enter is the arabic numeral 3. Notice that this is only one of the printed representations we use in our daily lives for the number 3. Another common printed representation we use for 3 is the roman numeral III. I mention this not because COMMON LISP uses roman numerals, but to point out that the distinction between printed representations of objects and the objects themselves is one you are already familiar with. Anyway, LISP interprets the numeral 3 as representing the number 3 and evaluates that form (that is, the numeric object 3). In LISP, numbers evaluate to themselves, so 3 evaluates to 3. LISP then must choose a printed representation for 3 and, in fact, chooses the arabic numeral 3 and prints that.

In this text, I will show a sample LISP interaction as:

```
> 3
3
```

The > is what I will use for the LISP prompt, and it is followed by an S-expression as you would type it to LISP. The line after that shows LISP's response.

In some LISPs, when you make a mistake, or when you make certain mistakes, LISP will enter a *debugger* (sometimes called a *break loop* or *break package*). The debugger is a LISP listener, just like the top level, except that some special commands are available to obtain information relevant to figuring out your error. We will look at this in more detail in later chapters. If you make a mistake while in the debugger, you may (depending on the implementation of COMMON LISP you are using) get into another debugger. The first debugger will remember the information relevant to your first mistake; the second one will have information relevant to your second mistake. This can go on for many levels of nested debuggers.

The debugger is recognizable because it uses a different prompt. For example, Kyoto COMMON LISP's (KCL's) top-level prompt is >, while its debugger prompt is >>. To get out of KCL's debugger, type :q. If you are several levels down in debuggers, you may have to do this repeatedly, or your COMMON LISP might have a single command to jump all the way back to the top level. For example Lucid's COMMON LISP uses :a to return to the top-level listener from any debugger level.

If the LISP you're using has a debugger, you can often force your way into it by typing the appropriate *interrupt key*. This may be the BREAK, RUB, or DEL key, or it may be some control character such as CTRL-C (this means typing the C key while holding down the CTRL key). Sometimes, for the interrupt key to work, it must be struck before any other character is typed on the line, and sometimes it must be typed more than once in succession.

Having returned to the top-level listener, you may want to terminate your LISP session. The way to get out of COMMON LISP varies with different implementations. To leave KCL, type (bye) followed by a carriage return. (It is important to type the parentheses as shown.) Other implementations may use (exit), (system:exit), CTRL-D, or something else.

Finally, you need to know how to *log off* your computing system. As was the case for the other system-dependent information discussed in this chapter, you must find out how to do that from your manual, your teacher, a consultant, or a friend.

Exercises

1.1 *(i)* What is the procedure for getting into your LISP? Find out and write it here:

_____

_____

_____

1.2 *(i)* What is the procedure for getting out of your LISP? Find out and write it here:

_____

_____

_____

1.3 *(i)* Get into LISP. What is the top-level listener's prompt? Write it here: ___.

1.4 *(d)* Get out of LISP and log off.

1.5 *(r)* Get back into LISP. Enter the numeral 3 and a carriage return. Note that LISP types 3 back and issues a prompt. Try 5 this time. Log off.

1.6 *(i)* Get back into LISP. Does it have an interrupt key? If so, write it here: ___ and get into the debugger.

1.7 *(i)* What is your debugger's first-level prompt? Write it here: ___.

1.8 *(i)* How do you get out of the debugger? Write it here:

_____

Do it! Are you back to the top level?

1.9 *(i)* Try going at least three levels deep in the debugger. Does the prompt change again? Write the answer here:

1.10 *(r)* While in the debugger, try typing a small numeral to LISP. LISP should echo it.

1.11 *(i)* How do you go back up a single level in the debugger? Write it here:

Do it.

1.12 *(i)* How do you go all the way to the top-level listener from deep in the debuggers? Write the answer here:

Do it.

1.13 *(d)* Exit LISP and log off your system.

1.14 *(u)* Copy all the answers you wrote here to the appropriate blanks in Appendix B.2.

CHAPTER 2

NUMBERS

In Chapter 1, you learned how to get into and out of your COMMON LISP top-level listener and how to recognize the top-level and debugger-level prompts, and you had your first experience with the LISP read-eval-print loop. You should recall that the read-eval-print loop operates in the following way: you type an S-expression, which is the printed representation of some form (some LISP object we intend to have LISP evaluate); LISP reads your S-expression and creates the form you (presumably) intended; LISP then evaluates the form—its value is some other object; finally, LISP prints the latter object, using some printed representation it chooses. Notice that LISP is an *object-oriented language* in the sense that it evaluates objects, not expressions. LISP is also object-oriented in that, unlike many programming languages, LISP has typed objects rather than typed variables.[1]

In this chapter, you will get more experience interacting with the LISP listener and distinguishing between objects and their printed representations. We will again use numbers, since you are already familiar with them.

Numbers are one type of COMMON LISP object, and there are several subtypes, including *integers* and *floating-point numbers*.

---

[1]It should be noted that these two senses of "object-oriented" are not exactly the sense in the expression "object-oriented programming," which is the subject of Part IV of this book.

Integers are used for whole numbers, such as 5 or 127. COMMON LISP recognizes arabic numerals as printed representations of integers, except that they cannot contain commas or blanks. Thus, we write 54325 rather than 54,325. For a negative integer, just precede the digits by a minus sign; for example, -5 or -4326. A positive integer may be preceded by a plus sign; +24 is recognized as the same object as 24. An integer may end with a decimal point as long as there are no digits after it: 12. is read as an integer; 12.0 is not.

Integers may be as large as you need, even several hundred or thousand digits long. The size is limited only by the size of the computer you are using.

The value of an integer is itself. So if you enter a numeral, such as −123, LISP will type it right back at you:

```
> -123
-123
```

Floating-point numbers are used for numbers with fractional parts such as 3.14156. A floating-point number looks like an integer except that it must include a decimal point with at least one digit after it; 12.0 is read as a floating-point number.

Floating-point numbers may also be written in a computerese form of *scientific notation*. This is done by following the digits of the number with an *exponent marker*, an optional sign, and some more digits. If the exponent marker is present, the decimal point is not necessary.

The exponent marker can be e, s, f, d, or l or any of these letters in uppercase. The exponent marker s or S indicates a short-float number, f or F indicates a single-float number, d or D indicates a double-float number, and l or L indicates a long-float number. These are various subtypes of floating-point numbers. These different types of numbers vary in the minimum number of bits used to represent them. The more bits used, the more digits will be represented. The number of bits used is implementation-dependent, but, in general, short-float numbers will use fewer bits than single-float numbers, single-float will use fewer than double-float, and double-float will use fewer than long-float. (Some implementations of COMMON LISP don't even distinguish these four different types.)

The exponent marker e (or equivalently, E) will be interpreted as the same as s, f, d, or l depending on a certain parameter setting of your COMMON LISP. We will use e as the standard exponent marker. So in COMMON LISP you may write as 0.34e-5 the number you would write in scientific notation as 0.34×10^{-5}.

The value of a floating-point number is itself, but COMMON LISP may choose a different printed representation than you use.

We can summarize the type hierarchy of COMMON LISP numbers that we have discussed so far, using the official names, in the following table. Note that the indentations are intended to show that integer and float are subtypes of number, and that short-float, single-float, double-float, and long-float are subtypes of float. There is no significance to the order of types that are at the same level.

```
number
     integer
     float
          short-float
          single-float
          double-float
          long-float
```

Exercises

From now on, unless otherwise mentioned, all exercises assume you are typing to the top-level COMMON LISP listener.

2.1 *(r)* Type some small positive and negative integers, one per line. Note that LISP types them back. Try typing some positive integers with the optional plus sign.

2.2 *(i)* Type some small floating-point numbers to LISP. Note the representation LISP uses in typing them back to you.

2.3 *(i)* Try the numbers -.6, .43e5, and 0.0000521347. Type them one per line and see how your LISP responds.

2.4 *(i)* Try the numbers 1.0e-5, 1.0s-5, 1.0f-5, 1.0d-5, and 1.01-5. What exponent markers does your COMMON LISP use in the numbers it prints? Write them here:_____.

2.5 *(i)* To see the difference between varying amounts of precision, try the number 1.1s-5, 1.12s-5, and so on, adding digits to the right until you exceed the ability of **short-float** numbers to represent them. Then try the last number using the next higher precision, and keep adding digits until that precision becomes inadequate, and so on.

2.6 *(i)* Try typing the numbers 3. and 3.0. Are they interpreted as integers or as floating-point numbers?

2.7 *(i)* Does LISP distinguish the numeral 0.0 from the numeral 0? Find out by typing 0, -0, .0, 0.0, and -0.0 and comparing what LISP types back to you.

2.8 *(i)* Type a number *preceded* by some blanks. Note that LISP ignores initial blanks (white space) on a line.

2.9 *(i)* Type the *two* numbers 54 and 325 on *one* line with one or more blanks between them. How does your LISP respond? Some LISPs expect only one S-expression per line; others will read more than one.

2.10 *(i)* Type 54,325 to LISP. How does it treat a numeral with a comma in it?

2.11 *(i)* Enter the characters 123.4.5e6e-7. If it causes an error message, write it here:_____.

2.12 *(i)* Type the characters 123;45 on a line. The semicolon is the *comment character*. LISP ignores it and everything after it on the line. If your LISP doesn't respond after you typed the carriage return, try using the interrupt key and returning to the top level. Then try typing ;45 on one line and 123 on the next line.

2.13 *(i)* What is your character erase (backspace) character? Some possibilities are BS, #, ←, CTRL-H (remember, that's pressing the H key while holding down the CTRL key), DEL, RUB, and RUBOUT. Write yours here:_____.
Enter some numbers, using the backspace character to change your mind. Note that it works.

2.14 *(i)* What is your line erase character? Some possibilities are BRK, ESC, CLEAR INPUT, @, and CTRL-U. Write it here:_____. Enter some numbers, using the line erase character to change your mind. Note how it works.

2.15 *(r)* Try entering an integer that is so long that it wraps around to the second line. That is, the digits should appear on your screen on two lines *before* you type a carriage return.

CHAPTER 3

LISTS

In Chapter 2, we discussed one type of LISP object—numbers and subtypes of numbers. In this chapter, we will begin discussing the most important type of LISP object, the *list*—what LISP was named for. We will start discussing the evaluation of lists in the next chapter. In this chapter, we will discuss the printed representation of lists; that is, list S-expressions. We can define the list S-expression as follows:

A left parenthesis followed by zero or more S-expressions followed by a right parenthesis is a list S-expression.

According to this definition, (1 2 3.3 4) is a list S-expression, since 1, 2, 3.3, and 4 are S-expressions (denoting numbers). Also () is a list S-expression, since it is a left parenthesis followed by zero S-expressions followed by a right parenthesis. We refer to the (zero or more) S-expressions in a list as *elements* or *members* of the list. So the first list has four members, which are 1, 2, 3.3, and 4, and the second list has no members (we call it *the empty list*). Since a list S-expression is itself an S-expression, a list can be a member of a list.[1] For example, (1 (2 3.3) 4) is a list with three members, the second of which is the list (2 3.3). Notice that the parentheses are part of the list; they are

---

[1] In this chapter, we will say "list" instead of "list S-expression" and say "list object" when we mean the object.

15

not merely grouping brackets as they are in algebra. For example, if you remove the inner set of parentheses from the three-member list (1 (2 3.3) 4), you get the four-member list (1 2 3.3 4), and the list ((1 2 3.3 4)) is different yet, because it is a list with one member, which is a list. Even () and (()) are different lists. The first is the empty list; the second is a list with one member, which happens to be the empty list.

If we typed a list to a LISP listener, it would read it, construct the list object it represents, and try to evaluate the list object. As I said above, we will discuss the evaluation of list objects in the next chapter, so at this stage, we are only interested in having LISP print the list back to us. You can prevent LISP from evaluating an object by *quoting* the S-expression you enter. You quote an S-expression by typing a *quote mark* in front of it. The quote mark is the single quote mark on your keyboard that you might use for an apostrophe. In this text, it will look like this: '. Notice that there is another single quote mark on your keyboard that points in the other direction. It is called a *backquote* and will look in this text like this: `. If you type a quoted list to LISP, it will type the list back to you:

```
> '(1 2 3.3 4)
(1 2 3.3 4)
> '(1 (2 3.3) 4)
(1 (2 3.3) 4)
> '((1 2 3.3 4))
((1 2 3.3 4))
```

Actually, the LISP listener is still going through its normal read-eval-print cycle, but when it reads a quoted S-expression, it constructs a quoted object, and *the value of a quoted object is the object itself*, so then it prints the list you typed in, using a printed representation it chooses. We will discuss quoted objects more completely in Chapter 9. The printed representation LISP chooses for a list is not always the same as the one you use. For example, LISP has its own peculiar way of printing the empty list:

```
> '()
NIL
> '(())
(NIL)
```

We will discuss NIL more in Chapter 6. For now, just think of it as a possible printed representation of the empty list.

The other way that LISP's printed representation of lists may differ from yours is in matters of spacing and line breaking. Anywhere within a list that one blank makes sense, you may have several blanks and even a carriage return, and blanks are optional on either side of a parenthesis. You may type spacing to please your own eye; LISP may choose different spacing. For example:

```
> '(1(2     3.3)
     ( 4 )5)
(1 (2 3.3) (4) 5)
```

It is important to remember that a list is one S-expression regardless of how many members it has. So the LISP listener will read one top-level list at a time. That is, after printing a value or upon initial entry to LISP, LISP prints a prompt. You now type a left parenthesis, perhaps preceded by a quote mark. You are typing a top-level list until the number of right parentheses you type equals the number of left parentheses you have typed. Your list may extend over several lines. Some LISPs will type a prompt at the beginning of each line. Others won't. When you finally type a right parenthesis to match that first left parenthesis and then type a carriage return, LISP will type the value of the list object whose printed representation you entered.

Miscounting parentheses can lead to a common, but very frustrating, experience. You have typed in too few right parentheses. You think you have entered an entire list and hit the carriage return. LISP, however, just types a prompt (or doesn't even do that), and you both just sit there staring at each other. LISP is waiting for you to finish your list. If you are too confused to finish it properly, it often works to just type several right parentheses—more than enough to do the job—and then the final carriage return. Some LISPs don't require you to type a carriage return after a list. They recognize when one is finished, automatically go to the next line, and output the value. These LISPs avoid the confusion discussed in this paragraph. Many modern LISP development environments also make typing lists easier by blinking the cursor on the matching left parenthesis just after you type each right parenthesis. If you are using such an environment, it pays to watch that cursor.

An easy way to count parentheses is to count 1 at the first left parenthesis, increase the count by 1 at each subsequent left parenthesis, and
decrease the count by 1 at each subsequent right parenthesis. When
you reach zero again, you are at the right parenthesis that matches the
first left parenthesis and your list is finished. The list below has the
appropriate numbers written below each parenthesis.

```
(1 ( ) (2 (3) 4) 5 ( ( (6) ) 7) )
1  2 1 2  3 2  1    2 3 4 3 2  1 0
```

Our hierarchy of COMMON LISP types is now

```
list
number
     integer
     float
          short-float
          single-float
          double-float
          long-float
```

Exercises

3.1 *(r)* Try all the interactions of this chapter for yourself.

3.2 *(i)* Enter some short unquoted lists and note the error messages.
We will discuss these errors later.

3.3 *(i)* Type a line containing just a right parenthesis. How does LISP
respond?

3.4 *(i)* Enter a quoted list with too many right parentheses. How
does your LISP respond?

3.5 *(i)* Enter some quoted lists that, by including carriage returns,
extend over several lines. Carefully observe how LISP behaves
until the list is finally finished. Note the format in which LISP
prints lists.

3.6 *(i)* Start entering a list that, by including carriage returns, extends over several lines, but stop before finishing the list. If you now decide that you don't want to enter this list after all, how do you erase it? Your character erase key may erase even into previous lines. Try that. If you are using some kind of Lisp Machine, you may have a CLEAR INPUT key. Press it. Otherwise, try pressing the interrupt character to get into the debugger (see Exercise 1.6); then get back to top-level LISP (see Exercise 1.8). Write your delete-current-list sequence here:_____.
You should now be able to delete the last character, delete the current line, or delete the current list.

3.7 *(d)* Experiment with lists with different spacing. Try spaces between the quote mark and the first open parenthesis. In each case, compare LISP's printed representation with yours.

CHAPTER 4

ARITHMETIC

In the last chapter, you learned how to type a list S-expression to the LISP listener. In this chapter, you will start evaluating list objects. As you will see, evaluating list objects is the basic operation involved in writing, testing, and using LISP. So this topic is very important.

> *The value of a list is the value obtained by applying the function named by the first member of the list to the values of the other members of the list.*

We will start exploring the evaluation of lists in the realm of arithmetic. Here, the *functions* we will be using are the usual arithmetic operators: addition, subtraction, multiplication, and division. The *symbols* that name these functions are, as usual, +, -, *, and /, respectively. So, for example, if we asked LISP to evaluate the list (+ 12 4), LISP would type back the value 16.

```
> (+ 12 4) 16
```

This format, in which arithmetic expressions are written as a list, with the name of the function (operator) as the first member and expressions that provide the arguments as the other members of the list, is called *Cambridge Prefix notation*: "Cambridge" because LISP was developed by John McCarthy and the Artificial Intelligence Group at

M.I.T. in Cambridge, Massachusetts; and "Prefix" because the function (operator) is written *before* its arguments (operands).[1] You may compare it with standard arithmetic "infix" notation, in which the operator is written between its operands (such as $12 + 4$), and with standard mathematical notation, in which functions are written before their operands but outside the parentheses [such as $f(x, y)$, which in Cambridge Prefix notation would be (f x y)].

Evaluating expressions involving subtraction, multiplication, and division works just like evaluating expressions involving addition:

```
> (- 12 4)
8
> (* 12 4)
48
> (/ 12 4)
3
```

One major advantage of Cambridge Prefix notation is that the notation is consistent regardless of how many arguments the function is given. In normal notation, to use the "unary" minus sign, you write it in front of its argument: -12. The "binary" minus sign is written between its two arguments: $12 - 4$. If you want to subtract a series of numbers, each from the previous result, you write the minus sign between every two numbers: $12 - 4 - 2 - 5$. In Cambridge Prefix notation, you always write the operator once, before all the operands, separate all with blanks, and enclose all in parentheses:

```
> (- 12)
-12
> (- 12 4)
8
> (- 12 4 2 5)
1
```

---

[1]The term "Cambridge Prefix" was patterned after the term "Polish Prefix," where the function is written before its arguments, but parentheses are not needed because the number of arguments of each function is fixed and known. The term "Polish Prefix" is used because the notation was invented by the Polish logician Jan Lukasiewicz. He also invented Polish Postfix notation, which is like Polish Prefix, but the function follows its arguments. Polish Postfix notation is used by some pocket calculators today.

All four arithmetic operators work the same way and can take one or more arguments.

If all the arguments to any of these arithmetic functions are integers, the result will be an integer. If any argument is a floating-point number, the result will be a floating-point number. There is one exception. If you try to divide an integer by an integer that does not go into it evenly, the result will be a third kind of number called a *ratio*. A ratio is written as two digit strings separated by / and optionally preceded by a + or -. There must be no space within the ratio. COMMON LISP always prints a ratio in simplest terms, but you needn't. Compare:

```
> (/ 12 4)
3
> (/ 12.0 8)
1.5
> (/ 12 8)
3/2
> 12/8
3/2
```

Expressions may be nested within expressions in the usual way. In mathematical notation, we might write $f(x, g(y))$; whereas in Cambridge Prefix notation, we'd write (f x (g y)). So the LISP version of $5 \times (3 + 4)$ is (* 5 (+ 3 4)), and the LISP version of $5 \times 3 + 4$ is (+ (* 5 3) 4). (Notice that we don't have to discuss operator precedence, since every operator, with its arguments, must be enclosed in its own list.) One of the roots of the equation

$$2x^2 + 7x + 5 = 0$$

is

$$\frac{-7 + \sqrt{7^2 - 4 \times 2 \times 5}}{2 \times 2}$$

and is written in LISP as

```
(/ (+ -7.0 (sqrt (- (expt 7 2) (* 4 2 5)))) (* 2 2))
```

Notice that (sqrt *number*) returns the square root of the *number* and that (expt *number₁ number₂*) is *number₁* raised to the power of *number₂*.

Numbers may be checked for equality with the function =. Just as with the arithmetic operators, = may be given zero, one, two, or more arguments, although the usual number is two. The arguments may also be any types of numbers; = cares only about numerical equality. = returns True if all its arguments are equal and False if any two of them are not equal. Peculiarly, LISP uses T as its printed representation of True and NIL as its printed representation of False. (Yes, LISP's printed representation of False is the same as its printed representation of the empty list—strange, often confusing, but true.) Some examples of the use of = are:

```
> (= 50 50.0 100/2)
T
> (= 50 50.0001)
NIL
> (= (+ 2 2) (* 2 2) (expt 2 2))
T
```

You will not be writing LISP programs until Part II. In Part I, you will be using LISP in a kind of "desk calculator" mode in which you type forms to the LISP listener and it immediately types back their values. This is not just a temporary technique, however. All LISP programmers use this "desk calculator" mode all the time to develop and test their programs. You will, too.

Exercises

4.1 *(r)* Check LISP's responses to the inputs:

```
(+ 12 4)        (- 12 4)
(* 12 4)        (/ 12 4)
(- 12)          (- 12 4)
(- 12 4 2 5)    (= 50 50.0 100/2)
(= 50 50.0001)  (= (+ 2 2) (* 2 2) (expt 2 2))
```

4.2 *(i)* Ask LISP to evaluate (notafunction 5 3). What is the error message when you try to evaluate a list that doesn't begin with the name of a function? Write it here:

4.3 *(d)* See what happens if you mistakenly leave out the blank between the operator and the first argument by typing (+2 3) and (*2 3) to LISP.

4.4 *(d)* See what happens if you mistakenly leave out the operator altogether, by typing (2 3) to LISP.

4.5 *(d)* Try the mistake (2 + 3).

4.6 *(d)* See what happens if you mistakenly leave out the parentheses, by typing

```
> + 2 3
```

or

```
> 2 + 3
```

to LISP.

4.7 *(i)* Try the operators +, *, and / with one and with more than two arguments.

4.8 *(i)* Try each of the four arithmetic operators with *no* arguments. For example, + applied to no arguments is written (+). You should get two numeric answers, and two error messages. What is COMMON LISP's error message when you give a function too few arguments? Write it here:

_____

4.9 *(i)* Try = with zero and with one argument.

4.10 *(i)* Ask LISP to evaluate (sqrt 4 9). What is the error message when you give a function too many arguments? Write it here:

_____

4.11 *(r)* Check LISP's responses to (/ 12 4), (/ 12.0 8), (/ 12 8), and 12/8.

4.12 *(d)* Try the other operators with mixtures of integers and floating-point numbers.

4.13 *(d)* Try doing arithmetic with a mixture of integers, floating-point numbers, and ratios.

4.14 *(r)* Check that LISP's response to (* 5 (+ 3 4)) is 35 and that its response to (+ (* 5 3) 4) is 19.

4.15 *(r)* Check that LISP's response to

(/ (+ -7.0 (sqrt (- (expt 7 2) (* 4 2 5)))) (* 2 2))

is -1.0.

4.16 *(d)* Have LISP calculate the other root of the equation

$$2x^2 + 7x + 5 = 0$$

namely:

$$\frac{-7 - \sqrt{7^2 - 4 \times 2 \times 5}}{2 \times 2}$$

Make sure the answer is -2.5.

4.17 *(d)* Using LISP, find the values of
a. $(25 + 30) \times 15/2$
b. 6×3.1416
c. The average of 5, 6.7, -23.2, 75, and 100.3

CHAPTER 5

STRINGS AND CHARACTERS

The kinds of COMMON LISP objects we have discussed so far are numbers (integers, floating-point numbers, and ratios) and lists. We are building up to a discussion of the object type *symbol*. Along with lists, symbols are the most important kind of objects in LISP because they are used for program variables, for function names (as was already briefly mentioned), and as data to allow LISP programs to manipulate symbolic data as well as numeric data. Just as there can be several different printed representations of a given number (for example, 5e2, 500.0, and 5000e-1), there can be different printed representations of a given symbol, and novice LISP users are often confused by this. To avoid such confusion, we will have to distinguish carefully between a symbol and the symbol's *name*. A symbol's name is an instance of another COMMON LISP object type, called a *string*. So before pursuing the discussion of symbols and symbol names, we will have to discuss strings, and since a string is made up of *characters* (another type of COMMON LISP object), we will have to discuss characters also.

A string is a vector (single-dimensional array) of characters and is both read and printed by LISP as a sequence of its characters surrounded by double quotes. For example, "This is a string." is a string. Like numbers, strings evaluate to themselves, so if you type a string to the LISP listener, it will print it back to you:

```
> "This is a string."
"This is a string."
```

A string can be as long as you like and can contain strange characters such as the CARRIAGE RETURN character.

Just as COMMON LISP has functions (such as +, -, *, /, =, sqrt, and expt) that operate on numbers, COMMON LISP also has functions that operate on objects of other types. For example, the function length will tell you the number of characters in a string:

```
> (length "This is a string.")
17
```

and string= returns True if its two argument strings are made up of the same characters and False if they have different characters.

```
> (string= "This is a string." "This is a string.")
T
> (string= "This is a string." "This is another string.")
NIL
> (string= "This is a string." "this is a string.")
NIL
```

To have LISP print a particular character in the string, use the form (char *string index*), where you type a string in place of *string* and an integer less than the length of the string in place of *index*. The index of the first character in the string is 0.

```
> (char "This is a string." 0)
#\T
> (char "This is a string." 1)
#\h
> (char "This is a string." 15)
#\g
>  (char "This is a string." 16)
#\.
```

Notice that a character is printed with a prefix of #\. This is also the way you type a character to LISP.

```
> '#\T
#\T
```

Just like numbers and strings, characters evaluate to themselves, so

```
> #\T
#\T
> #\.
#\.
```

Just as = tests for equality of numbers and `string=` tests for equality of strings, `char=` tests for equality of characters. Like =, but unlike `string=`, `char=` takes any number of arguments. For example:

```
> (char= (char "This is a string." 2)
         (char "This is a string." 5)
         #\i)
T
> (char= #\t (char "This is a string." 0))
NIL
```

Our hierarchy of COMMON LISP types is now:

```
character
number
      integer
      ratio
      float
              short-float
              single-float
              double-float
              long-float
list
string
```

Exercises

5.1 *(r)* Check LISP's value of the string `"This is a string."`.

5.2 *(i)* Look at LISP's value of the string `"a|b#c;d"`. Notice that the characters |, #, and ; are treated like ordinary characters in a string.

5.3 *(i)* Enter a string consisting of the alphabet repeated several times, so that the string is longer than a line of your terminal. Don't type a carriage return until after you have typed the closing " of the string. Notice that LISP prints the string back to you without omitting any characters.

5.4 *(i)* Enter the string "ab", but type a CARRIAGE RETURN between the a and the b. Notice that LISP also prints the CARRIAGE RETURN.

5.5 *(r)* Check that (length "This is a string.") evaluates to 17.

5.6 *(i)* What does LISP tell you is the length of the string "a|b#c;d"? Notice that each character printed between the quote marks is counted exactly once.

5.7 *(i)* What is the length of the string you typed in for Exercise 5.4? The CARRIAGE RETURN is counted as a single character.

5.8 *(r)* Check LISP's value of
```
(string= "This is a string." "This is a string.")
(string= "This is a string."
         "This is another string.")
```
and
```
(string= "This is a string." "this is a string.")
```

5.9 See what happens if you try to give string= more than two arguments.

5.10 *(r)* Check that the characters at index positions 0, 1, 15, and 16 of "This is a string." are #\T, #\h, #\g, and #\., respectively.

5.11 *(r)* Check that a character evaluates to itself by entering the characters #\T, #\h, #\g, and #\., one per line. Also try the characters #\|, #\#, and #\;.

5.12 *(i)* What is the character at index position 4 of

```
"This is a string."
```

LISP uses #\SPACE as the printed name of the space character, because using the actual space would be too confusing.

5.13 *(r)* Check LISP's value of

```
(char= (char "This is a string." 2)
       (char "This is a string." 5)
       #\i)
```

and

```
(char= #\t (char "This is a string." 0))
```

5.14 *(i)* Check that `#\SPACE` is LISP's way of printing the space character; evaluate the space character by typing an actual space after the `#\`. That is, type on one line a `#`, followed by a `\`, followed by an actual space, followed by a CARRIAGE RETURN.

5.15 *(i)* Check that `(char= #\space #\SPACE)` evaluates to True. Perhaps this is because LISP does not distinguish between lower- and uppercase letters; perhaps LISP converts the lowercase letters you type outside of quoted strings into uppercase letters. We will pursue this more in Chapter 6.

5.16 *(i)* What is the character at index position 1 of the string you typed in for Exercise 5.4? `#\NEWLINE` is LISP's name for what we have been calling the CARRIAGE RETURN character.

5.17 *(i)* How could you get the character `#\"` into the middle of a string? Just typing it there won't work because it would be considered the ending quote of the string. LISP has an *escape character* for this purpose, and it is the *backslash* character \ (sometimes called "bash"). Try this by evaluating the string `"a\"b"`.

5.18 *(i)* Convince yourself that when LISP printed `"a\"b"` to you in the previous exercise, it was also using \ as an escape character and not as a character actually in the string. Do this by asking LISP for the `length` of the string `"a\"b"` and by using `char` to ask LISP to show you each character in the string.

5.19 *(d)* How would you actually get the character \ into a string?

5.20 *(d)* To help convince yourself that the backslash used as an escape character within a string is not really part of the string, ask LISP to evaluate `(string= "a\"b" "\a\"\b")`.

5.21 *(i)* See what your LISP does if you ask it to evaluate

$$\text{(string= "a" \#\textbackslash a)}$$
$$\text{and}$$
$$\text{(char= "a" \#\textbackslash a)}$$

5.22 *(i)* See what your LISP does if you ask it to evaluate
(= 5 "five").

CHAPTER 6

SYMBOLS

We are finally ready to discuss *symbols*. Symbols are another COMMON LISP data type, like integers, floating-point numbers, ratios, characters, strings, and lists.

The subject of the possible printed representations of symbols is somewhat complicated, and we will discuss it in this and the next chapter. To begin with, however, we will use sequences of letters and the characters * and - to form the printed representations of symbols. For example, some symbols are written as `frank`, `pi`, and `*read-base*`.

A symbol may stand for something that we wish to store information about. For example, the symbol `frank` may represent some person. Symbols are also used as the variables of the LISP programming language. Treated as a variable, a symbol may have a value, in which case we say it is *bound* to that value, or it may not have a value, in which case we say that it is *unbound*. We will see later how to bind a value to a symbol, but some symbols are already bound to values when we start LISP. Some symbols that already have values are `pi`, `*read-base*`, `*print-base*`, and `*package*`. The value of `pi` is what you would expect—the value of the mathematical constant π. The values of `*read-base*` and `*print-base*` tell LISP what base you will be using to enter numbers and what base you want LISP to use to print numbers, respectively. We will discuss the significance of

33

package in the next chapter. To see the value of a symbol, just type
it as a form to the top-level LISP listener:

```
> pi
3.1415926535897936d0
> *read-base*
10
> *print-base*
10
> *package*
#<Package USER 4515050>
```

The most important symbols in LISP are T and NIL. We have already seen that LISP uses them as the printed representation of True
and False, respectively, and that NIL is also used as LISP's printed
representation of the empty list. Because of their importance, they are
bound to themselves as values:

```
> T
T
> NIL
NIL
```

Since we often use symbols to stand for people, places, and objects
of all sorts, we often want to talk to LISP about a symbol rather than
about the symbol's value. If we want to do this, we quote it:

```
> 'frank
FRANK
> 'pi
PI
```

LISP responded with the symbol spelled in uppercase letters because
COMMON LISP converts every lowercase letter you type into uppercase
in the process of interpreting your S-expression as the printed representation of some object. You could type in uppercase instead, but it's
more trouble. For example, it's easier to type T and NIL as t and nil
and the results are the same:

```
> t
T
> nil
NIL
```

We will see how to make use of lowercase letters soon. There are two important points here. One is that the value of a quoted symbol is the symbol itself. This is the same rule we saw with lists: *The value of a quoted object is the object itself.*

The other important point is that **frank** and **FRANK** are just two different printed representations of the same symbol. COMMON LISP allows you to use lowercase letters just because it's easier for you to type lowercase letters than uppercase letters. We can check this with the function **eql**, which is COMMON LISP's equality test for symbols:

```
> (eql 'frank 'FRANK)
T
> (eql 'frank 'pi)
NIL
> (eql 'pi 'PI)
T
```

Actually, **eql** is more general than an equality test for symbols. It takes *any* two LISP objects as arguments and returns True if they are identical (references to the same locations in computer memory), the same symbols, the same characters, or numerically equal numbers of the same numeric subtype; otherwise **eql** returns False.[1] For example:

```
> (eql #\a (char "This is a string." 8))
T
> (eql 50 50.0)
NIL
> (eql 5.0e1 50.0)
T
```

---

[1]Readers with some previous exposure to LISP may have expected the **eq** function. In COMMON LISP, **eq** tests implementation equality. Even **(eq 50 50)** might be False if the two integers are stored in different memory locations. In COMMON LISP, **eql** serves the purpose that **eq** served in earlier versions of LISP. Therefore **eq** shall not be mentioned again until Chapter 30.

Returning to our discussion of symbols, every symbol has a *print name*, or simply a *name*, which is a string of the characters used to print the symbol. The name of the symbol `frank` is the string `"FRANK"`. You can see the name of a symbol by using the function `symbol-name`:

```
> (symbol-name 'frank)
"FRANK"
> (symbol-name 'pi)
"PI"
```

A symbol name can be as long as you want, and it can contain any character in it. However, if you want to get an unusual character into a symbol name, you must either precede it with the escape character \ or enclose it between a pair of escape brackets ||. The normal characters, which can be included in a symbol name without using an escape character, are the 26 uppercase letters, the 10 digits, and the characters !, $, %, &, *, +, -, ., /, <, =, >, ?, @, [,], ^, _, {, }, and ~. As we have seen, uppercase letters are special because you can type them in lowercase. If you want to get a lowercase letter into a symbol name, you must precede it with an escape character or enclose it in escape brackets:

```
> 'f\rank
|FrANK|
> 'f|rank|
|Frank|
> '|frank|
|frank|
```

Although these symbols differ only in the cases of some of the letters of their names, they are, in fact, different symbols. We can see this by using `eql`:

```
> (eql 'f\rank 'f|rank|)
NIL
> (eql 'f|rank| '|frank|)
NIL
> (eql 'f\rank '|frank|)
NIL
```

In general, LISP's printed representation of an object is a character sequence that you could use to type the object to LISP. That way it is easier to have LISP read a file that it has written. That is why, in all three examples above, LISP used the escape brackets. To convince yourself that the escape brackets are not part of the name itself, you could do

```
> (symbol-name '|frank|)
"frank"
> (string= (symbol-name 'f|rank|) "Frank")
T
> (eql 'f\rank '|FrANK|)
T
```

We have now seen COMMON LISP objects that are integers, floating-point numbers, ratios, strings, characters, lists, and symbols. These are called different *types* or *data types*. You may be familiar with programming languages that have typed variables. COMMON LISP has typed objects. The COMMON LISP function `type-of` will tell you, for any object, what its type is. For example:

```
> (type-of '12)
FIXNUM
> (type-of '123456789)
BIGNUM
> (type-of '53e21)
SINGLE-FLOAT
> (type-of pi)
DOUBLE-FLOAT
> (type-of 'pi)
SYMBOL
```

FIXNUM and BIGNUM are two subtypes of integer that differ according to storage requirements. Notice carefully the difference between the type of the value of `pi` and that of `pi` itself.

Symbols are also used as names of functions. The symbols we have already seen used as names of functions are +, -, *, /, =, `length`, `char`, `char=`, `string=`, `eql`, `symbol-name`, and `type-of`. (Do you remember what each of them does?) For example:

```
> (type-of '+)
SYMBOL
> (type-of 'symbol-name)
SYMBOL
```

Finally, note that not only might we use a symbol to stand for something (we might use **frank** to stand for some person), but LISP itself uses symbols to stand for things. For example, COMMON LISP uses symbols to stand for the names of data types:

```
> (type-of "frank")
STRING
> (type-of (type-of "frank"))
SYMBOL
```

Our hierarchy of COMMON LISP types is now

```
character
number
     integer
            fixnum
            bignum
     ratio
     float
            short-float
            single-float
            double-float
            long-float
symbol
list
string
```

Exercises

6.1 *(r)* Check LISP's value of **pi**, ***read-base***, ***print-base*** and ***package***. Your COMMON LISP's printed representation of the value of ***package*** might be somewhat different from mine.

6.2 *(r)* Check LISP's value of **NIL** and **T**. Try typing them both in uppercase and in lowercase.

6.3 *(r)* Enter the quoted symbols **'frank** and **'pi**. Notice that a quoted symbol evaluates to the symbol itself.

6.4 *(i)* Enter the unquoted symbol `frank`. Write the error message you get here:_____.
That means that this symbol is not bound to a value.

6.5 *(r)* Check LISP's value of
`(symbol-name 'frank)`
and
`(symbol-name 'pi)`.

6.6 *(r)* Check LISP's value of
`(eql 'frank 'FRANK)`
`(eql 'frank 'pi)`
and
`(eql 'pi 'PI)`

6.7 *(r)* Check LISP's value of
`(eql #\a (char "This is a string." 8))`
`(eql 50 50.0)`
and
`(eql 5.0e1 50.0)`

6.8 *(i)* Check your LISP's value of `(eql "string" "string")`. This is implementation-dependent.

6.9 *(i)* See what LISP does if you ask it to evaluate `(eql "a" #\a)`. `eql` should report that two objects of different types are not the same.

6.10 *(r)* Check what LISP prints when you enter `'f\rank`, `'f|rank|`, and `'|frank|`.

6.11 *(r)* Check that `eql` considers no two of `'f\rank`, `'f|rank|`, and `'|frank|` to be the same.

6.12 *(r)* Check LISP's value of
`(symbol-name '|frank|)`
`(string= (symbol-name 'f|rank|) "Frank")`
and
`(eql 'f\rank '|FrANK|)`

6.13 *(d)* Try typing in the characters `'abc;de`. If necessary, review Exercise 2.12.

6.14 *(d)* Type a quoted symbol whose print name contains the character #\;.

6.15 *(r)* Check LISP's values of
(type-of '12)
(type-of '123456789)
(type-of '53e21)
(type-of pi)
and
(type-of 'pi)

6.16 *(r)* Check LISP's values of
(type-of '+)
(type-of 'symbol-name)
and
(type-of "frank")

6.17 *(i)* See what LISP considers the type of 10/3 and #\t.

6.18 *(i)* Check LISP's value of (type-of '(1 2 3)). We will discuss this in Chapter 8.

6.19 *(r)* Check LISP's value of (type-of (type-of "frank")). Make sure you understand this.

6.20 *(i)* What does LISP consider to be the type of the *value* of ***package***? We will discuss packages in the next chapter.

6.21 *(i)* Can a symbol's name begin with a digit? Evaluate (type-of '53g21), and compare that with the value of (type-of '53e21).

6.22 *(i)* Compare the types of '12 and '\12. The escape character causes LISP to treat the next character as an alphabetic character.

6.23 *(i)* The character #\# can appear as a normal character in the middle of a symbol name, but not at the beginning. Convince yourself of this by typing appropriate entries to LISP.

6.24 *(i)* See if the character #\: can be a normal character at the beginning of a symbol name or in the middle of a symbol name. Try it in both positions with the escape character before it.

6.25 *(d)* See if you can create a symbol whose name contains the `#\NEWLINE` character.

6.26 *(d)* See if you can create a symbol whose name contains the `#\SPACE` character.

CHAPTER 7

PACKAGES

COMMON LISP was designed to enable teams of programmers to cooperate on building a large system. To help keep them from getting in each other's way, COMMON LISP was designed so that each programmer could keep his or her own set of symbols. Each set of symbols is kept in what COMMON LISP calls a *package*. So that one programmer can make use of some of what another programmer does, the symbols a programmer intends others to use can be *exported* from its original package (called its *home package*) and *imported* into another package.

In the last chapter, you should have learned not to get confused by the printed representations of a symbol. A symbol can have several printed representations and still be the same symbol, with the same symbol name. In this chapter, you will see that several different symbols can have the same symbol name—as long as they are in different packages. So you need to be able to distinguish between a symbol, the symbol's name, the symbol's home package, and the symbol's printed representations.

Whenever you are interacting with COMMON LISP, you are "in" some particular package. You can tell which one you're in by checking the value of the symbol *package* (see Chapter 6):

```
> *package*
#<Package USER 4515050>
```

This indicates that I am in the user package. When you start running
COMMON LISP, you should also be in the user package, although the
printed representation your LISP uses may be slightly different from
the one mine uses.[1]

The LISP function describe is useful for finding out various things
about LISP objects. Among other things, it can tell us the home package of different symbols:

```
> (describe 'frank)
Symbol FRANK is in USER package.
It has no value, definition or properties
```

I will not bother showing some additional material printed by describe
because it is not relevant to our current discussion. You will see it when
you experiment with describe on your own system.

Most symbols already defined in COMMON LISP are in the lisp
package,[2] exported from that package, and automatically imported
into the user package. So, for example:

```
> (describe 'pi)
Symbol PI is in LISP package.
The value of PI is 3.1415926535897936d0
```

```
> (describe 'symbol-name)
Symbol SYMBOL-NAME is in LISP package.
The function definition of SYMBOL-NAME is
#<DTP-FUNCTION SYMBOL-NAME 11426436>: (SYMBOL)
```

```
> (describe 'describe)
Symbol DESCRIBE is in LISP package.
The function definition of DESCRIBE is
#<DTP-FUNCTION DESCRIBE 26354142>:
(SYS::ANYTHING &OPTIONAL SYS::NO-COMPLAINTS)
```

---

[1]The new COMMON LISP standard will use common-lisp-user instead of user.
Your COMMON LISP may already be following the new standard.

[2]The new COMMON LISP standard will use common-lisp instead of lisp.

You can move to a different package with the COMMON LISP function in-package:

```
> (in-package 'lisp)
#<Package LISP 5114210>


> (describe 'frank)
Symbol FRANK is in LISP package.
It has no value, definition or properties
```

Notice that this time **frank** is in the **lisp** package. This is a different symbol **frank** from the one in the user package. To refer to an internal symbol of one package when you are in another package, you must use its *qualified name,* which consists of the package name followed by two colons (::) followed by the symbol name. For example, when in the **lisp** package, you can refer to the **frank** that's in the **user** package as **user::frank**:

```
> (describe 'user::frank)
Symbol USER::FRANK is in USER package.
It has no value, definition or properties
```

If we now return to the **user** package, we can refer to the **frank** in the **user** package with its unqualified name, but we have to refer to the **frank** in the **lisp** package with its qualified name:

```
> (in-package 'user)
#<Package USER 4515050>


> (describe 'frank)
Symbol FRANK is in USER package.
It has no value, definition or properties


> (describe 'lisp::frank)
Symbol LISP::FRANK is in LISP package.
It has no value, definition or properties
```

We can, however, use the qualified name for a symbol in the package we're in. It's just redundant:

```
> (describe 'user::frank)
Symbol FRANK is in USER package.
It has no value, definition or properties

> 'user::frank
FRANK
```

It is important to realize that the package name and the double colon are not part of the symbol's name and that internal symbols in different packages may have the same names, but they are still different symbols:

```
> (symbol-name 'lisp::frank)
"FRANK"

> (symbol-name 'user::frank)
"FRANK"

> (string= (symbol-name 'lisp::frank)
           (symbol-name 'user::frank))
T

>(eql 'lisp::frank 'user::frank)
NIL
```

A symbol may be exported from its home package with the COMMON LISP function **export**. It then becomes an *external* symbol. The qualified name of an external symbol is the name of its home package, followed by a single colon, followed by its symbol-name.

```
> (export 'frank)
T

> (in-package 'lisp)
#<Package LISP 5114210>

> (describe 'user:frank)
Symbol USER:FRANK is in USER package.
It has no value, definition or properties
```

An easy way to tell that a symbol in another package has been exported is to type its qualified name to Lisp using the double colon and see what printed representation Lisp uses:

```
> 'user::frank
USER:FRANK
```

Lisp's use of the single colon indicates that **frank** is external in the **user** package.

```
> (in-package 'user)
#<Package USER 4515050>

> 'lisp::frank
LISP::FRANK
```

This shows that **frank** is still internal in the **lisp** package.

The **in-package** function will create a new package if necessary:

```
> (in-package 'test)
#<Package TEST 16431743>
```

Some versions of COMMON LISP print the package you are in just before the prompt. Others print it in some information line at the bottom of the screen.

In the **test** package, **lisp::frank** and **user:frank** are available if we use properly qualified names:

```
> 'lisp::frank
LISP::FRANK

> 'user:frank
USER:FRANK

> 'user::frank
USER:FRANK

> (describe 'lisp::frank)
Symbol LISP::FRANK is in LISP package.
It has no value, definition or properties
```

```
> (describe 'user:frank)
Symbol USER:FRANK is in USER package.
It has no value, definition or properties
```

If we want, we can import an external symbol from one package into another with the function import. The benefit of so doing is that we can then refer to it in the new package with an unqualified name even though its home package is still the original one.

```
> (import 'user:frank)
T
```

```
> (describe 'frank)
Symbol FRANK is in USER package.
 It is also interned in package TEST
It has no value, definition or properties
```

```
> (eql 'frank 'user::frank)
T
```

```
> (eql 'frank 'lisp::frank)
NIL
```

```
> 'user::frank
FRANK
```

It is an error to import a symbol into a package that already has a symbol with the same name. What you might do in such a case is examined in a few of the exercises at the end of this chapter.

When a symbol is in a package in such a way that you can refer to it with its unqualified name, it is said to be *interned* in the package. Normally, when you are interacting with COMMON LISP and you type a symbol to LISP, that symbol is automatically interned into the package you are in if it is not already there. That is why you never had to worry about this before. That is also one of the features that makes LISP easy to use interactively—you don't have to declare symbols before using them; just using a symbol causes LISP to construct it.

As I said above, standard symbols in the lisp package are external and are automatically imported into other packages (recall that we are still in the test package):

```
> 'lisp::pi
PI

> 'lisp::describe
DESCRIBE
```

Packages are another COMMON LISP data type.

```
> *package*
#<Package TEST 12356212>

> (type-of *package*)
PACKAGE
```

Every package has a name, which you may find with the function
`package-name`. A package's name may be the same string as some
symbol's name. Nevertheless, packages and symbols are different, even
if they have the same name:

```
> (package-name *package*)
"TEST"

> (string= (package-name *package*) (symbol-name 'test))
T

> (eql *package* 'test)
NIL
```

Although COMMON LISP has some printed representation of packages
to type to us, as mentioned above, different COMMON LISPs may use
different printed representations, and there is no printed representation
of a package that you may type to the COMMON LISP listener. That
is why you use the package name, but remember that a package and
its name are different objects.

The function `package-name` maps a package to its name. If a package already exists, the function `find-package` will map from a package
name to the package it names:

```
> (find-package "TEST")
#<Package TEST 12356212>

> (find-package "LISP")
#<Package LISP 6460611>
```

Packages may be created by **in-package**, as we have seen. A package may also be created by the function **make-package**. The difference is that **in-package** also changes the package we are in, whereas make-package doesn't.

```
> (make-package "foo")
#<Package foo 12760773>

> *package*
#<Package TEST 12356212>

> (in-package '|foo|)
#<Package foo 12760773>

> *package*
#<Package foo 12760773>
```

The functions **in-package**, **make-package**, and **find-package** all take as arguments either the string that is the package name or a symbol that has the same name as the package. But when using both a symbol and its name, remember that uppercase versus lowercase matters, even though COMMON LISP changes the case of letters you type in unless you escape them.

Our hierarchy of COMMON LISP types is now as shown in Figure 7.1.

Exercises

7.1 *(r)* Try all the interactions of this chapter for yourself. Be sure to do them all and in exactly the same order as they were presented in the text. Return to the **user** package when you are through.

7.2 *(i)* Try **describe** on some objects other than symbols.

```
            character
            number
                  integer
                        fixnum
                        bignum
                  ratio
                  float
                        short-float
                        single-float
                        double-float
                        long-float
            symbol
            list
            string
            package
```

Figure 7.1 The COMMON LISP type hierarchy as of this chapter.

7.3 *(i)* In the user package, evaluate (describe 'bill). Then export bill.   Then change to the test package, and try (describe 'bill) again. This bill will have test as its home package. Now try to import user:bill into the test package. Some COMMON LISPs will give you an error warning and a chance to *unintern* test::bill and replace it with user:bill. Other COMMON LISPs will just give you an error.

7.4 *(i)* In the test package, do (describe 'pi). You should find that pi is in the lisp package. Now evaluate (shadow 'pi) and (describe 'pi) again. You should now find that pi is in the test package. How would you now get LISP to describe the pi in the lisp package?

7.5 *(i)* Export test::pi.   Change into the foo package.   Do (describe 'pi). You should find that pi is in the lisp package. Now do (shadowing-import 'test:pi), and (describe 'pi) again. Now pi should be the one whose home package is test.

CHAPTER 8

BASIC LIST PROCESSING

In Chapter 3, we introduced the list S-expression and discussed how lists are typed to the LISP listener and how it prints them to us. Since then, you have had a lot of practice in having LISP evaluate lists.[1] In this chapter, we will start to discuss the use of lists as data objects— that is, *list processing*—what LISP was named for.

The basic function for creating lists is cons:

(cons *object list*) Takes two arguments. The first can be any LISP object. The second must be a list. Returns a list just like its second argument, but with the first argument inserted as a new first member. For example:

```
> (cons 'a '(b c))
(A B C)
> (cons 2 (cons 4 (cons 6 '(8))))
(2 4 6 8)
```

Notice that, just as with other functions we have seen, the argument forms are evaluated. The value of the first argument form becomes the first member of the new list and the value of the second argument form provides the remaining members.

---

[1]From now on, I will say "list" when I mean a list object, not a list S-expression.

The name "cons" comes from "construct," since it is the basic list constructor. Every LISP list can be constructed from the empty list and cons. For example:

```
> (cons 'c '())
(C)
> (cons 'b (cons 'c '()))
(B C)
> (cons 'a (cons 'b (cons 'c '())))
(A B C)
```

Notice that I used '() to represent the empty list, even though () and nil would be equivalent. This is a matter of good style. It clearly shows that I meant the argument form to evaluate to the empty list, not the symbol nil or the value False and that I did not mean to type a form that called some other function but accidently left something out.

The function cons is so basic that we can use it to provide a constructive definition of LISP lists:

1. nil is a list.

2. If o is any LISP object and l is a list, then (cons o l) is a list.

3. Nothing else is a list.

Compare this definition to the one on page 15. That one defined a list by its printed representation. This one defines a list as a data object by the way it is constructed.

The function cons constructs a list from an arbitrary object and a smaller list. We can recover those two arguments with the functions first and rest.[2]

(first *list*) Takes a list and returns its first member. If the argument list is (), returns NIL.

(rest *list*) Takes a list and returns a list just like it but omitting the first member. If the argument list is (), returns NIL.

-----

[2]Those with some previous experience with LISP may have expected a discussion of car and cdr here. I think that, with the inclusion of first and rest as standard COMMON LISP functions, it is finally time to retire car and cdr, except when doing destructive list manipulation on cons cells, which we won't do until Chapter 30.

For example:

```
> (first '(1 2 3))
1
> (rest '(1 2 3))
(2 3)
> (first (cons 'a '(b c)))
A
> (rest (cons 'a '(b c)))
(B C)
> (first '())
NIL
> (rest '())
NIL
```

The relationship among cons, first, and rest may be expressed as the LISP *identities*:

- (first (cons o l)) $\equiv o$

- (rest (cons o l)) $\equiv l$

- Unless l is (), (cons (first l) (rest l)) $\equiv l$

Here are some more examples:

```
> (first (rest '(1 2 3)))
2
> (cons (first (rest '(1 2 3))) (rest (rest '(1 2 3))))
(2 3)
> (first '(((((())))))) 
(((NIL)))
> (first (first '((A B) C)))
A
> (rest (first '((A B) C)))
(B)
> (cons '() '(A B C))
(NIL A B C)
```

```
> (cons '(a b c) '())
((A B C))
> (rest '(a))
NIL
> (cons nil nil)
(NIL)
```

Just as **string=** tests for character-by-character equality of strings, the function **equal** returns True if given two lists whose corresponding members are equal (according to the appropriate equality function) and False if given two lists of different lengths or if at least one pair of corresponding members are not equal.

```
> (equal '(a (b c) d) '(a (b c) d))
T
> (equal '(a (b c) d) '(a b c d))
NIL
> (equal '(a) '((a)))
NIL
> (equal '(a) (first '((a))))
T
```

The function **length**, which we have already used to tell us the number of characters in a string, can also tell us the number of members of a list:

```
> (length '(a (b c) d))
3
> (length '(a b c d))
4
> (length '())
0
> (length '(atom))
1
> (length '(alpha beta gamma))
3
> (length '(5 is a number "this is a string"))
5
> (length '((a list within a list)))
1
```

```
> (length '(()))
1
> (length '((((())))))
1
> (length '(()()()()()))
5
> (length '(an (interesting ((list) structure)))))
2
```

Finally, let us summarize what we know about the evaluation of lists:

- The first member of the list must be a symbol that names a function.

- The remaining members of the list are treated as argument forms and are evaluated.[3]

- The value of the list is the value of the function applied to the values of the argument forms.

Recall that by "form," we mean any COMMON LISP data object meant to be evaluated. For instance, in (* pi (expt 7 2)), the area of a circle whose radius is 7 units, the first argument form is a symbol and the second is a list both of whose argument forms are numbers.

Exercises

8.1 *(i)* How does LISP respond to giving cons a symbol instead of a list as its second argument; for example, (cons 'a 'b)? This value is another LISP object called a *dotted pair*, which is not used much. For the time being, if you see a dotted pair it will be because you have made a mistake.

8.2 *(i)* Compare your LISP's response to (cons 'a (cons 'b 'c)) with its response to (cons 'a (cons 'b '())). The former, sometimes called a *dotted list,* is not a true list because it was built on a symbol other than nil. Again, for the time being,

---

[3]The order in which the argument forms are evaluated can vary in different implementations of COMMON LISP.

if you ever see a dotted list it will be because you have made a mistake.

8.3 *(r)* Try all the interactions of this chapter for yourself.

8.4 *(d)* Using only the function cons, the quoted empty list '(), strings, numbers, and quoted symbols, type forms to the LISP listener that evaluate to each of the lists that appear in this chapter.

8.5 *(i)* Check LISP's value of (type-of '(1 2 3)) and of (type-of '()). COMMON LISP divides objects of type list into the empty list and objects of type cons. Conses are all nonempty lists (those constructed by the use of cons).

8.6 *(i)* While COMMON LISP is reading a top-level form that you are typing, the symbol * is bound to the last value LISP typed back and the symbol ** is bound to the second to the last value. Therefore, you can try applying a sequence of functions to the same argument without always retyping the argument form by doing this sort of thing:

```
> '(a b c)
(A B C)
> (first *)
A
> **
(A B C)
> (first (rest *))
B
> **
(A B C)
> (first (rest (rest *))))
C
```

Try this for yourself.

8.7 *(d)* Using the technique of Exercise 8.6 and the functions you learned in this chapter, type forms that evaluate to each of the symbols in the list (((a b) (c d) e) (f g) (h) i).

CHAPTER 9

THE SPECIAL FORM QUOTE

We have been using the quote mark, as in 'a or '(1 2 3), since Chapter 3. Actually, the quote mark is an abbreviation of a use of the LISP function quote, which is a different kind of function from those we have discussed so far. quote is a *special form*. Special forms are special in that their argument forms are given to them unevaluated and they control the evaluation of their argument forms themselves. quote is rather simple. It returns its unevaluated argument form as is—unevaluated.

(quote *f*) Returns the unevaluated form *f* unevaluated.

Note that the effect is just what you're used to. For any S-expression *s*, the value of (quote *s*) is the LISP object represented by *s*. (quote a) is exactly equivalent to 'a. '(1 2 3) is exactly equivalent to (quote (1 2 3)).

Exercises

9.1 *(r)* Enter 'a and (quote a). Note the equivalence.

9.2 *(r)* Enter '(1 2 3) and (quote (1 2 3)). Note the equivalence.

9.3 *(d)* Enter (quote 5e2), '5e2, and 5e2. Note that the value of quote is not the S-expression you type for the argument *as you type it,* but the LISP object *represented by* that S-expression and it is typed back to you in COMMON LISP's choice of printed representation.

9.4 *(d)* Enter (quote '(1 2 3)) and '(quote (1 2 3)). What does your LISP type back?

9.5 *(d)* Enter
'(1 2 '(a b) 3)
and
(quote (1 2 (quote (a b)) 3))

9.6 *(d)* Enter ''a and (quote (quote a)). Did you predict what happened?

Part II

PROGRAMMING IN PURE LISP

CHAPTER 10

DEFINING YOUR OWN FUNCTIONS

Although there are quite a few functions provided by the COMMON LISP system (some say that there are too many), you will want to define your own. Indeed, a LISP program is nothing but a collection of functions written by the LISP programmer.

To define a function, you use the special form **defun**:

(**defun** *fn varlist doc-string form*)

fn must be a symbol.

varlist must be an empty list or a list of symbols.

doc-string must be a string.

form can be any COMMON LISP form.

None of these are evaluated. **defun** returns *fn*, but its main use is that it has the side effect of defining *fn* to be the name of a function whose formal arguments are the symbols in *varlist*, whose definition is *form*, and whose documentation string is *doc-string*.

In LISP terminology, we call the formal arguments of a function *lambda variables*. This has historical significance because of the influence of A. Church's Lambda Calculus in the design of LISP. You may see the symbol **lambda** as part of your COMMON LISP's printed representation of functions, but we will not discuss this in too much detail.

Let's consider an example:

```
> (defun list3 (o1 o2 o3)
    "Returns a list of its three arguments in order."
    (cons o1 (cons o2 (cons o3 '()))))
LIST3
```

This has the effect of defining the function list3, which takes three LISP objects as arguments and returns a list whose members are those objects. After evaluating this defun, we can use list3 just as if it were a built-in LISP function:

```
> (list3 'a (cons 'b '()) 'c)
(A (B) C)
```

The documentation string provides documentation that can be retrieved from the function name with the COMMON LISP function documentation:

```
> (documentation 'list3 'function)
"Returns a list of its three arguments in order."
```

The choice of the symbols o1, o2, and o3 for the lambda variables of list3 is completely arbitrary. We could have chosen almost any three symbols, but nil and t, in particular, would have been very bad choices.

The steps in the evaluation of a list were summarized on page 57. Now that we have seen a programmer-defined function, we can give more details (almost all COMMON LISP functions are defined in LISP, so this really does apply to more than just programmer-defined functions).

When a function is called—that is, when LISP is asked to evaluate a list—the following happens:

1. LISP checks that the first member of the list is a symbol that is the name of a function.

2. The argument forms are evaluated (not necessarily left to right).

3. The values of the argument forms become the values of the corresponding lambda variables. (We say that the variables are *bound to* the values of the arguments.)

4. The form in the definition of the function is evaluated.

5. The lambda variables are unbound—returned to their previous states.

6. The value of the form in the definition becomes the value of the original form.

Let us follow the evaluation of (list3 'a (cons 'b '()) 'c) through the process:

1. list3 is a symbol that is the name of a function.

2. 'a evaluates to A, (cons 'b '()) to (B), and 'c to C.

3. o1 is bound to A, o2 to (B), and o3 to C.

4. (cons o1 (cons o2 (cons o3 '()))) is evaluated. Note that the symbols o1, o2, and o3 have values during this evaluation. The value of this form is (A (B) C).

5. o1, o2, and o3 return to their previous values (possibly none).

6. (A (B) C) is returned as the value of

$$(list3 \ 'a \ (cons \ 'b \ '()) \ 'c)$$

This is the first time that we have seen a symbol get a new value. *The primary method by which a symbol gets a value is to be bound as a lambda variable.* We should not use t or nil as lambda variables because we always want them to have themselves as values.

For another example of a programmer-defined function, let's define a function to interchange the two members of a two-member list:

```
> (defun switch (l)
    "Given a two-member list, returns a list just like it,
     but with the two members interchanged."
    (list2 (second l) (first l)))
SWITCH
```

In this definition, I've used a function named list2 and one named second even though I've never before said that such functions are available in COMMON LISP. This doesn't matter, because *we can use*

an undefined function in the definition of a function, as long as we
define it before actually calling it. The functions list2 and second
are just so obviously clear and useful in this context that it makes
sense to define switch this way and worry about defining list2 and
second later. It turns out that second is already defined in COMMON
LISP, but list2 isn't; so let's define it:

```
> (defun list2 (o1 o2)
    "Returns a list of its two arguments in order."
    (cons o1 (cons o2 '()))))
LIST2
```

We've now written a short program consisting of two functions, one
of which uses the other. We must test this program. One of the
beauties of LISP is that we can test programs "bottom up." That
is, it's a good idea to make sure that list2 works properly before
testing switch, because if list2 doesn't work, then surely switch
won't either. In most other programming languages, it is easy to run
a main program, but difficult to test a subprogram. In LISP, any
function can be tested directly from top-level LISP, and any form that
appears in a function definition may be evaluated directly by the top-
level listener, as long as you replace each lambda variable in it (or each
form that contains lambda variables) by sample values. So let's test
list2:

```
> (list2 (second '(a b)) (first '(a b)))
(B A)
> (list2 'b 'a)
(B A)
```

Now we can test switch:

```
> (switch '(a b))
(B A)
```

You could also do top-down testing, since the only effect of calling
an undefined function is to put you into the debugger. Some debuggers
will provide an easy way to specify the value the function call would
have returned, so you can simulate the undefined function, and go on
testing the other functions. Other debuggers make this process a bit
harder. In general, I advise bottom-up testing.

Exercises

10.1 *(r)* Define the function list3 as given in this chapter, and test it on several different groups of arguments.

10.2 *(r)* Check the values of o1, o2, and o3 both before and after a call to list3. Notice that, even though they have values within list3, they have no values either before or after.

10.3 *(i)* Define switch as given in this chapter and try it out *before* defining list2. The error occurs when LISP tries to evaluate the form (list2 (second l) (first l)). You should now make sure you know how to find the value to which the lambda variable l is bound. The method differs among implementations of COMMON LISP. It may be that the value of l was printed as part of the error message. (This is the case on the Texas Instruments Explorer Lisp Machine.) Chances are that you cannot find out merely by typing l to the debugger listener, because of various efficiencies used by COMMON LISP implementations to store the values of lambda variables. However, there should be something you can type to your LISP to make it tell you. For example, if you are using a Texas Instruments Explorer Lisp Machine, you can just read it in the error message or enter (eh-arg 0). If you are using Kyoto COMMON LISP, you enter :vv. If it is not obvious, see if your LISP has a help facility you can use in the debugger. If so, you will probably be told there. As a last resort, ask your instructor or a more experienced friend. After learning how to find the value of the lambda arguments, write the method here and in Appendix B.2:

_____.

Get out of the debugger and back to the top-level listener.

10.4 *(r)* Now define list2, test list2, and test switch again.

10.5 *(i)* You can observe LISP evaluating a set of functions by using the trace package. This consists of the two special forms **trace** and untrace. (trace $fn_1 \ldots fn_k$) turns on the tracing of functions $fn_1, \ldots, fn_k$. (untrace $fn_1 \ldots fn_k$) turns them off. Evaluate (trace switch first second list2) and (switch '(a b)). Note that when each function is called, its arguments are printed

and when it returns, its value is printed. Also note that each trace
print is labelled and/or indented so you can tell which value goes
with which call. Now evaluate

(untrace switch first second list2)

and (switch '(a b)) again. The tracing has been turned off.

10.6 *(i)* Try giving switch argument lists with fewer than two members and with more than two members. Make sure you understand why the values are what they are. Peculiar results are acceptable when the argument forms do not satisfy the conditions
spelled out in the documentation string, but we will see later how
we can get LISP to test these conditions for us.

10.7 *(d)* Redefine list3 using list2 and cons.

10.8 *(d)* Define the function list1 to be a function that takes one
argument and returns a list with the value of that argument as
its only member.

10.9 *(d)* Redefine list2 using list1 and cons.

10.10 *(d)* Test list3 while tracing list1, list2, and list3. Notice
that although you didn't redefine list3, it now uses your new
version of list2.

10.11 *(d)* Define the functions list4 through list10, each taking the
obvious number of arguments and returning a list of their values.
Each definition need be no longer than your current definition of
list2. Use the tracing facility to watch some of these in action.

10.12 *(i)* The COMMON LISP function list takes an arbitrary number
of arguments and returns a list of all of them. Try this function
with various numbers of arguments.

10.13 *(d)* Redefine switch to use list, and test this version.

10.14 *(d)* Define the function (sqr n) to return the square of the number n.

10.15 *(i)* COMMON LISP has the function third, which takes a list and
returns the third member of it. Try this out.

10.16 *(d)* Using **first**, **second**, **third**, and **list**, define the function
(**reverse3** l) to return the reverse of the three-member list, l.
For example, (**reverse3** '(a b c)) should evaluate to (C B A).

10.17 *(i)* You now know that COMMON LISP has the functions **first**,
second, and **third**. How many functions in this sequence are
defined?

CHAPTER 11

DEFINING FUNCTIONS IN PACKAGES

Recall from Chapter 7 that packages are used to enable teams of programmers to cooperate in building large COMMON LISP systems. By using different packages, different programmers can use symbols with the same names to name different functions. For example, programmers Bill and Sally may each want to define a function named main-function. If Bill defines all his functions in the bill package, and Sally defines all her functions in the sally package, Bill can have a function with the fully qualified name of bill::main-function, Sally can have a function with the fully qualified name of sally::main-function, and each can refer to his or her function within his or her own package as simply main-function. If Bill and Sally both export their main-function symbols, other programmers may choose to import either bill:main-function or sally:main-function and refer to that one as main-function.

Even if you will be the only person ever using the functions you define, you should consider yourself to be a member of a team of programmers building a large COMMON LISP system; the other members of the team are the people who wrote the implementation of COMMON LISP that you are using. You may not want to avoid using a certain symbol to name a function merely because a symbol with the same name was used for one of the many predefined COMMON LISP functions, and if you do use that symbol, you do not want to redefine the COMMON LISP function for fear of changing COMMON LISP. We will develop a particular programming style to make all this easy to do. In this chapter, we will experiment with the style. In the next chapter, we will see how to make it a habit.

First of all, make up a new package for defining your functions. Leave the lisp package for predefined COMMON LISP functions and the user package for using your functions and the predefined functions.[1] For now, let's say you will define your functions in the learn package. To define a function—say, a function named fn—do the following:

1. Go into the learn package.

2. Using describe, see if fn is a symbol inherited from another package.

3. If it is, shadow it. (See Exercise 7.4.)

4. Use describe again to make sure that fn is now a symbol in the learn package.

5. Define the fn function.

6. Test your fn function, using its unqualified name.

7. Check that the original fn function is still available, using its qualified name.

8. If your fn function is to be used outside the learn package, export your fn symbol.

In the following interaction, I will use this method to define last as a function that returns the third member of a three-member list, even though last is already used by COMMON LISP to name a different function.

---

[1]Recall that the new standard calls these packages common-lisp and common-lisp-user.

```
> (in-package 'learn)
#<Package LEARN 52200250>

> (describe 'last)
Symbol LAST is in LISP package.
 It is also interned in package GLOBAL
The function definition of LAST is
#<DTP-FUNCTION LAST 11424543>: (LIST)

> (shadow 'last)
T

> (describe 'last)
Symbol LAST is in LEARN package.
It has no value, definition or properties

> (defun last (l)
    "Returns the third element of a list
     that has three or more elements."
    (third l))
LAST

> (last '(a b c))
C

>(lisp:last '(a b c))
(C)

> (export 'last)
T

> (in-package 'user)
#<Package USER 2150061>

> (learn:last '(a b c d e))
C

> (lisp:last '(a b c d e))
(E)
```

In this book, we will often define our own versions of predefined
COMMON LISP functions as a way of studying what they do and how
they do it. So we will be using this technique often.

Some otherwise knowledgeable LISPers have gotten confused by a
subtlety in the use of packages when defining functions to compare
symbols. Say we wish to define the function isqmark to recognize a
question mark, and we want to define it in our learn package:

```
> (in-package 'learn)
LEARN

> (describe 'isqmark)
Symbol ISQMARK is in LEARN package.
It has no value, definition or properties

> (defun isqmark (o)
    "Returns True if O is the question mark symbol;
     False otherwise."
    (eql o '?))
ISQMARK

> (isqmark '?)
T

> (isqmark 'foo)
NIL
```

Now, say we want to export isqmark and use it in the user package:

```
> (export 'isqmark)
T

> (in-package 'user)
#<Package USER 2150061>

> (learn:isqmark '?)
NIL
```

The problem is really simple. When we defined isqmark, we were in the
learn package, so we actually defined it to return True if the argument

were `learn::?`. Now that we are testing `learn:isqmark` in the **user** package, we give it the argument `user::?`, which, of course is not the same symbol as `learn::?`. A quick test will show that `learn:isqmark` is really working correctly:

```
> (learn:isqmark 'learn::?)
T
```

What was probably intended for `isqmark` was not to recognize the symbol ? since there can be many such symbols, but to recognize *any* symbol whose print name is "?". If this was what was meant, it can be defined easily:

```
> (in-package 'learn)
#<Package LEARN 4434433>

> (defun isqmark (s)
    "Returns True if symbol S has the same name as '?;
     False otherwise."
    (string= (symbol-name s) "?"))
ISQMARK

> (isqmark '?)
T

> (in-package 'user)
#<Package USER 2150061>

> (learn:isqmark '?)
T
```

Exercises

11.1 *(r)* Try the interaction of this chapter for yourself. Be sure to do everything in exactly the same order as given here.

11.2 *(d)* Using the style of this chapter, define **reverse** to return the reverse of a four-member list. That is, (**reverse** '(a b c d)) should evaluate to (D C B A).

11.3 *(d)* Using the style of this chapter and the arithmetic functions you learned in Chapter 4, define and test the function (discrim a b c) to take three numbers $a, b,$ and c and return $\sqrt{(b^2 - 4ac)}$.

11.4 *(d)* Also in the **learn** package, define and test the function (quad-roots a b c), which returns a list of the two roots of the quadradic equation $ax^2 + bx + c = 0$:

$$\left(\frac{-b + \sqrt{(b^2 - 4ac)}}{2a} \quad \frac{-b - \sqrt{(b^2 - 4ac)}}{2a} \right)$$

See Exercises 4.15 and 4.16 for a specific numerical example. Be sure to use the **discrim** function where appropriate. Also make sure that **quad-roots** returns a list of two elements rather than a dotted pair (see Exercise 8.1).

CHAPTER 12

SAVING FOR ANOTHER DAY

So far, all your typing of LISP S-expressions has been directly to the top-level LISP listener. If you defined a function and found that you had made a mistake in it, you had to type it all in again. You also couldn't define a function and save it for another session. Both these problems are solved by typing your function definitions into a *file*. You can use a normal text file, editing it with the same editor that you use to type letters, papers, electronic mail, or programs in any other programming language. However, there are certain benefits if you use a special editor that is provided with your COMMON LISP or an Emacs editor such as GNU Emacs.[1] I will describe these benefits below.

Once you type a series of **defun** forms into some file, you should save it. First, you must choose a *name* for the file; on many systems, you must also choose an *extension.* The name can be any sequence of letters followed by digits. (Most systems have more complicated naming rules and allow other characters, but since these rules differ, let's use this one.) Let's say you choose **myfunctions** as the name of your file. The extension, if required by your system, will be the same

---

[1]Available from Free Software Foundation, 1000 Massachusetts Avenue, Cambridge, MA 02138, U.S.A.

for all LISP source files. Let's say the extension is `lisp`. There will also be a separator character between the name and the extension. This is often the period, so we'll use that. That makes the name of your file `myfunctions.lisp`. How you save a file depends on the editor you use.

You can choose to load your source file into COMMON LISP and use the functions defined there in "interpreted mode," or you can *compile* the file, load the compiled version into COMMON LISP, and use the compiled versions of the functions. Generally, compiled functions use less time and space to execute, but can be more difficult to debug. Therefore, you should debug the interpreted versions of your functions until you are quite confident of them. Then you should compile the file and use the compiled versions for efficiency. Often, you will find more bugs when you compile your file: the compiler will give you error messages and warnings. You should not consider your programming task complete until you have compiled your file without error messages or warnings. The compiler will automatically give the compiled version of your file the same name as your source file and a standard extension that is different from the standard extension of LISP source files.

Once you've saved your file, you can get the functions defined in it into your LISP by executing the form `(load "myfunctions")`.

(`load` *filename*) Reads the file whose name is given by the string *filename* and evaluates all the top-level forms in it. If *filename* contains an extension, that file will be read. Otherwise, `load` will either read the file whose name is given by *filename* and whose extension is the standard LISP source extension, or it will read the file whose name is given by *filename* and whose extension is the standard LISP compiled file extension, whichever is more recent.

If your system organizes its files as a directory hierarchy, then there will be a way for you to specify a "full path name" for your file that is system-dependent.

Once you've loaded your function definitions, you can test them. If you need to alter a function definition, return to the editor, edit your file, save it again, load it again, and continue testing. Modern LISP development environments, containing either a special LISP editor or an Emacs-type editor, make this process much easier.

If you have a modern LISP development environment, you will be able to do the following:

- Divide your screen into two windows, with an active editor open to your LISP source file running in one window and an active COMMON LISP listener running in the other.

- Move your cursor into the editor window and type and edit **defun** forms.

- Either copy a form from the editor window into the COMMON LISP window and evaluate it there, or directly evaluate a **defun** form in the editor window so that the function is defined in the environment of the COMMON LISP window.

- Move your cursor into the COMMON LISP window and interact with COMMON LISP as you've become used to; in particular, to test the functions defined in the file appearing in the editor window.

- Move your cursor into the editor window and save the file there. This need be done only every half hour or so, or just before terminating your session.

This process is the standard method experienced LISPers use to develop their LISP programs.

Certain standard styles are recommended when writing COMMON LISP source files:

defun forms: The first opening parenthesis of each **defun** form starts at the first character position of a line. The other lines are indented to show the structure of the form. Many editors will do the indenting automatically or semiautomatically.

Comments: Comments are preceded by the comment character ; and extend to the rest of the line. There are three levels of comments:

  - Comments outside any function definition start with ; ; ; and begin in the first character position on the line.

  - Comments inside a function definition, on their own line, start with ; ; and are indented with the rest of the definition.

  - Comments on the same line as LISP code begin with ; and are to the right of the LISP code.

Packaging details: Typically, each file will define functions in a separate package. It is helpful if the beginning of each of your files looks like the following:

```
;;; Establish the default package
;;; for symbols read in this file.
(in-package 'package-name)

;;; Shadow any symbols from automatically inherited
;;; packages that have the same names as symbols
;;; in this package.
(shadow '(symbol₁, symbol₂ ...))

;;; Shadow and import any symbols from other packages
;;; that are to be available as internal symbols
;;; in this package, but whose names conflict with
;;; symbols from automatically inherited packages.
(shadowing-import '(symbol₁, symbol₂ ...))

;;; Specify any packages all of whose external
;;; symbols are to be accessible
;;; as internal symbols in this package.
(use-package '(package-name₁, package-name₂ ...))

;;; Explicitly import any other symbols that are to
;;; be accessible as internal symbols
;;; in this package.
(import '(symbol₁, symbol₂ ...))

;;; Export the symbols from this package that are to
;;; be accessible to other packages.
(export '(symbol₁, symbol₂ ...))
```

Under the new COMMON LISP standard, you will be able to do this using the function **defpackage** as follows:

```
(defpackage package-name

    (:shadow symbol-names)

    (:shadowing-import-from package-name symbol-names)
```

$\vdots$

(:shadowing-import-from *package-name symbol-names*)

(:use *package-names*)

(:import-from *package-name symbol-names*)

$\vdots$

(:import-from *package-name symbol-names*)

(:export *symbol-names*))

(in-package *package-name*)

Exercises

12.1 *(p1)* Begin a file named **match**. Set it up so that the functions in it will be defined in the **match** package.

12.2 *(p1)* In your **match** file, define a function **variablep** that takes one symbol as an argument and returns T if the first character of the symbol's name is #\? and returns NIL otherwise. If you have a modern LISP development environment, develop and test this function using the two-window approach described in this chapter.

12.3 *(i)* Compile your **match** file by evaluating the form (**compile-file** "match").

12.4 *(i)* Load your **match** file using the **load** function. Can you tell that you've loaded the compiled file instead of the source file? Test **variablep** again.

12.5 *(p2)* Begin a file named **calculator**. Set it up so that the functions in it will be defined in the **calculator** package.

12.6 *(p2)* In your **calculator** file, define the function **combine-expr** to take an arithmetic operator, an operand, and a list representing an arithmetic expression and return the expression with the operator and operand applied to the first member of the expression. For example, (**combine-expr** '+ 3 '(5 - 6 * 8)) should evaluate to ((3 + 5) - 6 * 8).

CHAPTER 13

PREDICATE FUNCTIONS

Predicate functions are functions that return either True, represented by LISP as T, or False, represented by LISP as NIL. The predicate functions that we have seen so far are the equality functions =, char=, string=, eql, and equal.

Another basic set of predicate functions are those that check the type of their arguments. The names of these functions are typically formed from the type followed by the letter p. Some type-checking functions for the types we have seen so far are numberp, integerp, floatp, characterp, symbolp, stringp, packagep, and listp. Each one returns T if its argument is of the proper type and NIL if it isn't. For example:

```
> (numberp 5)
T
> (integerp 5)
T
> (floatp 5)
NIL
> (characterp "a")
NIL
> (stringp "a")
T
```

```
> (symbolp '\5)
T
> (packagep (in-package 'test))
T

> (listp "a list?")
NIL
> (listp '(a list?))
T
```

To compare numbers, COMMON LISP has the standard set of numeric predicates including < and >, as well as =, which we've seen before.

To combine the results of predicate functions, COMMON LISP has the logic operators **and** and **or**. Like the arithmetic operators +, -, *, and /, **and** and **or** take an arbitrary number of arguments. However, **and** and **or** are special in that they don't always evaluate all their argument forms; they stop as soon as they can definitely determine the final answer:

(**and** *forms*) Takes an arbitrary number of argument *forms* and evaluates them one at a time left to right. As soon as one of them evaluates to False, returns False. If none of them evaluates to False, returns True.

(**or** *forms*) Takes an arbitrary number of argument *forms* and evaluates them one at a time left to right. As soon as one of them evaluates to True, returns True. If none of them evaluates to True, returns False.

The fact that **and** and **or** stop as soon as they determine their answer is not only useful for saving computer time; it is extremely useful if an error would result from blindly evaluating all the arguments. For example:

- Dividing by zero would produce an error, but the form
  (or (= y 0) (> (/ x y) 100)) will always return T if x/y is greater than 100, even if $y = 0$.

- It is an error to apply **length** to any argument type we know about so far except for strings and lists, but the form

```
(and (or (stringp x) (listp x)) (> (length x) 5))
```

will always return T or NIL without producing an error.

Even with the few predicates mentioned so far, we can define many additional functions, as should be clear from the complicated forms in the previous examples. In particular, we can define other simple and useful functions such as <=:

```
(defun <= (x y)
  "Returns T if the first number is less than or equal to
   the second number; NIL otherwise."
  (or (< x y) (= x y)))
```

Notice that this function will cause an error if x or y is not a number. COMMON LISP provides a way to test that lambda variables are bound to objects of the proper type. For now, this is all right because the documentation clearly says that the two arguments must be numbers, and we would not want to confuse a value of NIL meaning that one of the arguments was not a function with NIL meaning that the first number is greater than the second. Later we will see how to produce our own error messages.

Exercises

13.1 *(r)* Try out numberp, integerp, floatp, characterp, symbolp, stringp, packagep, and listp. Be sure to try each with a variety of arguments. In particular, try out the interaction shown at the beginning of this chapter. At the end of these tests, you should be in the test package.

13.2 *(r)* To impress upon yourself the fact that and evaluates its argument forms in order and only until a final answer is evident, evaluate (and nil nil nil), (and nil t nil), (and foo nil), (and nil foo), (and t foo), and (and foo t).

13.3 *(r)* To impress upon yourself the fact that or evaluates its argument forms in order and only until a final answer is evident, evaluate (or t t t), (or t nil t), (or foo t), (or t foo), (or nil foo), and (or foo nil).

13.4 *(d)* Define a function that takes two numbers x and y and returns T if $x/y > 100$, and NIL otherwise. Test your function. It should work even if $y = 0$.

13.5 *(d)* Define a function that takes any LISP object and returns T if the object is a string containing more than five characters or a list containing more than five members. Test your function with various arguments.

13.6 *(d)* Make sure you are in the **test** package. In that package, define the function <= as shown in this chapter. Before you do, however, check that lisp:<= is an inherited symbol in the **test** package, and shadow it. Test your <= function. Compare it with lisp:<=. In particular, try both on three or more arguments. We will discuss how to define functions that take an arbitrary number of arguments in Chapter 20.

13.7 *(i)* NIL is such an important symbol that LISP has a special predicate to recognize it, called **null**. Try defining **null** in the **test** package; remember to shadow lisp:null. The value of (null object) should return T if object is NIL and NIL otherwise.

13.8 *(i)* What is the value of (listp '())? Of (listp 'nil)? Remember that '(), 'nil, (), and nil are all the same.

13.9 *(i)* Define a function (in the **test** package) that returns T if its argument is a nonempty list and NIL otherwise. LISP calls this function lisp:consp because it is the recognizer of just those objects that are returned by calls to **cons**. Make sure that your function does not cause an error regardless of the type of its argument.

13.10 *(i)* We discussed **and** and **or** in this chapter. Define **not** (in the **test** package, shadowing lisp:not) to return T when its argument is NIL, and NIL when its argument is T. Compare your **not** with your **null**. Compare them with lisp:not. Try giving them an argument that is neither T nor NIL.

13.11 *(i)* COMMON LISP defines the function (atom object) to be (not (consp object)). Test **atom** on various arguments. Does COMMON LISP consider a string to be an atom?

13.12 *(u)* In this book, we will use the terms *element* or *elemental object* to mean those LISP objects that are testable with `eql`; that is, symbols, characters, numbers, and packages.[1] (Remember, `eql` will say that two numbers are the same only if they have the same value and are of the same type.) Define the function `elementp` to return True if its argument is an element by this definition. Put this definition in a file named `util`, in which all symbols will be in the `util` package. Make `elementp` an external symbol in that package.

13.13 *(p1)* In your file `match`, which you began for Exercise 12.1, define the function (`match-element e1 e2`) to return T if its two arguments are `eql` or if either of them is a variable as recognized by `match::variablep`.

13.14 *(p1)* Can you use `match-element` to compare two numbers? Try (`match-element 5 5`) and (`match-element 5 6`). Modify `variablep` so that it returns `NIL` if its argument is not a symbol, instead of causing an error.

---

[1]The COMMON LISP standard does not actually say that packages may be compared with `eql`, but that seems to be the case.

CHAPTER 14

CONDITIONAL EXPRESSIONS

One of the two most powerful features of any programming language is the *conditional*—a way of saying, "*if* this *then* that *else* this other." COMMON LISP has two principal conditionals, if and cond.

(if *test then else*) If *test* evaluates to True, returns the value of *then*; otherwise, returns the value of *else*. For example:

```
> (if t 'yes 'no)
YES
> (if nil 'yes 'no)
NO
```

Just as **and** and **or** don't evaluate all their arguments when they can determine their answers early, if never evaluates all its arguments. It always evaluates the *test* argument, but then either evaluates the *then* argument or the *else* argument, whichever will determine the value of the if form. For example, the form

```
(if (= y 0) 9999999999 (/ x y))
```

89

will return the value of x/y if y is not zero and the large number 9,999,999,999 if $y = 0$ and will not produce an error in either case.

A simple function that we can define using if is:

```
(defun absval (n)
  "Returns the absolute value of the argument,
   which must be a number."
  (if (< n 0) (- n) n))
```

The function if is very convenient if you want to choose one of two possible computations based on a single test, but for multiple tests and more than two choices, it gets cumbersome. For example, the function sign, which returns -, 0, or + depending on the sign of its argument, can be written using if, but it looks like this:

```
(defun sign (n)
  "Takes a numeric argument
   and returns - if it is negative,
   0 if it is zero, and + if it is positive."
  (if (< n 0)
        '-
      (if (= n 0) 0 '+)))
```

For multiple tests and the choice of one of three or more computations, COMMON LISP has the function cond:

(cond $(p_1\ e_1)$ ... $(p_n\ e_n)$) Evaluates the p_i in order until one of them, p_j say, evaluates to True. Then returns the value of e_j. If no p_i evaluates to True, returns NIL.

Each list $(p_i\ e_i)$ is called a cond *pair*. The first member of a cond pair is called its *test, predicate,* or *condition.* The second member of a cond pair is called its *expression* or *then* part. Notice that

- At most one *then* part will be evaluated.

- No *test* will be evaluated after the first one that evaluates to True.

- The value of a cond form is always the value of the last form within it that is evaluated.

Using cond, we can write a much clearer version of sign:

```
(defun sign (n)
  "Takes a numeric argument
   and returns - if it is negative,
   0 if it is zero, and + if it is positive."
  (cond ((< n 0) '-)
        ((= n 0) 0)
        ((> n 0) '+)))
```

Notice that the double open parentheses at the beginning of each cond pair are there because the first is the open parenthesis of the cond pair itself and the second is the open parenthesis of the test form.

In most programming languages, if-then-else is a kind of statement. In LISP, cond (as well as if) is an expression, but it is like if-then-else. Notice the similarity:

```
if b1 then s1            (cond (p1 e1)
else if b2 then s2             (p2 e2)
else if b3 then s3             (p3 e3)
else s4                        (t  e4))
```

Since t always evaluates to True, if p1, p2, and p3 evaluate to NIL, the value of the cond form will be the value of e4, just as s4 will be executed if b1, b2, and b3 are false.

Exercises

Do the exercises of this chapter in the package ch14.

14.1 *(r)* Check LISP's value of (if t 'yes 'no) and (if nil 'yes 'no).

14.2 *(d)* Using if, define a function that takes two numbers x and y, and returns x/y if $y \neq 0$, but returns the number 9,999,999,999 if $y = 0$. It should not cause an error message in either case.

14.3 *(r)* Define absval as given in this chapter. Try it out with positive and negative integers, with floating-point numbers, and with zero.

14.4 *(r)* Define and test sign using if.

14.5 *(r)* Define and test sign using cond.

14.6 *(r)* Define and test `absval` using `cond`.

14.7 *(p1)* In your `match` file, define the function `dont-care` to return True if its argument is a question-mark symbol and `NIL` in any other case. You might want to review the discussion of `isqmark` that starts on page 74. Make sure that (`dont-care 5`) returns `NIL` rather than causing an error.

14.8 *(p1)* Also in your `match` file, redefine (`match-element e1 e2`) so that it returns True if the two arguments are `eql` or either argument is `?`; if either argument is a variable (as recognized by `variablep`), `match-element` should return a two-member list whose first member is the variable and whose second member is the other argument; otherwise, `match-element` should return `NIL`. Some test examples are

```
> (match-element 'a 'a)
T
> (match-element 'a '?)
T
> (match-element '? 'a)
T
> (match-element 'a '?x)
(?X A)
> (match-element '?x 'a)
(?X A)
> (match-element 'a 'b)
NIL
```

Save this new version of the file.

CHAPTER 15

RECURSION

At the beginning of Chapter 14, I said that one of the two most powerful features of any programming language is the *conditional*. The other is a method for repeating a computation over and over until some condition is found. This gives us a lot of computation for a relatively small amount of text. One such method is called *recursion*.

The definition of a LISP function contains a form. The first element of the form also names a function. Some arguments of the form may be embedded forms, which also involve functions. We say that these functions are *used by* the function being defined, or that the function being defined *uses* these functions. For example, the function `absval`, defined on page 90, uses the functions < and -. A function that uses itself is called a *recursive function*. The use of recursive functions is called *recursion*.

Does it make sense to use a function in its own definition? Sure! Remember what I said on pages 65–66: *we can use an undefined function in the definition of a function, as long as we define it before actually calling it.* When we define a function using itself, it is undefined only until we finish the definition. By the time we call it, it is already defined. So everything is OK.

To continue the discussion, let's look at an example. We will define addition using only the most primitive arithmetic functions. These are (zerop *n*) Equivalent to (= *n* 0).

(1+ *n*) Equivalent to (+ *n* 1).

(1- *n*) Equivalent to (- *n* 1).

Using only these three functions (plus **defun** and **if**), let's define the
function **sum** to be a function that returns the sum of two nonnegative
integers:

```
(defun sum (n1 n2)
  "Returns the sum of two nonnegative integers."
  (if (zerop n1) n2
      (sum (1- n1) (1+ n2))))
```

Let's trace the evaluation of (sum 3 5):

```
> (trace sum)
(SUM)

> (sum 3 5)
(1 ENTER SUM: 3 5)
  (2 ENTER SUM: 2 6)
    (3 ENTER SUM: 1 7)
      (4 ENTER SUM: 0 8)
      (4 EXIT SUM: 8)
    (3 EXIT SUM: 8)
  (2 EXIT SUM: 8)
(1 EXIT SUM: 8)
8
```

Evaluating (sum 3 5) causes the evaluation of (sum 2 6), which
causes the evaluation of (sum 1 7), which causes the evaluation of
(sum 0 8), which finally returns 8. What if we evaluated (sum 10000
100)? The rather short definition of **sum** would cause a lot of computation.

Each call of **sum** causes another, recursive, call of **sum**, until finally
sum is called with a first argument of 0. This causes a value to be
returned, and the computation terminates. When defining a recursive
function, we must make sure that, for every intended set of arguments,
the computation will eventually terminate. A recursive function whose

evaluation never terminates is called *infinitely recursive*. The process is called *infinite recursion*. If you ask LISP to evaluate a form that causes infinite recursion, LISP will not return to you until it encounters a time or space limit, or you get tired of waiting and press the interrupt key. If you never press the interrupt key, your entire LISP session might be terminated by the operating system. Needless to say, defining an infinitely recursive function is a mistake.

It is easy to avoid defining an infinitely recursive function if you observe the standard pattern of recursive function definitions:

1. Every recursive function is of the form

   (defun *fn* *varlist* (cond *cond-pairs*))

   or of the form

   (defun *fn* *varlist* (if *test then else*))

2. The *test* of the first cond pair, or the *test* of the if, always tests for a termination condition.

3. The *then* part of the first cond pair, or the *then* of the if, gives a result that does not require a recursive call of the function being defined.

4. The *then* part of the last cond pair, or the *else* of the if, uses the function being defined.

5. If cond is used, the cond pairs should be in increasing order of the amount of work they might require. (I call this the "law of laziness.") Specifically, all cond pairs that use the function being defined should come after all those that don't.

6. Each recursive call of the function being defined must somehow bring the computation closer to the termination condition.

Our definition of sum obviously satisfies points 1–5. To see that it also satisfies point 6, note that the termination condition is that the first argument is zero, that each time sum is called the first argument is decremented by 1, and that since the first argument is both an integer and positive, repeatedly subtracting 1 from it will eventually cause it to be zero.

Before calling a recursive function, you should be sure that it will terminate. Usually this is fairly easy. Also, it is usually fairly easy to convince yourself that the definition is correct. This involves checking termination, checking that every case is considered, and checking that every case is correct. In our **sum** example, we already checked termination. A nonnegative integer is either zero or it isn't. The test is for whether **n1** is zero, so the only two possible cases are covered by the *then* part and the *else* part. The first case is correct because for any n_2, $0 + n_2 = n_2$, and that is what the *then* part returns. The second case is correct because if a nonnegative integer is not zero, it must be positive, and for any positive n_1 and any n_2, $n_1 + n_2 = (n_1 - 1) + (n_2 + 1)$. Since all cases are handled correctly, our definition of **sum** must be correct!

Although you now know that the **sum** function must be called with a nonnegative integer as its first argument, it is possible that later, when **sum** is incorporated into a large program, it will be called by accident with a negative integer or a nonintegral number. That program will then get into an infinite recursion, and it might not be obvious what has caused it. To protect future users of such a function, Com- mon Lisp allows *assertions* to be put into function definitions between the documentation string and the form that defines the body of the function. The form of an assertion is

(**assert** *assertion* (*variables-to-change*) *string mentioned-variables*)

When the function within which this **assert** appears is called, the form *assertion* is evaluated. If it evaluates to True, nothing happens and the function call takes place normally. However, if *assertion* evaluates to False, an error is forced; LISP prints an error message and gives the user the choice of aborting the computation or replacing the current values of the variables listed as *variables-to-change*. If the user chooses the latter, the function is retried with the new values. The error message printed contains the *string*. Anywhere in the *string* that you want to mention the value of some variable, put ~S and put the variable next in the group of *mentioned-variables*. For example, a reasonable assertion for **sum** is provided in the definition:

```
(defun sum (n1 n2)
  "Returns the sum of two nonnegative integers."
  (assert
    (and (integerp n1) (>= n1 0))
    (n1)
    "N1 must be a nonnegative integer, instead it's ~S."
    n1)
  (assert
    (integerp n2)
    (n2)
    "N2 must be an integer, instead it's ~S."
    n2)
  (if (zerop n1) n2
      (sum (1- n1) (1+ n2)))))
```

Exercises

Do the exercises of this chapter in the package ch15.

15.1 *(r)* Test the functions zerop, 1+, and 1-, each on several different arguments.

15.2 *(r)* Define sum the way it is defined the first time in this chapter. Read it carefully to make sure it is correct. Try it out with several examples. Use at least one example for each case (here, zero and positive), and try the examples in the same order as specified by the "law of laziness."

15.3 *(r)* Trace your function sum and follow it closely while evaluating (sum 3 5). Turn off the trace.

15.4 *(i)* Try sum with some large integers as its first argument. Can you find an integer so large that an error occurs? Write the error message here:

_____.

This is the same error you will get if a function you write is infinitely recursive. The error occurs when a large number (but not an infinite number) of recursive calls have been made.

15.5 *(d)* LISP has probably put you into the debugger. Have LISP tell you the current values of n1 and n2, either by evaluating them or by the technique you learned when doing Exercise 10.3. Their current values are what they are bound to in the most recent call of **sum**.

15.6 *(d)* Get out of the debugger and back to the top-level listener. (See Exercise 1.8.) Notice that the computation is aborted.

15.7 *(i)* Sometimes a computation that we ask LISP to do takes so long that we suspect infinite recursion. In that case, interrupt LISP, get into the debugger, and examine where LISP is and what is happening. In many LISPs, you interrupt a computation by pressing the same interrupt key as used to get into the debugger when the top-level LISP listener is waiting for input (see Chapter 1), but in some LISPs a different interrupt key is used. Once LISP is interrupted, it enters the same debugger you saw in Chapter 1 and in Exercise 15.5 above. There are now two different ways to leave the debugger: jump back to the top level without completing the computation ("abort" the computation), as you did in Exercise 15.6 above, or continue (or "resume") the computation from where it was interrupted. Look in your manual or ask your instructor or a more experienced friend for the following information:

a. The key to interrupt a computation: _____

b. The way to continue a computation after an interruption: ___

c. The way to abort the computation after an interruption: ___

Also write these answers in Appendix B.2.

15.8 *(i)* Try **sum** with a first argument large enough that there is a noticeable time lapse before the value is printed, but not so large that an error is caused. Now do this again, but before LISP prints the value, press the interrupt key. Examine the current values of n1 and n2 to see how far the computation has gone. Leave the debugger by continuing the computation. Check that the answer is correct and has not been affected by the interruption.

15.9 *(i)* Try the same **sum** example, and again press the interrupt key before it finishes. Look at n1 and n2 again. Are you in the same place you were before? (The chances of that are slim.) Now get back to the top level without finishing the computation.

15.10 *(i)* Ask LISP to evaluate (sum -4 3). You are now in an infinite recursion. (What element of the argument that sum terminates has broken down?) Press the interrupt key to see how far LISP has gotten. Return to LISP's top level without finishing the computation (especially since you never would finish).

15.11 *(i)* Redefine sum, using the assertions shown in this chapter. Try (sum -4 3) again. Resume the computation, using 2 as the new value of n1. Try (sum -4 3) again, but this time abort the computation.

15.12 *(i)* Define a different version of sum as follows:

```
(defun sum2 (n1 n2)
  "Returns the sum of two nonnegative integers."
  (assert
    (and (integerp n1) (>= n1 0))
    (n1)
    "N1 must be a nonnegative integer, but it's ~S."
    n1)
  (assert
    (integerp n2)
    (n2)
    "N2 must be an integer, instead it's ~S."
    n2)
  (if (zerop n1) n2
      (1+ (sum2 (1- n1) n2)))))
```

Does sum2 always give the same answer as sum for the same arguments? Trace (sum2 3 5). Note carefully the difference between the ways sum and sum2 compute the answer. sum accumulates its answer in one of its arguments "on the way down" and does no computation "on the way up." sum2 seems to peel apart the problem on the way down, collects a "stack" of computations, and then constructs the answer on the way up. This latter approach is actually more common than the former among recursive functions.

15.13 *(d)* Using only zerop, 1-, and either sum or sum2 (and, of course, defun, cond or if, and assert), define product to be a recursive function that multiplies two nonnegative integers. Make sure that your function works correctly. Trace **product** and your summing function to see how they work together.

15.14 *(d)* Using only **zerop**, **1-**, and **product** (and, of course, ...), define the function (**power n i**) to return the value of n^i assuming that n and i are nonnegative integers. Remember, defining a new function includes designing it, convincing yourself that it will work, typing it into the LISP file, carefully reading it for typing errors, possibly editing it, trying it with an adequate set of examples, and repeating the last three steps until it's correct.

15.15 *(i)* Compile your **sum** function by evaluating (**compile 'sum**), and do Exercise 15.4 again. Many COMMON LISP compilers greatly improve both the time and the space used by recursive functions.

CHAPTER 16

RECURSION ON LISTS, PART 1—ANALYSIS

In the last chapter, we wrote recursive functions that operated on integers. We saw that recursive functions must be written so that every recursive call brings one of the arguments closer to the termination condition. With integers, the termination condition is usually **zerop**, and either **1-** (for positive integers) or **1+** (for negative integers) will always bring an integer closer to zero.

In this chapter, we will start writing recursive functions that operate on lists. The function **rest** will always return a list one member shorter than its argument list. The shortest list is the empty list **()**, so the termination condition for lists is **null**. For our first function, let's write our own version of **length**, which will be limited to lists, but, like **lisp:length**, will return the number of members a list has.

First, we will go into the package **ch16**, and shadow **lisp:length**.

```
> (in-package 'ch16)
#<Package CH16 60277265>

> (shadow 'length)
T
```

Then, we will define **ch16::length**, using the same pattern we used in the last chapter:

Termination condition: The length of () is 0.

Recursive case: The length of a nonnull list is one more than the
length of the rest of the list.

So our definition is

```
(defun length (l)
  "Returns the number of members in the argument list."
  (assert (listp l) (l)
          "L must be a list, instead it is ~S." l)
  (if (null l) 0
      (1+ (length (rest l)))))
```

Notice that this definition will always terminate and that every case
(there are only two) is correct, so the definition must be correct. Let's
try it:

```
> (length '())
0
> (length '(a b c d e))
5
```

There was only one *then* part and one *else* part in length because
length always recurses all the way to the null termination condition.
Often there is a second termination condition that can allow the recursive function to stop before () is reached. This condition usually
involves some property of the first member of the list. A good example
of this is

```
(defun member (obj l)
  "Returns True if OBJ is eql to a member of the list L,
  NIL otherwise."
  (assert (listp l) (l)
          "L must be a list, instead it is ~S." l)
  (cond ((null l) '())
        ((eql obj (first l)) t)
        (t (member obj (rest l)))))
```

This time, we used cond instead of if because there are three possible outcomes, not just two. The basic pattern, however, is the same. The test for () is first because null is always the final termination condition for lists. The only cond pair involving recursion is last. The definition must be correct because it always terminates and every case is correct: o is not a member of an empty list; o is a member of any list whose first member is eql to o; and if the first member of a nonempty list is not eql to o, o is a member of the list if and only if it is a member of the rest of the list. Since a list has only a first part and a rest part, there is no other place for o to hide. (Remember, we do not consider X to be a member of the list ((A) B (C X D) E).)

The execution of member stops as soon as it can return True and returns NIL only when it searches the whole list. Some functions reverse this pattern. Consider:

```
(defun number-listp (l)
  "Returns T if all members of the list L are numbers,
  NIL otherwise."
  (assert (listp l) (l)
          "L must be a list, instead it is ~S." l)
  (cond ((null l) ???????????????)
        ((not (numberp (first l))) nil)
        (t (number-listp (rest l)))))
```

Again, the test for () is first. As soon as we find one member that is not a number, we can return NIL without looking any further. If (first l) is a number, we can return T only if (number-listp (rest l)) is T. But what should we return if l is ()? Is () a list of all numbers? Asked just like that, the answer is not obvious, but consider (number-listp '(5)). Since 5 is a number, the value of (number-listp '(5)) is the value of (number-listp '()). But the value of (number-listp '(5)) *should be* T. Therefore, the value of (number-listp '()) *must be* T. This is a common situation: we want to define a function on lists, but it's not obvious what its value should be for (), so we write it to handle the other cases properly and look at the definition to see what its value should be for (). Our resulting definition is

```
(defun number-listp (l)
  "Returns T if all members of the list L are numbers,
   NIL otherwise."
  (assert (listp l) (l)
          "L must be a list, instead it is ~S." l)
  (cond ((null l) t)
        ((not (numberp (first l))) nil)
        (t (number-listp (rest l)))))
```

The use of (not (numberp ...)) makes this definition awkward. At the cost of bending our rules a bit, we could write

```
(defun number-listp (l)
  "Returns T if all members of the list L are numbers,
   NIL otherwise."
  (assert (listp l) (l)
          "L must be a list, instead it is ~S." l)
  (cond ((null l) t)
        ((numberp (first l)) (number-listp (rest l)))
        (t nil)))
```

This reads so much better that we will stick with it. Considerations of readability often lead us to interchange the last two **cond** pairs, and readability is important because we want our functions to reflect how we think about our problems.

Now let us write a function to test if two lists have the same length. An easy way is

```
(defun same-length1 (l1 l2)
  "Returns T if the lists L1 and L2 have the same length,
   NIL otherwise."
  (assert (listp l1) (l1)
          "L1 must be a list, instead it is ~S." l1)
  (assert (listp l2) (l2)
          "L2 must be a list, instead it is ~S." l2)
  (= (length l1) (length l2)))
```

The trouble with this definition is that both lists must be examined in their entirety. If one list has 5 members and the other has 10,000, this seems like a lot of extra work. Let's try a different version that stops as soon as the shorter list is exhausted. This is the same method you would use to compare two piles of stones if you didn't know how to count. Keep throwing away a pair of stones, one from each pile, until either pile is empty. If the other pile is now empty, both piles had the same number of stones in them. Otherwise, they didn't.

```
(defun same-length2 (l1 l2)
  "Returns T if the lists L1 and L2 have the same length,
  NIL otherwise."
  (assert (listp l1) (l1)
          "L1 must be a list, instead it is ~S." l1)
  (assert (listp l2) (l2)
          "L2 must be a list, instead it is ~S." l2)
  (cond ((null l1) (null l2))
        ((null l2) nil)
        (t (same-length2 (rest l1) (rest l2)))))
```

The only difference between **same-length2** and the pattern we saw earlier is that here we are recursing on two arguments simultaneously. Even though the *then* part of the first **cond** pair is not a constant, it is a form whose evaluation does not involve recursion.

Exercises

Do the exercises of this chapter in the package **ch16**, except where otherwise instructed.

16.1 *(r)* Shadow **lisp:length** and then enter the definition of **length** given in this chapter. Test it with several examples. Trace some small examples.

16.2 *(r)* Try evaluating **(length "abc")**. Observe the error message. Abort the computation. Now do it again, but this time, specify that you want to replace the bad value of L with **'(a b c)**. The correct answer should now be returned.

16.3 *(i)* The form **(check-type** *variable type-specifier***)** may be used in a function definition instead of **assert** if the only assertion to be checked is the type of a variable. For example, in the definition of **length**, instead of the form

```
(assert (listp l) (l)
        "L must be a list, instead it is ~S." l)
```

you may use (check-type l list). Here, the *type-specifier* is the type name list. Redefine length using check-type instead of assert. Try Exercise 16.2 again. From now on, use check-type instead of assert whenever it is more appropriate.

16.4 *(r)* Shadow lisp:member and then enter the definition of member given in this chapter. Test it and trace some examples. Try out (member 'x '((a) b (c x d) e)).

16.5 *(i)* Compare the behavior of ch16::member with that of lisp:member when the first argument is eql to a member of the second argument. LISP actually considers any object other than NIL to represent True, so lisp:member returns a useful value rather than just T when it succeeds. Rewrite ch16::member so that it behaves the way lisp:member does.

16.6 *(i)* Write the function (before *e1 e2 l*) so that it returns True if the element *e1* occurs before the element *e2* in the list *l*. Remember, by "element" I mean an object that can be compared with eql. Since COMMON LISP does not recognize element as a type, we cannot use (check-type a element) to assert that a must be an element, but we can use

```
(check-type a (satisfies util:elementp))
```

where util:elementp is the predicate you defined in the util file for Exercise 13.12. The type-specifier (satisfies *predicate*) is satisfied by any value that satisfies the given *predicate*. You will need to load your util file before trying out the function before. Do not use if or cond in your definition of before, but use member twice.

16.7 *(r)* Enter the definition of number-listp and test it.

16.8 *(r)* Enter the definitions of same-length1 and same-length2. Test them and compare traces.

16.9 *(i)* The COMMON LISP function (time *form*) evaluates *form*, returns what *form* evaluates to, and prints how much time it took for the evaluation of *form*. Use time to compare the running times of same-length1 and same-length2 when one argument has 5 members and the other has 10, and again when one has 5 members and the other has 100.

16.10 *(d)* Define the function (count *e l*) to return the number of times that the element *e* appears as a member of the list *l*. You may have to shadow lisp:count before redefining it. (Hint: Two of three cond pairs will cause recursion.)

16.11 *(d)* Define the function (equal-lelt *l1 l2*), where *l1* and *l2* are lists of elements (all members are elements) and equal-lelt returns T if the corresponding members of *l1* and *l2* are eql, but NIL if they are not. (Hint: In my version, only the third of four cond pairs causes recursion.)

16.12 *(d)* Shadow lisp:nth and then define the function (nth *n l*), where *n* is an integer and *l* is a list, to return the *n*th member of *l*. Compare ch16::nth with lisp:nth.

16.13 *(i)* Define (allbut *n l*), where *n* is an integer and *l* is a list at least *n* members long. allbut should return a list whose members are the members of *l* omitting the first *n*. For example, (allbut 3 '(a b (c d) e f)) should be (E F). COMMON LISP already has the function nthcdr, which works just like allbut. Try nthcdr with several examples.

16.14 *(i)* Define the function (assoc *e al*), where *e* is an element and *al* is a list all of whose members are lists. The function should return the first element of *al* whose first member is eql to *e*. For example:

```
(assoc 'Mary
        '((John black hair brown eyes)
          (Mary blond hair blue eyes)
          (Sue red hair hazel eyes)))
```

should return (MARY BLOND HAIR BLUE EYES). We are treating *al* as an *association list* in that we can *associate* a list of properties

with each element that is the first member of a member list of
al. COMMON LISP already has `lisp:assoc` defined, so shadow it
before you write your version, and use the COMMON LISP version
in the future whenever you need its functionality.

16.15 *(p1)* In your `match` file (see Exercise 14.8), define the function
(`matchlelt` *l1 l2*) to be like `equal-lelt` except to consider the
symbol ? (recognized by `dont-care`) to be `eql` anything. For
example, (`matchlelt` '(a ? c d e) '(a b c ? e)) should return T.

CHAPTER 17

RECURSION ON LISTS, PART 2—SYNTHESIS

In Exercise 15.12, we saw that there were two kinds of recursive functions. One kind might perform some computations "on the way down," but once it finds an answer, it just returns it and does no computation "on the way up." The other kind collects a "stack" of pending computations on the way down and constructs its answer on the way up. If you look carefully at the functions we dealt with in Chapters 15 and 16, you will see that the only ones that did any contruction on the way up returned numbers. We will now consider recursive functions that construct lists.

Remember that the basic list construction function is cons, which builds a list from an object and a list. cons will be at the heart of recursive list construction functions. Remember also that the basic list—on top of which all others are built—is (), the empty list.

The simplest recursive list construction function is

```
(defun copy (l)
  "Returns a copy of the list L."
  (check-type l list)
  (if (null l) '()
      (cons (first l) (copy (rest l)))))
```

Notice that `copy` pulls apart the list on the way down and puts it back together on the way up, thus showing the basic pattern of list synthesis functions. `copy` is useful enough that it is already defined in COMMON LISP (under the name `lisp:copy-list`).

Let's next write a function that strings together two lists: `(append '(a b c) '(d e f))` should return `(A B C D E F)`, and `(append '() '(d e f))` should return `(D E F)`.

```
(defun append (l1 l2)
  "Returns a list consisting of the members of L1
  followed by the members of L2."
  (check-type l1 list)
  (check-type l2 list)
  (if (null l1) l2
      (cons (first l1) (append (rest l1) l2)))))
```

Compare this with `sum2` in Exercise 15.12. Note the analogies:

append	sum2
null	zerop
cons (first l1)	1+
rest	1-

LISP lists have a strange asymmetry about them: the first member is easier to get at than the last. This asymmetry becomes apparent when we try to write a function to reverse a list. `(reverse '(a b c))` should be `(C B A)`. It is not as easy to write as `copy` was, but we can use `append`:

```
(defun reverse (l)
  "Returns a copy of the list L
  with the order of members reversed."
  (check-type l list)
  (if (null l) '()
      (append (reverse (rest l))
              (list (first l))))))
```

The second argument of the recursive call of `append` must be `(list (first l))` rather than just `(first l)` because both arguments of `append` must be lists.

A second way of writing `reverse` is interesting because it illustrates a common pattern. It is easy to write a function `reverse2`, which

takes two lists and appends the reverse of its first argument to its
second argument:

```
(defun reverse2 (l1 l2)
  "Returns a list consisting of
   the members of L1 in reverse order
   followed by the members of L2 in original order."
  (check-type l1 list)
  (check-type l2 list)
  (if (null l1) l2
      (reverse2 (rest l1)
                (cons (first l1) l2)))))
```

Notice that the relation of **reverse2** to **sum** (Chapter 15) is exactly
the same as that of **append** to **sum2**.

Given **reverse2**, we can easily write a second version of **reverse**,
called **reverse1**:

```
(defun reverse1 (l)
  "Returns a copy of the list L
   with the order of members reversed."
  (check-type l list)
  (reverse2 l '()))
```

Notice that **reverse1** does nothing on its own. It just initializes
reverse2's second argument to be (). There seldom would be a reason
to call **reverse2** directly, with a nonnull second argument. It really
just serves as a "helper function" for **reverse1**. This is a common
situation—the helper does all the work—and actually a fundamental
element of LISP programming style. *Each function does as little work
as possible,* passing the bulk of the work to some other function, but,
if necessary, doing some processing of the data first.

Comparing **reverse** with **reverse1** (we include **reverse1**'s helper,
of course), we see that **reverse** is very inefficient. Look at the recursive form (append (reverse (rest l)) (list (first l))). The
recursive call to **reverse** pulls (rest l) apart and pastes it together
in reverse order only to have **append** pull it apart and paste it together
again. **reverse1**, on the other hand, "visits" each member of its list
only once.

So far, we have essentially been copying lists. A simple modification
makes substitutions in a list:

```
(defun sub-first (new old l)
  "Returns a copy of the list L with the element NEW
   replacing the first occurrence of the element OLD."
  (check-type new (satisfies util:elementp))
  (check-type old (satisfies util:elementp))
  (check-type l list)
  (cond ((null l) '())
        ((eql (first l) old) (cons new (rest l)))
        (t (cons (first l)
                 (sub-first new old (rest l))))))
```

Notice that a third cond pair has appeared. The pattern is a combination of what we saw in the last chapter and what we have been seeing
in this chapter. As soon as we find old as the first member of l, we
can return a value. If we never find it, we eventually get to the null
list and return NIL. In either case, we paste back the earlier members
on the way up.

If you have forgotten the significance of the type-specifier
(satisfies util:elementp), review Exercise 16.6. We could define
our own element type to make checking for the correct type easier.
The form for defining a new type is

(deftype *symbol* () *documentation-string* '*type-specifier*)

Evaluating such a form makes *symbol* the name of a type that is equivalent to the given *type-specifier*. You have to supply the () and the
quote mark exactly as shown. They are there for more sophisticated
options that are beyond the scope of this book. The *documentation-
string* is like the documentation string of functions and is retrievable
from the *symbol* by evaluating (documentation *symbol* 'type). This
is the same documentation function we saw earlier, but its second argument specifies that we want the documentation of the *symbol* as a
type name, rather than as a function. We can define our element type
by evaluating

```
(deftype element ()
  "Elements  are objects testable by EQL,
   namely symbols, characters, numbers, and packages."
  '(satisfies util:elementp))
```

Then, our definition of `sub-first` can be

```
(defun sub-first (new old l)
  "Returns a copy of the list L with the element NEW
   replacing the first occurrence of the element OLD."
  (check-type new element)
  (check-type old element)
  (check-type l list)
  (cond ((null l) '())
        ((eql (first l) old) (cons new (rest l)))
        (t (cons (first l)
                 (sub-first new old (rest l))))))
```

We can use lists to represent sets. Let a *set* of elements be a list of elemental objects in which no two elements are `eql` and for which order is irrelevant. A list in which order is irrelevant but elements can appear more than once is called a *bag*. Let's write a function to turn a bag into a set. I will assume that we have defined the type `bag` to be equivalent to the type `list`. (Note that there is no way to differentiate a single bag from a single list; we just treat them differently.)

```
(defun makeset (b)
  "Returns a set containing
   just those elements of the input bag B."
  (check-type b bag)
  (cond ((null b) '())
        ((member (first b) (rest b))
         (makeset (rest b)))
        (t (cons (first b) (makeset (rest b))))))
```

Note that both the second and third `cond` pairs involve recursion, but only the third pair involves explicit list construction. The second pair just recurses down the bag ignoring the first element. Compare this with your definition of `count` from Exercise 16.10.

The union of two sets s_1 and s_2 is a set that contains every element in s_1 or in s_2, and only those elements. The definition of `union` is similar to that of `makeset`.

```
(defun union (s1 s2)
  "Returns the union of the sets S1 and S2."
  (check-type s1 set)
  (check-type s2 set)
  (cond ((null s1) s2)
        ((member (first s1) s2)
         (union (rest s1) s2))
        (t (cons (first s1) (union (rest s1) s2))))))
```

Here again, I assume that we have defined the type **set**. However, defining **set** is more involved than defining the type **bag**. Since the only difference between a bag and a list is how we treat them, not what they are, it is all right to make **bag** a synonym of the type **list**. However, the list (A B C A C) is obviously not a set because it has repeated elements. There are at least three possible solutions to this problem. First, we can just make **set** a synonym of the type **list**. The trouble with this solution is that if someone gives **union** a list with repeated elements, we will not be able to detect the error. Some programmers advocate this solution and just don't worry about the extra elements.

The other two solutions to the problem of defining the **set** type both use (**satisfies setp**) as the type-specifier, but they differ in the definition of **setp**. In the first of these, we can define **setp** to examine its argument to make sure that it is a bag (a list) without repeated elements. The definition of this **setp** is left as an exercise. The problem with this solution is that lists will need to be examined a huge number of times to make sure they are sets. We will also address this in the exercises.

The third solution to the definition of the **set** type relies on the fact that every set must be the result of an execution of the **makeset** function. If we can label every object produced by **makeset**, then all **setp** has to do is check for the label. Since every object that **makeset** produces is a list, we can label them by putting the symbol **:set** as the first member of each of these lists. The symbol **:set** is a symbol in the special package called the *keyword* package. This package has an empty name (notice it before the colon) and has the special property that all its symbols evaluate to themselves, just like numbers, characters, and strings. We use a symbol in the keyword package to label sets, because we don't expect to get confused by lists of such symbols. The definition of this `setp` is also left as an exercise, but let's examine the revised definition of `makeset`. The problem is that if we try to modify `makeset` as a single function, the label will keep getting in our way. (Try it!) The solution is to divide `makeset` into a main function and a helper function. The helper function will look like our original `makeset`, and it will do all the work (as is usual for helpers).

```
(defun makeset (b)
  "Returns a set containing
   just those elements in the input bag B."
  (check-type b bag)
  (cons :set (make-unlabelled-set b)))

(defun make-unlabelled-set (b)
  "Returns a list containing
   the elements in the input bag B, without duplicates."
  ;; Assumes that B has already been checked to be a bag.
  (cond ((null b) '())
        ((member (first b) (rest b))
         (make-unlabelled-set (rest b)))
        (t (cons (first b)
                 (make-unlabelled-set (rest b))))))
```

I have used a comment to point out that `make-unlabelled-set` is doing no type-checking of its own. It shouldn't be called by any function other than `makeset` anyway, so not doing the type checking will make it faster than checking the type unnecessarily. The problem with this solution is the necessity of doubling all the set functions, but it may be worthwhile if we are going to make a package out of our set functions; put them in a file; make only the main functions, not the helpers, external; and use them in many other places.

Exercises

Do the exercises of this chapter in the package ch17 except where otherwise instructed.

17.1 *(r)* Enter the definition of `copy` and test it, first checking to see if your implementation of COMMON LISP has a function named copy (one of mine does, and one doesn't) and, if so, shadowing it.

17.2 *(i)* Is a list eql to a copy of itself? Find out using the technique of Exercise 8.6: enter a quoted list and then evaluate

```
(eql * (copy *))
```

Now try it using equal instead of eql. A list and its copy are equal to each other, but not eql. We will pursue this in the next chapter.

17.3 *(i)* Define the identity function as

```
(defun identity (object)
  "Returns its argument unmodified."
  object)
```

but first shadow lisp:identity since, amazingly enough, it is a standard COMMON LISP function. Compare the values of (copy '(a b c)) and (identity '(a b c)). Although they seem to do the same thing, if you now redo Exercise 17.2 using (eql * (identity *)) instead of copy, you will notice again that two lists can look the same without being identical.

17.4 *(r)* Shadow lisp:append, and then enter and test the function append as shown in this chapter.

17.5 *(d)* Define (firstn *n* *l*), where *n* is an integer and *l* is a list at least *n* members long. firstn should return a list whose members are the first *n* members of *l*. For example:

```
(firstn 3 '(a b (c d) e f))
```

should be

```
(A B (C D))
```

17.6 *(i)* Enter a quoted list, and then evaluate

```
(eql (firstn (length *) *) (firstn (length *) *))
```

The moral is that **firstn** makes a copy of its list.

17.7 *(i)* Enter a quoted list, and then evaluate

(eql (nthcdr 0 *) (nthcdr 0 *))

nthcdr, which you first met in Exercise 16.13 does not make a copy of its list. Is this also true if you replaced 0 by some positive integer?

17.8 *(i)* Enter two quoted lists, and then evaluate

(eql (nthcdr (length **) (append ** *)) *)

Note that **append** does not make a copy of its second argument. What about its first argument?

17.9 *(r)* Define and test **reverse** (after shadowing **lisp:reverse**) and **reverse1**. Compare their running times on some long list. (See Exercise 16.9.)

17.10 *(r)* Define and test **sub-first**.

17.11 *(u)* Add to your **util** file, which you created for Exercise 13.12, the definition of the type **element**, and make **element** an external symbol of the **util** package. Use this type wherever it is useful in future projects and exercises.

17.12 *(d)* Define **subst*** to be like **sub-first** but to replace *all* top-level occurrences of **old** by **new**. For example,

(subst* 'x 'y '(a b y (x y) z y))

should evaluate to

(A B X (X Y) Z X)

17.13 *(u)* Create a file named **set**, the symbols of which should be in the package named **set**. In this file, define a predicate **setp** that returns True if its one argument is a list of objects, no two of which are **eql**, and False otherwise. Make sure that **setp** returns False when given a nonlist, rather than causing an error.

17.14 *(u)* In your `set` file, shadow `'lisp:set`, and define `set` to be a type of object that satisfies `setp`. Make `set` an external symbol of the `set` package.

17.15 *(u)* Define `makeset` in the `set` file, and test it. To do this, you should define the type `bag` in your `util` file and make `bag` an external symbol in the `util` package. Also specify in your `set` file that you will use all external symbols of the `util` package in the `set` package. Make `makeset` an external symbol in the `set` package.

17.16 *(u)* Add the definition of `union` to the `set` file, and export it. Be sure to shadow `lisp:union` in that file. Test `set:union`.

17.17 *(i)* Evaluate (`union '(a b c d )` `'(b d e f))` while tracing `setp`. Note the inordinate number of times the sets are checked.

17.18 *(u)* Redefine `makeset` in the `set` file so that every set is represented by a list whose first member is `:set`.

17.19 *(u)* Redefine `setp` in the `set` file so that it just checks that the first member of a list that represents a set is `:set`.

17.20 *(u)* Define `set:first` and `set:rest` in your `set` file to return the element that happens to be listed first in a set, and the set without that element, respectively. Make these external symbols in the `set` package and shadow `lisp:first` and `lisp:rest`. Go through all the definitions in your `set` file; make sure to type `lisp:first` and `lisp:rest` explicitly wherever necessary.

17.21 *(u)* Define (`insert e s`) in your `set` file to return a set just like s, but with e added as an additional element. If e is already in s, s should be returned unchanged. Make `insert` an external symbol in the `set` package.

17.22 *(u)* Define `empty` in your `set` file to be a function that returns True if its one argument is a set with no elements, and returns False otherwise. Make `empty` an external symbol in the `set` package.

17.23 *(u)* Redefine **set:union** to use the new representation of sets. Define the help function **union-unlabelled-sets** as an internal function. Again evaluate (**union** '(a b c d) '(b d e f)) while tracing **setp**.

17.24 *(u)* The intersection of two sets s_1 and s_2 is the set consisting of those elements that are in s_1 and also in s_2. Define **intersection** in your **set** file, with **intersection** an external symbol in the set package. Shadow **lisp:intersection**.

17.25 *(u)* The relative complement of two sets s_1 and s_2 is the set consisting of those elements of s_1 that are not also in s_2. Define **complement** in your **set** file, with **complement** an external symbol in the **set** package.

17.26 *(u)* A set s_1 is a subset of a set s_2 if every element of s_1 is a member of s_2. Define (**subsetp** *s1 s2*) in your **set** file to return True if the set s_1 is a subset of the set s_2, and False otherwise. Make **subsetp** an external symbol in the **set** package, and shadow **lisp:subsetp**.

17.27 *(u)* Two sets are equal if they have exactly the same elements. Define (**equal** *s1 s2*) in your **set** file to return True if s_1 and s_2 are equal sets, and False otherwise. Make sure that it does not matter if one set has its elements in a different order than the other set, and make sure that the order of the two arguments of **set-equal** is irrelevant. Make this **equal** an external symbol in the **set** package and shadow **lisp:equal** in that package.

17.28 *(d)* The cross product of two sets s_1 and s_2 is the set s_3, which consists of all pairs such that the first of each pair is a member of s_1 and the second of each pair is a member of s_2. In the **ch17** package, define (**xprod** *s1 s2*) to return the cross product of the sets s_1 and s_2. For example,

```
(xprod '(:set a b) '(:set c d e))
```

should evaluate to

```
(:SET (A C) (A D) (A E) (B C) (B D) (B E))
```

or any other ordering of these six pairs. Where appropriate, use the functions whose names are external symbols in the **set** package, but do not use any function whose name is an internal symbol in the **set** package. Hint: Use a help function **xprod1** that takes an object and a set and returns a list of pairs. For example,

$$(\text{xprod1 'a '(:set c d e)})$$

would return

$$(\text{:SET (A C) (A D) (A E)})$$

17.29 *(p1)* A *substitution* is an association list (see Exercise 16.14), in which the first member of each sublist is a variable and the other member of each sublist is a *term* the variable is *bound to.* Add to your **match** file the function (**boundp v subs**) that returns True if the variable *v* (as recognized by **variablep**) is bound to anything in the substitution *subs,* and False otherwise. You may use the LISP function **assoc** in this definition. You will have to shadow **lisp:boundp** in your **match** file.

17.30 *(p1)* Add to your **match** file a function (**bound-to v subs**) that returns the term that the variable *v* is bound to in the substitution *subs,* or NIL if *v* is unbound in **subs**.

17.31 *(p1)* Add to your **match** file a function (**match** *pat lst*), where *pat* and *lst* are both lists of elements. **match** should return a substitution—a list of all pairs (**V A**) where **V** is a variable in **pat** and **A** is the corresponding element in **lst**. If the *n*th member of **pat** is not a variable, it must be **eql** to the *n*th member of **lst**. Otherwise, **match** should return NIL. If no element of **pat** is a variable but each is **eql** to its corresponding element of **lst**, **match** should return ((T T)). If a variable occurs more than once in **pat**, its corresponding elements in **lst** must be the same. For example:

```
> (match '(a b c) '(a b c))
((T T))
> (match '(a b c) '(a c b))
NIL
```

```
> (match '(a ?x c) '(a b c))
((?X B) (T T))
> (match '(a ?x c ?x) '(a b c d))
NIL
> (match '(a ?x c ?x) '(a b c b))
((?X B) (T T))
> (match '(a ?x c ?y) '(a b c d))
((?Y D) (?X B) (T T))
```

The order of pairs in your answer needn't be the same as above. (Hint: You may find it useful to define a help function (match1 pat lst pairs).)

17.32 *(p1)* In your match file, define (substitute pat subs), where pat is a list like the first argument of match, subs is substitution, and substitute returns a list like pat except every variable in pat that is bound in *subs* is replaced by the element it is bound to. For every appropriate pat and lst, it should be the case that (substitute pat (match pat lst)) = lst. Shadow lisp:substitute in your match file.

17.33 *(p2)* In your calculator file, which you created for Exercise 12.5, revise the function combine-expr so that the first member of the list it returns is in Cambridge Prefix notation. That is, (combine-expr '+ 3 '(5 - 6 * 8)) should now evaluate to ((+ 3 5) - 6 * 8)).

17.34 *(p2)* Write the function enclose-expression to take a list representing an arithmetic expression in normal infix notation and return a list whose one member is the expression transformed into Cambridge Prefix notation. For now, assume that the only operators in the expression are + and -. For example, (combine-expression '(5 + 3 - 2)) should evaluate to ((- (+ 5 3) 2)). Add this function to your calculator file. (Hint: Use your new version of combine-expr in the recursive step of your function.)

17.35 *(p2)* A term is one of the operands of addition or subtraction. For example, in the expression $5 - 4 + 3$, the first term is 5, and in the expression $5 * 3/2 + 7 - 8$, the first term is $5 * 3/2$. Define

the function `enclose-term` to take a list like (5 - 4 + 3) or
(5 * 3 / 2 + 7 - 8) and return it with the first term collected
as the first member and expressed in Cambridge Prefix notation.
That is

$$(\texttt{enclose-term ’(5 - 4 + 3))}$$

should return

$$(5 - 4 + 3)$$

and

$$(\texttt{enclose-term ’(5 * 3 / 2 + 7 - 8))}$$

should return

$$((/ (* 5 3) 2) + 7 - 8)$$

For now, assume the only operators in the expression given to
`enclose-term` are +, -, *, and /. Add `enclose-term` to your
`calculator` file.

17.36 *(p2)* A factor is one of the operands of multiplication or division.
For example, in the expression $5 * 4 + 3$, the first factor is 5,
and in the expression $5^{3^2}/7 - 8$, the first factor is 5^{3^2}. Define
the function `enclose-factor` to take a list like (5 * 4 + 3) or
(5 ^ 3 ^ 2 / 7 - 8) and return it with the first factor collected
as the first member. That is,

$$(\texttt{enclose-factor ’(5 * 4 + 3))}$$

should return

$$(5 * 4 + 3)$$

and

$$(\texttt{enclose-factor ’(5 ^ 3 ^ 2 / 7 - 8))}$$

should return

$$((^{\char`\^} 5 (^{\char`\^} 3 2)) / 7 - 8)$$

Add `enclose-factor` to your `calculator` file.

CHAPTER 18

RECURSION ON TREES

We have been treating lists as linear arrangements of unstructured elements. That is, we have been considering both (A B C) and ((A B) ((C)) (D)) as simply lists with three members, and all our recursive functions on lists have recursed only down the **rest** parts of the lists. We now want to consider the entire structure of lists whose members are also lists and allow recursion down the **first** parts as well. Lists looked at in this way are often called *trees,* and the atoms in the lists (remember that every nonempty list is a cons, and an atom is any LISP object other than a cons) are called the *leaves* of the tree. For example, Figure 18.1 shows the list ((A B) ((C)) (D)) drawn as a tree. In this drawing, every rectangle is called a *node* of the tree and represents a *subtree* of every tree higher in the drawing. A line going down and to the left represents the application of the **first** function to the higher tree, and a line going down and to the right represents the application of the **rest** function. So the node at the very top represents the tree ((A B) ((C)) (D)), and the two nodes immediately below it, read left to right, represent (A B) and (((C)) (D)), respectively. We consider the atoms, which are leaves of the tree, to be trees themselves. That way, trees form a *recursive data structure* in which every tree is either an atom or is constructed (using **cons**) from two subtrees. As we shall see, recursive functions operating on trees follow closely this view of trees as recursive data structures.

123

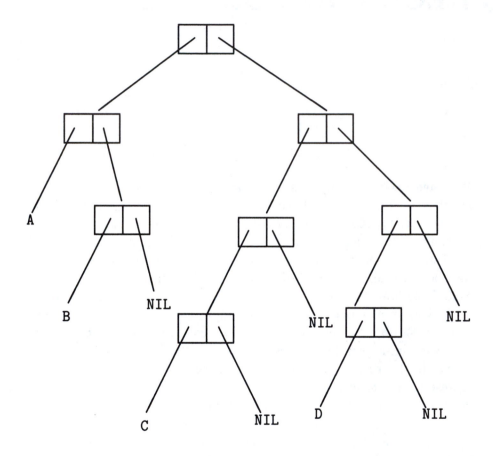

Figure 18.1 The list ((A B) ((C)) (D)) drawn as a tree.

To focus on a concrete example of recursion on trees, consider the statement in Exercise 17.2 that a list and its copy are **equal** to each other, but not **eql**. We would like to be able to say that ((A B) ((C)) (D)) and ((A B) ((C)) (D)) are equal as LISP trees, even if they are not identical. We can define precisely what we mean by "equal as LISP trees" by writing a LISP predicate function that takes two trees as arguments and returns T if they are equal as LISP trees and **NIL** otherwise. Remember, we have already written such functions for "equal as lists of elements" (**equal-lelt** of Exercise 16.11) and for "equal as sets" (**set-equal** of Exercise 17.27). Since this function will be "equal as trees," we will call it **tree-equal**.

Let's consider the cases. A tree, as a recursive data structure, is either a cons (a nonempty list) or an atom. We know that COMMON LISP has different equality predicates for different kinds of atoms, so for now let's use the predicate **atom-equal** as an equality predicate for any kind of atom and worry about defining it later.

A cons consists of a first part and a rest part, both of which are trees, so we can say that two conses are **tree-equal** if and only if their first parts are **tree-equal** and their rest parts are also **tree-equal**. This gives us

```
(defun tree-equal (t1 t2)
  "Returns T if T1 and T2 are trees with:
        1.   the same structure,
        2.   equal corresponding leaves
              (according to atom-equal);
  NIL, otherwise."
  ;; T1 and T2 can be any objects.
  (cond ((both_T1_and_T2_are_atoms
          (atom-equal t1 t2))
         ((both_T1_and_T2_are_conses
          (and (tree-equal (first t1) (first t2))
               (tree-equal (rest t1) (rest t2)))))))
```

Let's assume that, like **eql**, **atom-equal** can take any LISP objects as arguments without giving an error message and that it will surely return False if given one atom and one cons. Under these assumptions, we can simplify our reasoning as follows. If T1 is an atom, it is **tree-equal** to T2 if and only if it is **atom-equal** to T2. If T1 is not an atom, but T2 is, they are not **tree-equal**. If neither is an atom, they are both conses and have **first** parts and **rest** parts. If their **first** parts are **tree-equal**, T1 and T2 are **tree-equal** if and only if their **rest** parts are. Otherwise they are not **tree-equal**. This reasoning gives us:

```
(defun tree-equal (t1 t2)
  "Returns T if T1 and T2 are trees with:
      1. the same structure,
      2. equal corresponding leaves
         (according to atom-equal);
   NIL, otherwise."
  ;; T1 and T2 can be any objects.
  (cond ((atom t1) (atom-equal t1 t2))
        ((atom t2) nil)
        ((tree-equal (first t1) (first t2))
         (tree-equal (rest t1) (rest t2)))
        (t nil)))
```

Will this function always terminate? Since it is written to follow the recursive structure of trees closely, it is easy to see that it will terminate. A tree is either an atom or a cons. If either T1 or T2 is an atom, one of the first two **cond** pairs will be taken and recursion will stop. If both T1 and T2 are conses, the function will definitely recurse on their **first** parts and may recurse on their **rest** parts also (if their **first** parts are **tree-equal**). But both the **first** part subtree and the **rest** part subtree of a tree have fewer nodes than the tree itself (since they don't contain the top node of the tree). So we must eventually come to the leaves of the tree (trees with only one node). But a leaf is an atom, and as we have seen, recursion will stop as soon as either T1 or T2 is an atom. Therefore every recursion will eventually bottom out, and the function will always terminate. (Surprisingly, it is possible to create a tree that contains itself as a subtree by using the functions called "destructive list manipulation functions." Don't use any such functions until we discuss them later in this book!)

The moral of this discussion is that just as zero is the base case for recursion on integers and **NIL** is the base case for recursion on lists, the set of atoms is the base case for recursion on trees. We can formalize the above definition of trees as recursive data structures as follows:

1. Every atom is a tree.

2. If t1 and t2 are trees, then (cons t1 t2) is a tree whose **first** part is t1 and whose **rest** part is t2.

3. Nothing else is a tree.

Compare this with the definition of lists in Chapter 8.

Lists are just special cases of trees, such that the only atomic list is NIL. In general, the result of (cons o1 o2) is called a *dotted pair*, and is printed as (O1 . O2). Some people stress the idea that the list (A B) is also the dotted pair (A . (B . NIL)), but we will reserve the term "dotted pair" only for those nonatomic conses that cannot be considered lists. As an analogy to the fact that (A . (B . NIL)) is printed as (A B), COMMON LISP prints conses of the form (A . (B . C)) as (A B . C), and we refer to these as "dotted lists." We may refer to the normal lists that we are already familiar with as "strict lists" when the distinction is important. There are also "mixed lists." For example, (A (B C) . D) is a dotted list whose second element is a strict list. On the other hand, (A (B . C) D) is a mixed list whose second element is a dotted pair. Dotted pairs were mentioned in Exercise 8.1, where I said, "For the time being, if you ever see a dotted pair it will be because you have made a mistake." Although you know what they are, you still won't use them much.

It is interesting to note that the set of trees includes every possible COMMON LISP object, since it includes all conses and all atoms, and an atom is anything that is not a cons. (That is why I didn't bother to use **check-type** in the definition of **tree-equal**.) Figure 18.2 shows this organization of the COMMON LISP objects. Note that **element** is not an official COMMON LISP data type, but was defined on page 112. Also note that the type list does not appear in this hierarchy, because lists include both nonempty strict lists, which are conses, and the empty list NIL, which is a symbol.

One useful tree for storing information is called a *binary search tree*. We can define a binary search tree to be one of the following: (1) empty, represented by NIL; (2) a tree of one elemental member, represented by that element; or (3) a tree containing one *root* element and two binary search subtrees, represented by a list of three members—the root element, the *left* subtree, and the *right* subtree. In the last case,

```
tree
      atom
            element
                  character
                  number
                        integer
                              fixnum
                              bignum
                        ratio
                        float
                              short-float
                              single-float
                              double-float
                              long-float
                  symbol
                  package
            nonelemental atom
                  string
      cons
            dotted list
            mixed list
            nonempty strict list
```

Figure 18.2 An organization of COMMON LISP types as kinds of trees.

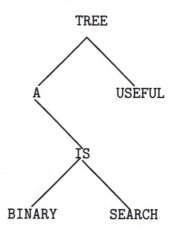

Figure 18.3 The binary search tree represented by the list (TREE (A NIL (IS BINARY SEARCH)) USEFUL).

all the elements in the left subtree must come (in some ordering) before the root element, and all the elements in the right subtree must come (in some ordering) after the root element. No two elements of a binary search tree should be **eql**. For example, Figure 18.3 depicts a binary search tree that would be represented by the list (**TREE (A NIL (IS BINARY SEARCH)) USEFUL**). In this case, the elements of the tree are symbols alphabetically ordered according to their names. This ordering can be tested for with the COMMON LISP function **string<**. First, let's define the type bstree:

```
(deftype bstree ()
  "A bstree is a Binary Search Tree.
   See the predicate bstreep for details."
  '(satisfies bstreep))
```

We will define the predicate **bstreep** to be a quick check that is just enough to make sure that a bstree is either an element or a list of three members, the first of which is an element.

```
(defun bstreep (tree)
  "A bstree is either an element, or a three-member list,
   the first of which is an element."
  (or (typep tree 'util:element)
      (and (listp tree)
  (= (length tree) 3)
  (typep (first tree) 'util:element)))))
```

(typep *object type*), which we haven't used before, returns True if the *object* is of the given *type*. We need to use it here because we don't have the function elementp and type-of would give us the one principal type of the object, such as symbol or character.

We can now define a function to build a binary search tree:

```
(defun bstree-insert (elt tree)
  "Returns the binary search tree TREE
   with the element ELT inserted in the proper place."
  (check-type elt util:element)
  (check-type tree bstree)
  (cond
   ((null tree) elt)
   ((eql elt (bstree-root tree)) tree)
   ((string< elt (bstree-root tree))
    (list (bstree-root tree)
          (bstree-insert elt (bstree-left tree))
          (bstree-right tree)))
   (t (list (bstree-root tree)
            (bstree-left tree)
            (bstree-insert elt (bstree-right tree))))))))
```

This definition uses the functions bstree-root, bstree-left, and bstree-right, which we haven't yet defined. However, the definitions of these functions are straightforward given the representation we decided on above:

```
(defun bstree-root (tree)
  "Returns the root element
        of the binary search tree TREE,
   NIL if TREE is empty."
  (check-type tree bstree)
```

```
    (if (atom tree) tree
        (first tree)))

(defun bstree-left (tree)
  "Returns the left subtree
        of the binary search tree TREE,
   NIL if TREE is empty or has an empty left subtree."
  (check-type tree bstree)
  (if (atom tree) '()
      (second tree)))

(defun bstree-right (tree)
  "Returns the right subtree
        of the binary search tree TREE,
   NIL if TREE is empty or has an empty right subtree."
  (check-type tree bstree)
  (if (atom tree) '()
      (third tree)))
```

Notice that in all three functions, there is no need to distinguish the empty from the elemental tree.

Some example calls to **bstree-insert** are

```
> (bstree-insert 'tree '())
TREE
> (bstree-insert 'useful (bstree-insert 'tree '()))
(TREE NIL USEFUL)
> (bstree-insert 'a
                 (bstree-insert 'useful
                                (bstree-insert 'tree
                                               '())))
(TREE A USEFUL)

> (bstree-insert
   'is
   (bstree-insert 'a
                  (bstree-insert 'useful
                                 (bstree-insert 'tree
                                                '()))))
(TREE (A NIL IS) USEFUL)
```

To determine if an element is in a binary search tree, compare it with the root. If they are **eql**, the element is there. If the element is earlier in the sort than the root, look in the left subtree. Otherwise, look in the right subtree. Of course, no element is in the empty tree. This reasoning is embodied in the function **bstree-member**:

```
(defun bstree-member (elt tree)
  "Returns True
        if ELT is stored in the binary search tree TREE;
   False otherwise."
  (check-type elt util:element)
  (check-type tree bstree)
  (cond ((null tree) nil)
        ((eql elt (bstree-root tree)) t)
        ((string< elt (bstree-root tree))
         (bstree-member elt (bstree-left tree)))
        (t (bstree-member elt (bstree-right tree)))))
```

On page 18, you learned to check for balanced parentheses in a list S-expression by counting 1 at the first left parenthesis, increasing your count by 1 at each subsequent left parenthesis, and decreasing your count by 1 at each right parenthesis. An interesting question might be: for any given list, what is the largest number you say when you count its parentheses in this way? Of course, the answer might be different depending on whether you represent the empty list as **NIL** or as (). If we draw a tree by drawing the left lines (applications of the **first** function) as vertical lines going down one level, and the right lines (applications of the **rest** function) as horizontal lines, this question is the same as the question of what is the deepest level in the tree (counting the first level as 0). The tree drawn in Figure 18.1 can be redrawn in this way, as shown in Figure 18.4.

If we let **depth** be the maximum level of a tree, we can sketch the LISP definition of **depth** as

```
(defun depth (tree)
  "Returns the depth of the argument TREE."
  (if (atom tree) 0 ; an atomic tree has a depth of 0
      (1+ the_maximum_depth_of_the_members_of_tree,
          viewed_as_a_nonempty_list)))
```

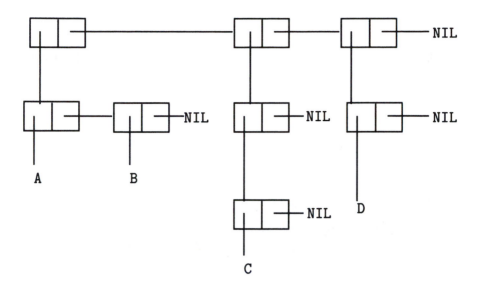

Figure 18.4 Another way of drawing ((A B) ((C)) (D)) as a tree.

To get the maximum depth of the members of a list, we need to write another function:

```
(defun max-depth-members (list)
  "Returns the maximum depth
   of the members of the argument LIST."
  (check-type list list)
  (if (null list) 0 ; the max depth of the members of ()
      (max (depth (first list))
           (max-depth-members (rest list)))))
```

COMMON LISP already has the function **max**, so all we need to do to finish our "program" for finding the depth of a tree is to complete the definition of **depth**:

```
(defun depth (tree)
  "Returns the depth of the argument TREE."
  (if (atom tree) 0 ; an atomic tree has a depth of 0
      (1+ (max-depth-members tree))))
```

Notice the interesting recursive structure of **max-depth-members** and **depth**. They each call the other, and **max-depth-members** calls itself as well.

Exercises

Do the exercises of this chapter in the package ch18 except where otherwise instructed.

18.1 *(r)* Evaluate

```
(eql '((a b) ((c)) (d)) '((a b) ((c)) (d)))
```

Notice that, although the two lists look the same, they are not eql.

18.2 *(i)* COMMON LISP has a kind of conditional function, typecase, that will evaluate one of a number of forms depending on the type of an object.

$$(\text{typecase } key \; (type_1 form_1) \; \ldots \; (type_n form_n))$$

will evaluate the first $form_i$ whose $type_i$ is the type of the value of *key* and will return that value. If none of the $type_i$ is correct, the value of the typecase will be NIL. For example:

```
(typecase key
  ((or symbol character number package) 'element)
  (string 'composite))
```

will have the value ELEMENT if key is an elemental object, COMPOSITE if key is a string, and NIL if key is any other COMMON LISP object. Use typecase and the type util:element from your util file to define atom-equal to be a function that returns True when its two arguments are atoms of the same type and are equal according to the proper equality predicate and False otherwise.

18.3 *(r)* Define tree-equal as given in this chapter. (Make sure you shadow lisp:tree-equal first.) Trace tree-equal and atom-equal while evaluating

```
(tree-equal '((a b) ((c)) (d)) '((a b) ((c)) (d)))
```

It should return True.

18.4 *(i)* Try **tree-equal** with all sorts of trees with various types of leaves. In particular, try some trees with strings at the leaves.

18.5 *(i)* COMMON LISP's **equal** function actually works the way your **tree-equal** should work. Try **equal** on the same examples you just tested **tree-equal** on. Also try **lisp:tree-equal** on those examples. You should notice some differences between the behavior of **lisp:equal** and **lisp:tree-equal**.

18.6 *(i)* Try

      (eql 5 5.0)   (= 5 5.0)
      (lisp:tree-equal 5 5.0) (ch18::tree-equal 5 5.0)
      (equal 5 5.0)   (equalp 5 5.0)

The function **equalp** is like **equal** but it uses = to compare numbers instead of **eql**. It is COMMON LISP's most general, and most generous, equality test. Compare **equal** and **equalp** on uppercase versus lowercase characters and strings.

18.7 *(i)* Look in the manual in Appendix B and find some destructive list manipulation functions. Don't use them!

18.8 *(d)* Play with constructing some dotted pairs. Notice how LISP prints them.

18.9 *(r)* Enter '(a . (b . nil)) and '(a . (b . c)). Notice how LISP prints them.

18.10 *(d)* Enter '(a (b c) . d) and '(a (b . c) d). Try to construct both of these by typing nested forms using only **cons** and quoted symbols.

18.11 *(i)* Ask LISP to evaluate some dotted pairs and dotted lists by typing them to the top level. For example, try

              (a . b)
          (first . '(a b))

and

           (cons 'a . 'b)

18.12 *(d)* Load the `util` file you created for Exercise 17.11. Compare
(`typep` *object* `'util:element`) with (`type-of` *object*) for several elemental and nonelemental LISP objects.

18.13 *(u)* Add the definition of the `bstree` type and of the `bstreep`
function to a new file named `bstree`, declare everything in that
file to be in the `bstree` package, and export the symbols `bstree`
and `bstreep`.

18.14 *(u)* Enter the functions `bstree-insert`, `bstree-root`,
`bstree-left`, and `bstree-right` in your `bstree` file. Delete
the `bstree-` prefix from all four functions, and export their new
names. Test these functions with the examples from the text and
with some examples of your own.

18.15 *(u)* Add the definition of `bstree-member` to your file, but omit
the `bstree-` prefix, and export its name. Be sure to shadow
`lisp:member`.

18.16 *(i)* Return to the LISP listener with `ch18` as the package. Load
the file with your five bstree functions. Notice that in package
`ch18` the names of the five bstree functions are

> `bstree:insert` `bstree:root`
> `bstree:left`   `bstree:right`
> `bstree:member`

Test them by evaluating

```
(bstree:member
 'is
 (bstree:insert
  'is
  (bstree:insert
   'a
   (bstree:insert 'useful
                  (bstree:insert 'tree '()))))))
```

while tracing `bstree:insert` and `bstree:member`. Your file constitutes an implementation of a binary search tree data type.

18.17 *(u)* Add the function `build-from-list` to your `bstree` file so that `(build-from-list elist)` assumes that `elist` is a list of elemental members and builds a binary search tree whose elements are precisely the members of `elist`. For example:

```
> (build-from-list
    '(a binary search tree is a useful tree))
(TREE (A NIL (IS BINARY SEARCH)) USEFUL)
```

Make `build-from-list` an external symbol of the package `bstree`.

18.18 *(u)* Add the function `inorder` to your `bstree` file so that `(inorder tree)` returns a list of all the elements in the binary search tree `tree` in alphabetical order. For example:

```
> (inorder '())
NIL
> (inorder 'tree)
(TREE)
> (inorder
    (build-from-list
     '(a binary search tree is a useful tree)))
(A BINARY IS SEARCH TREE USEFUL)
```

Make `inorder` an external symbol of the package `bstree`. (Hint: Contemplate the form `(append ____ (cons ____ ____)).)`

18.19 *(i)* Back in the `ch18` package, define the function **tree-sort** to take a list of symbols and sort them alphabetically, using `bstree:build-from-list` and `bstree:inorder`. Approximately how many calls to **string<** are made when sorting a list in this way, as a function of the length of the list?

18.20 *(r)* Define **depth** (and its auxiliary function). Test it out on various examples, including strict lists, dotted pairs, dotted lists, and mixed lists. If the depth of `'(a . (b c))` confuses you, remember that `'(a . (b c)) = (cons 'a '(b c)) = '(a b c)`. You should test a group of functions "bottom up." That is, test `max-depth-members` before `depth`, since `depth` will certainly not work if `max-depth-members` has a typo in it.

18.21 *(d)* Shadow `lisp:copy-tree` and define `copy-tree` to take a tree and make a copy of it at all levels. No two corresponding nonatomic subtrees of a tree and its copy, at whatever level, should be `eql`, but all should be `equal`.

18.22 *(d)* Define `subst`. `(subst new old tree)` should return a copy of `tree` with every subtree `equal` to `old` replaced by `new`. (First shadow `lisp:subst`, which is like this `subst`, but tests with `eql` instead of with `equal`.)

18.23 *(i)* Define `flatten` to take a tree and return a list of atoms that have the same left-to-right order as the atoms in the original tree. For example, `(flatten '(a ((b) (c d) e) (f ((g)))))` should be `(a b c d e f g)`. (You might find `typecase` useful, especially since `null` is an official COMMON LISP type consisting only of the object `nil`.)

18.24 *(d)* What is the value of `(flatten '(a () b))`? The two possible answers are `(A B)` and `(A NIL B)`. Whichever way your `flatten` works, write `flatten2` to work the other way. They should give the same answers on all lists not containing the empty list as a sublist.

18.25 *(p1)* Revise the functions `match` and `substitute` in your `match` file so that a pattern can be a list with sublists and a variable can occur at any level of the pattern.

18.26 *(p1)* Let a *rule* be a list of two patterns, called the Left-Hand Side and the Right-Hand Side. Define the type `rule` and the functions `lhs` and `rhs` so that, when given a rule, they return the appropriate patterns. Add them to your `match` file.

18.27 *(p1)* Define `(apply-rule tree rule)`, where `tree` is an arbitrary tree and `rule` is a rule. If `(lhs rule)` matches `tree`, `apply-rule` should return

```
(substitute (rhs rule) (match (lhs rule) tree))
```

Otherwise, `apply-rule` should return `tree` itself. Test examples like

```
(apply-rule '(I am depressed)
            '((I am ?x) (Why are you ?x ?)))

(apply-rule '(Man Socrates)
   '((Man ?x) (Mortal ?x)))
```

Add apply-rule to your match file.

18.28 *(p2)* In your calculator file, which you last modified for Exercise 17.36, define the function prefix to take an infix arithmetic expression whose only operators are +, -, *, and /, and return the expression in Cambridge Prefix notation. Assume expressions that are atoms or lists of fewer than three members needn't be altered. (Hint: Use enclose-expression, but make sure that every time it is called, the expression has had its first term enclosed.)

18.29 *(p2)* Again revise the functions in your calculator file so that prefix can take an arithmetic expression including any of the operators +, -, *, /, or ^.

CHAPTER 19

THE EVALUATOR

I have said that a form is a LISP object intended to be evaluated and that a list form must begin with a function name. We have now had practice writing functions that build and return lists. If the list returned by such a function were a form, could we somehow evaluate it? What normally happens to such a returned list? Either it is printed by the LISP listener, or it is returned to some function that passes it as an argument to some other function where it is bound to a variable. If the LISP listener prints a form, we can just type it back as the next line. Since LISP evaluates and prints the value of every form we type in, this will cause LISP to evaluate a form it has just built. What if a variable inside a function is bound to a form? To evaluate it, we would need to pass it to some evaluator. LISP obviously has such an evaluator, and, marvelously enough, it lets us use it.

I say "marvelously enough" because there is great power in programmers' having the ability to use the evaluator of the programming language they are using. Given that, and the ability to write programs that build source code of that programming language, we can write a program that "writes" and "runs" its own programs! LISP programs (functions) can obviously build LISP source code (the source code just consists of LISP lists), so LISP programmers have this power. We can use it, if we want, to extend LISP into a completely different programming language.

LISP's evaluator is the function eval, a function of one argument.
It gets its single argument evaluated, and it evaluates it one more time
and returns that value. For example:

```
> (eval 5)
5
> (eval ''a)
A
> (eval '(car '(a)))
A
> (eval '(cons 'a '(b c)))
(A B C)
> (eval (list (second '(+ - * /)) 5 4 3))
-2
```

Normally, when we type a list to the LISP listener or include one in
a function definition, we have a choice of two extremes: if we quote the
list, none of its members will be evaluated; if we don't quote it, each
of its members except the first will be evaluated and the list itself will
be evaluated. These extremes are illustrated in the two interactions
below:

```
> '(cons pi (list "are" "squared"))
(CONS PI (LIST "are" "squared"))
> (cons pi (list "are" "squared"))
(3.1415926535897936d0 "are" "squared")
```

What if, however, we want some of the members of the list to be
evaluated and other members not to be? One way of doing this is
to use list to construct the list, quote the members we don't want
evaluated, and not quote the members we do want evaluated. Another
way is to quote all members, but wrap a call to eval around those
members we want evaluated. So, for example:

```
> (list 'cons pi '(list "are" "squared"))
(CONS 3.1415926535897936d0 (LIST "are" "squared"))
> (list 'cons (eval 'pi) '(list "are" "squared"))
(CONS 3.1415926535897936d0 (LIST "are" "squared"))
```

A more convenient way of doing this is to use the COMMON LISP
backquote character. This is the single quote character on your keyboard other than the one you have been using for the quote character.

In this text, the backquote character will look like ', whereas the regular quote character looks like '. The backquote works just like the
quote, except that if you backquote a tree, any subtree, no matter how
deep, that is preceded by a comma is evaluated. For example:

```
> '(cons ,pi (list "are" "squared"))
(CONS 3.1415926535897936d0 (LIST "are" "squared"))
> '(cons pi ,(list "are" "squared"))
(CONS PI ("are" "squared"))
> '("me" ("and" ,(list "my" "shadow")))
("me" ("and" ("my" "shadow")))
```

If the comma is followed by @, then what comes after must evaluate to
a list, and it is "spliced" into the outer list. For example:

```
> '(cons pi ,@(list "are" "squared"))
(CONS PI "are" "squared")
> '("me" ("and" ,@(list "my" "shadow")))
("me" ("and" "my" "shadow"))
```

We will be using backquote in a function definition below.

To get an idea of how to use **eval**, we will look at how the equivalent
of infinite lists can be constructed using the technique known as *lazy
evaluation*. For example, say we want to have a list of all the natural
numbers. Since that is an infinite list, and we can't really construct
it, instead we will construct a list containing a few natural numbers
and a "promise" to construct the rest. A promise will look like a list
whose **first** member is the keyword :**promise** (see page 114 if you've
forgotten about keywords) and whose **rest** is a form that will evaluate
to some more of the list, again ending with a promise. For example, the
function **natural-numbers-from** will return an infinite list of natural
numbers, consisting of just one natural number and a promise of the
rest:

```
(defun natural-numbers-from (n)
  "Returns an infinite list of the natural numbers
   starting from N using the lazy evaluation technique."
  (check-type n integer)
  '(,n :promise natural-numbers-from ,(1+ n)))
```

Some lists generated by this function are

```
> (natural-numbers-from 0)
(0 :PROMISE NATURAL-NUMBERS-FROM 1)
> (natural-numbers-from 5)
(5 :PROMISE NATURAL-NUMBERS-FROM 6)
```

To use these lists, we need to write the functions lazy-first and
lazy-rest. These functions will act like first and rest unless they
bump into the keyword :promise, in which case they will redeem the
promise once before doing their usual thing:

```
(defun lazy-first (list)
  "Returns the first member of LIST,
   redeeming a promise if necessary."
  (check-type list list)
  (if (eql (first list) :promise)
      (first (eval (rest list)))
      (first list)))

(defun lazy-rest (list)
  "Returns the rest of the LIST,
   redeeming a promise if necessary."
  (check-type list list)
  (if (eql (first list) :promise)
      (rest (eval (rest list)))
      (rest list)))
```

A few examples may clarify this:

```
> (lazy-first (natural-numbers-from 0))
0
> (lazy-rest (lazy-rest (natural-numbers-from 0)))
(:PROMISE NATURAL-NUMBERS-FROM 2)
> (lazy-first
    (lazy-rest (lazy-rest (natural-numbers-from 0))))
2
```

The name "lazy evaluation" comes from the fact that only those members of the list that are actually accessed are computed.

For a final example of using eval, consider the function prefix you
have stored in the file named calculator. The value of

$$\text{(prefix '(7 + 12 / 4 - 2 * 3))}$$

is (- (+ 7 (/ 12 4)) (* 2 3)). We could easily define the function compute to compute arithmetic expressions written in normal syntax as follows:

```
(defun compute (expr)
  "Returns the value of the arithmetic expression EXPR.
   EXPR is to be a list containing an expression
   in normal, infix notation."
  (check-type expr list)
  (eval (prefix expr)))
```

The value of (compute '(7 + 12 / 4 - 2 * 3)) should then be 4.

Exercises

Do the exercises of this chapter in the package ch19 except where otherwise instructed.

19.1 *(d)* Evaluate (cons 'first '('(a))). Then type the value back to the LISP listener exactly as it printed it to you.

19.2 *(r)* Have LISP evaluate

    a. (eval 5)

    b. (eval a)

    c. (eval 'a)

    d. (eval ''a)

    e. (eval (first (a))) (eval (first '(a)))

    f. (eval '(first (a)))

    g. (eval '(first '(a)))

    h. (eval (cons 'first '((a))))

    i. (eval (cons 'first '('(a))))

19.3 *(r)* Try for yourself all the examples of using backquote shown in this chapter.

19.4 *(r)* Define `natural-numbers-from` as shown in this chapter. Check the values of

```
(natural-numbers-from 0)
and
(natural-numbers-from 5).
```

19.5 *(r)* Define `lazy-first` and `lazy-rest` as shown in this chapter. Check the values of

```
(lazy-first (natural-numbers-from 0))
(lazy-rest (lazy-rest (natural-numbers-from 0)))
and
(lazy-first
   (lazy-rest (lazy-rest (natural-numbers-from 0))))
```

19.6 *(i)* Define (`lazy-nth` *n list*) to return the *n*th member of the *list,* redeeming promises where necessary. Compare this with `nth` (Exercise 16.12). Check the value of

```
(lazy-nth 15 (natural-numbers-from 0))
```

To check that *n* is a positive integer, you can use

```
(check-type n (and integer (satisfies plusp)))
```

19.7 *(d)* The Fibonacci numbers are the sequence $0, 1, 1, 2, 3, 5, 8, \ldots$, where each number after the first two is the sum of the previous two numbers. A general Fibonacci sequence may be generated from any two numbers *n* and *m* and is the sequence $n, m, n + m, n + 2m, 2n + 3m, \ldots$, where again each number after the first is the sum of the previous two. Define the function (`fibonacci-from` *n m*) to return the infinite list of Fibonacci numbers generated from *n* and *m* using the technique of lazy evaluation. Using `lazy-nth`, check that the seventh Fibonacci number is 8 and that the twentieth is 4,181.

19.8 *(d)* Define the function (`relatively-prime` *n integers*) where *n* is a positive integer and *integers* is a list of positive integers, to return False if (= (`mod` *n i*) 0) for any integer *i* in *others* and True otherwise. ((`mod` *n m*) is the remainder after dividing *n* by *m*.)

19.9 *(d)* Using `relatively-prime`, define the function (`primes-from` *n others*), where *n* is a positive integer and *others* is a list of all primes less than *n*, to return an infinite list of prime numbers equal to or greater than *n*, using the technique of lazy evaluation. (Hint: If (`relatively-prime` *n others*), then *n* is the first prime on the desired list; otherwise the list is generated by (`primes-from` (1+ *n*) *others*).)

19.10 *(p2)* Define `compute` as in this chapter, and store it on the file named `calculator`. Check that

$$(\text{compute } '(7 + 12 \; / \; 4 \; - \; 2 \; * \; 3))$$

evaluates to 4.

19.11 *(p2)* Modify the functions in your `calculator` file so that

```
(prefix '(((5)))) = 5
(prefix '((5 + 3) / 4)) = (/ (+ 5 3) 4)
(prefix '(4 * (10 - 7))) = (* 4 (- 10 7))
(prefix '(2 ^ (5 + 4) * 3)) = (* (^ 2 (+ 5 4)) 3)
```

19.12 *(p2)* Modify your `prefix` function so that

$$(\text{compute } '(2 \; \hat{} \; 10 \; - \; 24))$$

evaluates to 1000.

19.13 *(p2)* Modify the functions in your `calculator` file to handle unary + and unary -.

19.14 *(p2)* The COMMON LISP function (`fboundp` *s*) returns True if the symbol *s* is the name of a defined function. Modify the functions in your `calculator` file so that if the first member of the list given to `prefix` is the name of a LISP function or if the first member of any sublist of that list is the name of a LISP function, that list or sublist is not modified.

19.15 *(d)* Redo Exercise 4.17 using `compute`.

19.16 *(p2)* Redo Exercise 11.4 using `compute`. Store `discrim` and `quad-roots` on the file `calculator`.

CHAPTER 20

FUNCTIONS WITH ARBITRARY NUMBERS OF ARGUMENTS

In Chapter 19, we defined `compute` so that we could use (`compute` '(7 + 12 / 4 - 2 * 3)) instead of (- (+ 7 (/ 12 4))(* 2 3)). This is an improvement, but it would be even better if we could use the form (`compute` 7 + 12 / 4 - 2 * 3). There are two problems here. First, this would require `compute` to be a function with an arbitrary number of arguments. (As defined in Chapter 19, `compute` is a function of one argument.) Although the form shown here gives `compute` nine arguments (`compute` is the first element of a ten-element list), we sometimes would want to evaluate something as simple as (`compute` 7 + 3), where `compute` is given three arguments. All the functions we have defined so far have a fixed number of arguments. The second problem is that `compute`, as used here, must not have its arguments evaluated. Although there is no problem evaluating 7 and 12 (they evaluate to themselves), +, /, -, and * are also arguments, and they are not bound to any values. Moreover, we don't want to evaluate them; `prefix` must examine them as is. Every function we've defined so far gets its arguments evaluated.

We will discuss how to solve the first of these two problems in this chapter. We will discuss the second in Chapter 23. In this chapter, our goal for `compute` will be to be able to use forms such as (`compute` 7 '+ 12 '/ 4 '- 2 '* 3) and (`compute` 7 '+ 3).

We have already discussed and used functions that have arbitrary numbers of arguments. They were all functions already provided in COMMON LISP, such as +, =, `list`, `and`, and `cond`. To define your own function to take an arbitrary number of arguments, add to the end of the list of lambda variables the *lambda-list keyword* `&rest` and follow it by another lambda variable of your own choosing. This last lambda variable is referred to as a *rest* parameter. After the previous lambda variables (if any) are bound to their corresponding actual arguments, the *rest* parameter is bound to a list of the remaining actual arguments. If there are no other lambda variables before `&rest`, the *rest* parameter is bound to a list of all the actual arguments. Notice this means that if there is only a *rest* parameter, the function may have zero or any number of arguments, whereas if there are n regular lambda variables and a *rest* parameter, the function may have n or more arguments.

The simplest example of a function with a *rest* parameter is the definition of `list`:

```
(defun list (&rest objects)
  "Returns a list of all its arguments
   in the given order."
  objects)
```

Here, `objects` is the *rest* parameter, and there are no other lambda variables. So when `list` is called—for example, when (`list` 'a 'b 'c) is evaluated—`objects` is bound to a list of the arguments (evaluated, of course). Since `objects` is the form in the function definition, `list` returns what `objects` is bound to—the list of arguments. Thus, this `list` behaves exactly like the `lisp:list` you have been using.

Simple examples of functions that require one or more arguments, and that therefore are defined with one regular lambda variable and a *rest* parameter, are the arithmetic comparison functions <, <=, >, and >=. As an example, we will define <=, which we defined on page 85 as a function of exactly two arguments. There we assumed that < and = were already defined. Here we will assume only that - and `minusp` are defined. (`minusp` n) is True if the number n is less than zero and False if it isn't. It is often convenient when defining a function of an arbitrary number of arguments to first define a version that takes two arguments. For <=, it's convenient to first define a two-argument greater-than function:

```
(defun greaterp (x y)
  "Returns T if the number X is greater than the number Y;
   NIL otherwise."
  (check-type x number)
  (check-type y number)
  (minusp (- y x)))
```

We can now define <= as

```
(defun <= (x &rest numbers)
  "Returns T if x is less than or equal to the first
   number in the list NUMBERS, and each number in that
   list is less than or equal to the next;
   NIL otherwise."
  (cond ((null numbers) t)
        ((greaterp x (first numbers)) nil)
        (t (eval '(<= ,@numbers)))))
```

The definition of compute that I said was the goal of this chapter is

```
(defun compute (&rest expr)
  "Returns the value of the arithmetic expression EXPR.
   EXPR is to be a list containing an expression
   in normal, infix notation,
   except that operators must be quoted."
  (check-type expr list)
  (eval (prefix expr)))
```

Compare this definition with the one in Chapter 19.

Exercises

Do the exercises of this chapter in the package ch20 except where otherwise instructed.

20.1 *(r)* Shadow lisp:list and define list as shown in this chapter. Test it. How does it compare with lisp:list?

20.2 *(r)* Shadow `lisp:<=` and define **greaterp** and `<=` as shown in this chapter. Test them and compare `ch20::<=` with `lisp:<=`.

20.3 *(p2)* Redefine the function **compute** in your **calculator** file as shown in this chapter and test it.

20.4 *(d)* Redo Exercise 4.17 using the latest version of **compute**.

20.5 *(p2)* Redefine the functions **discrim** and **quad-roots** in your **calculator** file to use the newest version of **compute** and test them. Remember that every one of the arbitrary number of **compute**'s arguments will be evaluated.

CHAPTER 21

MAPPING FUNCTIONS

Occasionally, we want to write a function that takes a list and returns a list just like the old one except that some operation has been performed on every element. For example, consider using a list of numbers to represent a vector and writing a function to add 1 to every element of the vector.[1] We could do this as follows:

```
(defun scalar-add1 (vector)
  "VECTOR is a list of numbers.
   Returns a list just like it,
   except that each number in it is incremented by 1."
  (check-type vector list)
    (typecase vector
    (null '())
    (cons (cons (1+ (first vector))
                (scalar-add1 (rest vector))))))
```

The only trouble with this definition is that it is not clear that the same operation is being performed on every element of the list with no possibility of skipping an element or stopping early. It would be clearer if we could simply say "add 1 to every element." Assuming we had a

---

[1]COMMON LISP actually has an **array** data type, but using lists to represent arrays provides nice examples for this chapter.

function `apply-to-each` that took a function and a list and returned
a list of the results of applying the function to each element of the list,
we could define `scalar-add1` as

```
(defun scalar-add1 (vector)
  "VECTOR is a list of numbers.
   Returns a list just like it,
    except that each number in it is incremented by 1."
  (check-type vector list)
  (apply-to-each The_function_whose_name_is_1+ vector))
```

That is much clearer. However, we must discuss the COMMON LISP
version of *The_function_whose_name_is_1+*.

In COMMON LISP, functions form their own data type of objects.
When we evaluate a form like (`defun fn ...`), the effect is to create
a new function object and associate it with the symbol `fn` so that `fn`
becomes the *name* of the newly created function. The COMMON LISP
function `symbol-function` takes a symbol that names a function and
returns the function it names, just as `symbol-name` returns the name
of the symbol. So, one way to express *The_function_whose_name_is_1+*
is (`symbol-function '1+`). However, a more general technique is
to use the *special form* `function`. `function` is a special form (as is
`quote`) that takes an unevaluated LISP object and tries to *coerce* it
into a function object. If successful, it returns that function; otherwise it produces an error. In particular, if its argument is a symbol
that names a function, `function` returns the function that the symbol
names. Thus, another way to express *The_function_whose_name_is_1+*
is (`function 1+`). Finally, just as (`quote a`) may be written as
`'a`, (`function fn`) may be written as `#'fn`. So the ultimate way,
and the way normally used by COMMON LISPers, to express
The_function_whose_name_is_1+ is `#'1+`.[2] So our next version of
`scalar-add1`, then, is

```
(defun scalar-add1 (vector)
  "VECTOR is a list of numbers.
   Returns a list just like it,
    except that each number in it is incremented by 1."
```

---

[2]This discussion follows the new COMMON LISP standard. Current implementations may not be as strict about what a function object is, but they allow the use
of `function` and `#'` as described, and LISPers should get used to using them.

```
(check-type vector list)
(apply-to-each #'1+ vector))
```

COMMON LISP already has a function like `apply-to-each` called `mapcar`. The name is a concatenation of "map" and "car." In mathematics, a *map* of one set onto another is a correspondence between the elements of each set. `mapcar` takes a function and a list, and produces another list such that the function forms the correspondence between the elements of the two lists. `car` is the original LISP name for the `first` function, and, as you can see by looking at the first version of `scalar-add1` above, `mapcar` replaces a recursion in which the function is always applied to the first member (the `car`) of the list. It is useful to think of `mapcar` as implementing a parallel control structure in which each member of the argument list is mapped into a member of the result list in parallel. Our final version of `scalar-add1` is thus

```
(defun scalar-add1 (vector)
  "VECTOR is a list of numbers.
   Returns a list just like it,
   except that each number in it is incremented by 1."
  (check-type vector list)
  (mapcar #'1+ vector))
```

What if the function we want to map down a list takes more than one argument? We will consider two cases: the case where only one argument varies and the case where all the arguments vary. As an example of the first case, consider the function (`subst*` *new old l*) defined in Exercise 17.12. We can rephrase what `subst*` does: apply to each element of *l* a function that returns *new* if the element is `eql` to *old* but returns the element itself otherwise. This function takes only one argument, but must use the values of *new* and *old*. We can do this by using *closures* of *lambda expressions*.

A *lambda expression* is a list of the form (`lambda` *lambda-list form*), where *lambda-list* is just like the list of lambda variables (possibly including a *rest* parameter) provided to `defun`, and *form* is any LISP object that can be evaluated. A lambda expression can be used as the first member of a list form, and it acts just as if some function `fn` were defined as (`defun fn` *lambda-list form*) and `fn` were the first member of the list form. For example:

```
> ((lambda (x y) (+ x y))
   4 5)
9
> ((lambda (new old elt) (if (eql old elt) new elt))
   'a 'x 'b)
B
> ((lambda (new old elt) (if (eql old elt) new elt))
   'a 'x 'x)
A
```

A *closure* is a kind of function object in which a *free* variable is bound to the value it was given in some outer environment. A closure can be created by the function special form applied to a lambda expression. For example, in the lambda expression

```
(lambda (elt) (if (eql old elt) new elt))
```

the variables old and new are *free*. The function #'(lambda (elt) (if (eql old elt) new elt)), is a closure in which old and new have the values they were bound to in the environment surrounding the lambda expression. Of course, if the closure is made at the top level, the free variables will be unbound in the outer environment, but if the closure is made within a function body, the free variables may have values, especially if they themselves are lambda variables of the function. For example, subst* may be defined as

```
(defun subst* (new old l)
  "Returns a list like L,
   with every member EQL to OLD replaced by NEW."
  (check-type l list)
  (check-type new util:element)
  (check-type old util:element)
  (mapcar #'(lambda (elt)
              (if (eql old elt) new
                  elt))
          l))
```

The closure will actually be created each time subst* is called. In each case, new and old will be bound to the first and second actual arguments of subst*. Then the closure will be formed with new and old bound to those values, and this closure will be applied to each member of the list l.

COMMON LISP's mapcar may be given one or any number of lists, as if it were defined as

```
(defun mapcar (function list &rest more-lists) ...)
```

It must be given as many lists as the number of arguments the function takes. The lists are taken to be a list of first arguments, a list of second arguments, and so on. The function is applied to the first of each list, the second of each list, and so on. For example:

```
> (mapcar #'cons '(a c e g) '((b) (d) (f) (h)))
((A B) (C D) (E F) (G H))
```

If the lists are of different lengths, the result list will be of the same length as the shortest list. The remaining members of the longer lists will be ignored:

```
> (mapcar #'+ '(1 2 3 4) '(5 6 7) '(8 9 10 11 12 13 14))
(14 17 20)
```

Exercises

Do the exercises of this chapter in the package ch21 except where otherwise instructed.

21.1 *(r)* Define scalar-add1 according to the first version in this chapter. Test it.

21.2 *(r)* Redefine scalar-add1 using mapcar. Test it.

21.3 *(r)* Check LISP's values of

```
((lambda (x y) (+ x y)) 4 5)
((lambda (new old elt) (if (eql old elt) new elt))
 'a 'x 'b)
```

and

```
((lambda (new old elt) (if (eql old elt) new elt))
 'a 'x 'x)
```

21.4 *(r)* Define `subst*` as in this chapter. Test it.

21.5 *(d)* Using `mapcar`, define (`scalar-plus` *n vector*) to return the results of adding the number *n* to every element of the list *vector*.

21.6 *(d)* Using `mapcar`, define (`scalar-times` *n vector*) to return the results of multiplying every element of the list *vector* by the number *N*.

21.7 *(d)* Define `copy` (see page 109) using `mapcar`. Make sure you check that a copy of a list is `equal` to, but not `eql` to the original. (Hint: Consider the `identity` function you learned about in Exercise 17.3.)

21.8 *(d)* If we consider *vector1* to be a column of *n* elements and *vector2* to be a row of *m* elements, the product of the two vectors is a matrix of *n* rows and *m* columns whose *i*th row is each element of *vector2* multiplied by the *i*th element of *vector1*. A matrix can be represented as a list of rows, each of which is a list. For example, the product of the column (1 2) and the row (3 4 5) would be the matrix ((3 4 5) (6 8 10)). Define (`vector-product` *vector1 vector2*) to be the product of the column vector *vector1* and the row vector *vector2* as described here.

21.9 *(p2)* Redefine the function `prefix` in your `calculator` file so that if the first member of a list given to `prefix` is the name of a LISP function, the arguments of that function are converted from infix to Cambridge Prefix form, if necessary. Remember that the first member of an infix expression could be a unary `+` or `-`.

21.10 *(p2)* Redefine the function `discrim` in your `calculator` file to take advantage of your revised `prefix`.

CHAPTER 22

THE APPLICATOR

In Chapter 19, we looked at **eval**. It is a function of one argument that gets its argument evaluated and evaluates it again. **eval** is the heart of **lisp**, but it is sometimes inconvenient to use.

Recall that on page 110, we defined (**append** l1 l2) to return the concatenation of the lists l1 and l2. That is, **append** returns a list consisting of the members of l1 followed by the members of l2. The function **lisp:append** actually takes an arbitrary number of list arguments and concatenates them all together. Let's see how we could define that version of **append**. As usual, we will first define a two-argument **append** and use that in our definition of our final **append**. Let's call the **append** that takes two arguments **append2** and define it as we defined **append** on page 110:

```
(defun append2 (l1 l2)
  "Returns a list consisting of the members of L1
   followed by the members of L2."
  (check-type l1 list)
  (check-type l2 list)
  (if (null l1) l2
      (cons (first l1) (append2 (rest l1) l2))))
```

To plan our definition of **append**, notice the following facts about how **lisp:append** works: **lisp:append** of no arguments evaluates

159

to (), lisp:append of one argument evaluates to its argument unchanged, and lisp:append of more than one argument copies all its argument lists but the last. So a plan for writing **append** is as follows: let lists be a list of the argument lists; if lists is empty, return (); if lists has just one list in it, return that list; otherwise, return the concatenation (using **append2**) of (first lists) with the concatenation (using **append**) of all the lists in (rest lists). A first attempt at defining **append** is

```
(defun append (\&rest lists)
  "Returns a list whose members are the concatenation of
   the members of the lists in LISTS in the order given."
  (cond ((null lists) '())
        ((null (rest lists)) (first lists))
        (t (append2 (first lists)
                    (append (rest lists))))))
```

That's close, but wrong! The form (append (rest lists)) calls **append** with one argument that is a list of lists, rather than with zero or more arguments each of which is a list. We could, of course, define a help function that takes one list of lists and returns the concatenation of them, but that would be an overabundance of concatenators. What we really want is to evaluate a form with **append** as its first member and the rest of the lists as its **rest**. It would seem that we could do this by changing (append (rest lists)) to (eval '(append ,@(rest lists))). However, there is a slight problem. (rest lists) is not a list of all but the first argument forms originally used in the call to **append**, but a list of all but the first actual arguments. If the original call were

(append '(a b c) '(d e) '(f g h))

'(append ,@(rest lists)) would be (append (d e) (f g h)), and evaluating this would require evaluating (d e) which would involve a call to the undefined function d. Instead, we must quote each element of (rest lists). That is, we must produce a list just like (rest lists) but in which each element list is replaced by 'list (which, remember, is actually the list (quote list)). We can do this by

(mapcar #'(lambda (l) (list 'quote l)) (rest lists))

So this version of `append` is

```
(defun append (&rest lists)
  "Returns a list whose members are the concatenation of
   the members of the lists in LISTS in the order given."
  (cond ((null lists) '())
        ((null (rest lists)) (first lists))
        (t (append2
             (first lists)
             (eval
               '(append ,@(mapcar
                            #'(lambda (l) (list 'quote l))
                            (rest lists)))))))))
```

This works, but LISP has a much easier way. Instead of any form like

```
(eval '(fn ,@(mapcar #'(lambda (l) (list 'quote l))
                     arguments)))
```

we can use (`apply` *fn arguments*). `apply` is a function of two arguments. The first must be a function object or a symbol that names
a function. The second must be (that is, must evaluate to) a list of
arguments for the function. `apply` applies the function to the arguments and returns the value. Back on page 21, I said that the value of
a list is the value obtained by applying the function named by the first
member of the list to the values of the other members of the list. `apply`
is the LISP's function that applies functions to arguments. (+ 12 4)
evaluates to 16, as does (`apply` #'+ '(12 4)).

Our final version of `append` is

```
(defun append (&rest lists)
  "Returns a list whose members are the concatenation of
   the members of the lists in LISTS in the order given."
  (cond ((null lists) '())
        ((null (rest lists)) (first lists))
        (t (append2 (first lists)
                    (apply #'append (rest lists))))))
```

`apply` is easy to use when you have a list of all the arguments. If
you have each argument separately, `funcall` is often easier to use.
`funcall` takes one or more arguments. The first must be a function

object or a symbol that names a function. The others are arguments for the function. `funcall` applies the function to the arguments and returns the result. Compare:

```
> (apply #'cons '(a (b)))
(A B)
> (funcall #'cons 'a '(b))
(A B)
```

Of course, if you have the function and the arguments separately, why not just use a normal form with the function as the first member of the list, such as

```
> (cons 'a '(b))
(A B)
```

The answer is that `funcall` allows you to *compute* the function, whereas the first member of a list form must be a lambda expression or a symbol that names a function. With `funcall`, you can do things like

```
> (funcall (third '(first rest cons)) 'a '(b))
(A B)
```

In COMMON LISP, `apply` is actually midway between `funcall` and `apply` as we have so far described it. `apply` can take one or more arguments, not just two. The first and last arguments are as we have described them so far. However the intermediate arguments can be initial arguments for the functions, as for `funcall`. For example:

```
> (funcall #'+ 1 2 3 4)
10
> (apply #'+ '(1 2 3 4))
10
> (apply #'+ 1 '(2 3 4))
10
> (apply #'+ 1 2 '(3 4))
10
> (apply #'+ 1 2 3 '(4))
10
> (apply #'+ 1 2 3 4 '())
10
```

Let's consider defining `vector-sum` to take an arbitrary number of vectors and return their sum. All the vectors should be the same length, and the ith element of the result should be the sum of the ith elements of all the argument vectors. Notice that we can get the result we want by evaluating a form like (`mapcar #'+` $vector_1 \ldots vector_n$) but the vectors will be gathered in the *rest* parameter of `vector-sum` as a list. The solution is

```
(defun vector-sum (&rest vectors)
  "Returns a vector that is the sum of
   all the argument vectors."
  (apply #'mapcar #'+ vectors))
```

Notice that `#'+` is the first argument of `mapcar` and that `vectors` is a list of the rest.

Exercises

Do the exercises of this chapter in the package `ch22` except where otherwise instructed.

22.1 *(r)* Define `append2` as shown in this chapter and test it.

22.2 *(r)* Verify that `lisp:append` of no arguments evaluates to `()`, `lisp:append` of one argument evaluates to its argument unchanged, and `lisp:append` of more than one argument copies all its argument lists but the last.

22.3 *(r)* Shadow `lisp:append` and define `ch22::append` the way it is done the first time in this chapter. Test it until you understand the error.

22.4 *(r)* Redefine `append` to use (`eval` `` `(append ,@(rest lists)))``). Test it.

22.5 *(r)* Redefine `append` to use

```
(mapcar #'(lambda (l) (list 'quote l)) (rest lists))
```

Test this version.

22.6 *(r)* Finally, redefine `append` using `apply` and test this version.

22.7 *(r)* Try evaluating (+ 12 4), (eval (cons '+ '(12 4))), and (apply '+ '(12 4)).

22.8 *(d)* Define the function xprod of Exercise 17.28, using mapcar and apply.

22.9 *(d)* Redefine depth from page 133 to use apply and mapcar. (Note that lisp:max can take an arbitrary number of arguments.) Test it. Compare it with the version on page 133.

22.10 *(r)* Check and compare LISP's value of

```
(apply #'cons '(a (b)))
(funcall #'cons 'a '(b))
(cons 'a '(b))
((third '(first rest cons)) 'a '(b))
(funcall (third '(first rest cons)) 'a '(b))
(funcall #'+ 1 2 3 4)
(apply #'+ '(1 2 3 4))
(apply #'+ 1 '(2 3 4))
(apply #'+ 1 2 '(3 4))
(apply #'+ 1 2 3 '(4))
(apply #'+ 1 2 3 4 '())
```

22.11 *(r)* Define vector-sum as in this chapter and test it.

22.12 *(u)* In COMMON LISP, if mapcar's lists are of different lengths, mapcar stops as soon as the shortest is exhausted. A different solution would be to consider the shorter lists to be extended, by repetition of the last member, until all lists have the same length as the longest. Call this version mapcar-ext. Using mapcar-ext, scalar-plus of Exercise 21.5 could be defined as

```
(defun scalar-plus (n vector)
  "Returns a copy of the vector VECTOR,
   with every element incremented by N."
  (mapcar-ext #'+ (list n) vector))
```

Define mapcar-ext as suggested here and add it, as an external symbol, to your util file. (Hints: I used two help functions, of

which one knows the length of the longest list and the other is a
special-purpose **rest** function. In writing these three functions,
I used **mapcar**, **apply**, **max**, **length**, and some other functions.)

22.13 *(d)* Using your **mapcar-ext** define and test **scalar-plus** as shown
above.

CHAPTER 23

MACROS

At the beginning of Chapter 20, I identified two problems that keep us from defining a better version of `compute`. One was the need to define a function that takes an arbitrary number of arguments; that problem was solved in that chapter. The other problem was the need to define a function that gets its arguments unevaluated. We will learn how to do that in this chapter.

As you should know by now, the basic operation of COMMON LISP is to evaluate a form. The COMMON LISP listener reads an S-expression, constructs the form it expresses, evaluates the form, and prints a representation of the value. Applying a function involves binding the formal parameters to the actual arguments and evaluating the form that is the body of the function definition. We have also seen that COMMON LISP has functionlike objects called *special forms* that act like functions but get their arguments unevaluated. We have seen the two special forms `quote` and `function`, and actually `if` is also a special form, although I have not previously mentioned that fact. We cannot define our own special forms, but we can define *macros,* which are another kind of functionlike object that get their arguments unevaluated.

Although a special form is different from a function in that it gets its arguments unevaluated, it is like a function in that it returns a value. When COMMON LISP evaluates a list, if its first member is

167

the name of a function or of a special form, the value of the list is
simply the value returned by the function or the special form. Macros
are like special forms in not getting their arguments evaluated, but
they are different from both special forms and from functions in what
they return. Instead of returning a simple value, a macro returns a
form that is automatically evaluated again by COMMON LISP. That
is, if COMMON LISP goes to evaluate a list, and its first member is
a symbol that names a macro, COMMON LISP "calls" the macro, the
macro returns a form, COMMON LISP evaluates the form, and that
value, finally, is the value of the original list.

You can define a macro just as you define a function, except that you
use defmacro instead of defun. The two have the same syntax. Later
we will learn some facilities that defmacro has that defun doesn't.
So, for example, let's define a function and a macro that are almost
identical:

```
> (defun pluslist-f (x y)
    "Returns a list that represents
     the sum of the numbers x and y."
    (check-type x number)
    (check-type y number)
    '(+ ,x ,y))
PLUSLIST-F
> (defmacro pluslist-m (x y)
    "Returns the sum of the numbers x and y."
    (check-type x number)
    (check-type y number)
    '(+ ,x ,y))
PLUSLIST-M
> (pluslist-f 4 5)
(+ 4 5)
> (pluslist-m 4 5)
9
```

Notice that, whereas the value returned by the function is the value
of the form that calls the function, the value "returned" by the macro
is evaluated again before becoming the value of the form that called
the macro. We say that the macro returns a *macro expansion,* which is
evaluated again by COMMON LISP. A very significant point is that the
macro expansion is evaluated outside the environment of the macro

definition. That is, when the expansion of (pluslist-m 4 5) was being computed, x and y had values—namely, 4 and 5, respectively. However, when the expansion (+ 4 5) was being evaluated, x and y no longer had values. The macro finishes when it returns its expansion. Then the expansion is evaluated. To see the expansion returned by a macro, give a form that calls a macro to the function macroexpand:

```
> (macroexpand '(pluslist-m 4 5))
(+ 4 5)
T
```

The two lines following my call of macroexpand were the *two* values returned by macroexpand.[1] The first is the expansion of the argument form; the second is True, indicating that the argument form was indeed a macro call. If the argument form is not a macro call, the first value will be the form itself and the second will be False:

```
> (macroexpand '(pluslist-f 4 5))
(PLUSLIST-F 4 5)
NIL
```

Since the arguments of pluslist-m are numbers, it is not clear whether pluslist-m is getting them evaluated or unevaluated. In fact, it is getting them unevaluated, which will be clear in a definition of if that includes the keywords then and else as dummies:

```
> (shadow 'if)
T
> (defmacro if
    (condition then then-clause else else-clause)
    "If CONDITION evaluates to True,
     evaluates and returns THEN-CLAUSE,
     otherwise evaluates and returns ELSE-CLAUSE."
    '(lisp:if ,condition ,then-clause ,else-clause))
IF
> (if t then 'yes else 'no)
YES
```

---

[1]COMMON LISP provides a facility that can be used to have a function return more than one value, and several facilities for making use of such *multiple* values. These facilities can safely be ignored by the novice LISPer, and we will not have a chance to discuss them in this book.

```
> (macroexpand '(if t then 'yes else 'no))
(LISP:IF T (QUOTE YES) (QUOTE NO))
T
```

Notice that the five argument forms of if (including then and else) were not evaluated. In particular, during the evaluation of the body of the definition of if, then-clause was bound to the actual argument (quote yes) not to the value of that form, which is yes.

The definition of if also illustrates the most common use of macros—to define new COMMON LISP forms as "syntactic sugar" for (variants of) old forms. In this way, we can eventually change the entire look of COMMON LISP itself. The use of macros merely as functions that get their arguments unevaluated is actually a secondary use although this is the only way a programmer can define such functions.

So, remembering that defmacro, like defun, can take *rest* parameters, we can define the compute we desired in Chapter 20 as

```
(defmacro compute (&rest expr)
  "Returns the value of the arithmetic expression EXPR.
  EXPR is to be a list containing an expression
  in normal, infix notation."
  (prefix expr))
```

A few final points about macros are important to remember:

- Macros are not functions and so cannot be used by mapcar, apply, or funcall.

- Macro calls are expanded during compilation, so macro definitions must precede their use in files, and if you redefine a macro, you must recompile the functions that use it.

- Some implementations of COMMON LISP expand macro calls when source files are loaded. In these implementations, macros cannot be traced, macro definitions must precede their use in files, and if you redefine a macro, you must reload the functions that use it.

- Some implementations of COMMON LISP replace a macro form by its expansion in an interpreted (uncompiled) function the first time the macro form is evaluated. In these implementations, a traced macro will produce tracing output only when the macro is actually called, not after its form has been replaced. If you redefine a macro in one of these implementations, you must reload the functions that use it, if you have already used those functions. Even if **symbol-function** shows you function definitions, it may not be obvious that a replacement has taken place because your COMMON LISP may print the macro form even though its been replaced.

Exercises

Do the exercises of this chapter in the package **ch23** except where otherwise instructed.

23.1 *(r)* Define **pluslist-f** and **pluslist-m** as shown in this chapter and test them.

23.2 *(r)* Evaluate
(macroexpand '(pluslist-m 4 5))
and
(macroexpand '(pluslist-f 4 5)).

23.3 *(i)* Try evaluating (pluslist-m (+ 3 4) 5). Notice that, since a macro gets its argument forms unevaluated, the **check-type** that we supplied is too restrictive.

23.4 *(i)* Redefine **pluslist-m** without using any **check-type**, and try evaluating (pluslist-m (+ 3 4) 5) again. Also evaluate (macroexpand '(pluslist-f (+ 3 4) 5)).

23.5 *(r)* Shadow **lisp:if** and define and test the **if** macro shown in this chapter.

23.6 *(p2)* Redefine the function **compute** in your **calculator** file to be a macro as shown in this chapter.

23.7 *(d)* Redo Exercise 4.17 using your latest version of **compute**.

23.8 *(p2)* Redefine the functions **discrim** and **quad-roots** in your **calculator** file to use the newest version of **compute**, and test them.

23.9 *(d)* Shadow `lisp:and` and define your own `ch23:and` as a macro that works exactly like `lisp:and`.

Part III

PROGRAMMING IN IMPERATIVE LISP

CHAPTER 24

ASSIGNMENT

Up to now, everything we have done with LISP has been done using
what is called "pure" LISP. That is, with a few minor exceptions, we
have used LISP as a pure *applicative* (or *functional*) programming language. In an applicative programming language, the only thing one
can do is *apply* functions to their arguments and get back their values.
Doing that does not change the environment of the programming system. After evaluating (cons 'a (rest '(x b c))), everything is the
same as it would have been had we not done it. Some ways we have
seen for changing the environment have included defining a function,
turning tracing on or off, and changing packages with in-package.
Changing the environment is called *side-effecting*. Functions like defun
and in-package are used principally for their side effects rather than
for their values. Although applicative programming has become more
popular recently, LISP, or rather the pure subset of LISP, was the first
applicative programming language.

Even though any program that can be written in any programming language can be written in pure LISP, LISPers often find the
nonpure facilities of LISP helpful. These facilities are based on the
facilities of *imperative* programming languages. These languages have
the *statement* as their basic structure, instead of the form. Statements
are orders to do something. That's why these languages are called

imperative. The imperative features of COMMON LISP are the subject of Part III of this book.

The most basic imperative statement is the *assignment* statement, which assigns a value to a variable. LISP, of course, uses assignment *functions* rather than assignment statements. COMMON LISP has eight different assignment functions: `defconstant`, `defparameter`, `defvar`, `set`, `setq`, `psetq`, `setf`, and `psetf`.

(`defconstant` *symbol value documentation*) makes *value* the value of the *symbol* and makes it illegal to give *symbol* any other value. *documentation* is a string that describes what *symbol* is supposed to stand for; it is retrievable by (`documentation` *symbol* `'variable`). `defconstant` is used to define constants that never change and are, therefore, most often put into program files before any macros or functions are defined. The symbol `pi` is a predefined constant. If we wanted to define the constant `e`, the base of the natural logarithms, we could do

```
> (defconstant e 2.6931471806d0
      "The base of the natural logarithms")
E
> e
2.6931471806d0
> (documentation 'e 'variable)
"The base of the natural logarithms"
```

`defparameter` is like `defconstant`, except that trying to change the value of the *symbol* does not cause an error. Presumably, however, parameters remain unchanged during the run of a program and change only at the beginning of a new run. `defparameter` forms typically appear in files after any `defconstant` forms and before any macro or function definitions.

`defvar` is like defparameter, except that *symbol*'s value is expected to change during the run of the program; the *value* is only an initial value. We refer to the symbol defined by `defvar` as a *global variable* because every function in the same package can access it and change its value. `defvar` forms typically appear in files after any `defparameter` forms and before any macro or function definitions. A peculiar feature of `defvar` is that if the *symbol* already has a value, `defvar` does not evaluate its *value* argument and does not give the *symbol* a new value.

This can lead to frustration: you load a file with some `defvar` forms, test the program, which results in changes to the values of the global variables, edit the program, and reload the file—the global variables are not reinitialized to the values in the `defvar` forms, because they already have values.

`defconstant`, `defparameter`, and `defvar` all are typically executed at the top level of LISP and are usually found in files, rather than being typed interactively to the LISP listener. The other five assignment functions `set`, `setq`, `psetq`, `setf`, and `psetf` are most often found within function definitions or are typed interactively to the LISP listener. They should not be used as top-level forms in files, except temporarily while debugging a file to avoid the problems with `defvar`.

(`set` *symbol value*) evaluates both its arguments. The first argument must evaluate to a symbol; the other can evaluate to any LISP object. `set` returns the value of its second argument, but its main purpose is to bind the symbol to that value.

```
> (set 'a 'b)
B
> a
B
> (set (third '(a b c d)) (+ 5 3))
8
> c
8
```

`set` is actually not used very much.

(`setq` x y) is almost exactly equivalent to (`set` 'x y). The difference is that `set` can be used to change the values of global variables and cannot be used to change the values of lambda variables, whereas `setq` can be used to change the value of any kind of variable.

`setf` is a macro. (`setf` x y) expands to (`setq` x y). However, `setf` is a generalized `setq` that can be used in circumstances where `setq` cannot be used. We will see some of these circumstances later. Older dialects of LISP did not have `setf`, and there is a controversy among users of COMMON LISP. Some believe that with `setf` available, `setq` should never be used again. Others believe in using `setq` in all circumstances where `setf` would expand into `setq` anyway. Although, as a longtime LISPer, I find myself using `setq`, I basically agree with

the first group and so will not use setq in this book after this chapter.
I recommend the same for you. If you never use setq, it will not
become a habit, and setf will seem perfectly natural.

setq and setf (but not set) can take an arbitrarily long sequence
of *symbol value* pairs. Each symbol is bound to the value that follows
it, and all the binding is done serially, so that the earlier symbols can
be used in the later value-forms. For example:

```
> (setq x0 1 x1 1 x2 (+ x1 x0) x3 (+ x2 x1) x4 (+ x3 x2))
5
> x3
3
> x4
5
```

A way to exchange the values of two variables is

```
> (setf temp x1 x1 x4 x4 temp)
1
> x1
5
> x4
1
```

psetq and psetf are exactly like setq and setf, respectively, except
that all the bindings are done in parallel. For example, another way
to exchange the values of two variables is

```
> (psetf x1 x4 x4 x1)
NIL
> x1
1
> x4
5
```

As we shall see, COMMON LISP has a large and flexible enough set
of imperative constructs that none of the assignment functions need
be used very often, but understanding them provides a base for all the
imperative constructs.

Exercises

Do the exercises of this chapter in the package **ch24** except where
otherwise instructed.

24.1 *(r)* Try typing the atom **x** to the LISP listener. Does it have a
value?

24.2 *(r)* Evaluate (**set** '**x** (+ 5 3)). What value does **set** return?
What value does **x** have now?

24.3 *(r)* Evaluate (**setq x** '**y**). What value does **x** have now?

24.4 *(d)* Evaluate (**set x** (+ 9 2)). What value does **x** have now?
What value does **y** have now?

24.5 *(d)* What is the value of (**eval x**)? Why?

24.6 *(i)* Do several parts of Exercise 8.7 again. Now do

```
(setq list '(((a b) (c d) e) (f g) (h) i))
```

Now redo all of Exercise 8.7 by typing in forms such as

```
(first (first (first list)))
```

and

```
(first (first (rest list)))
```

After each one, check that the top-level value of **list** hasn't
changed.

24.7 *(r)* Evaluate

```
(defconstant e 2.6931471806d0
    "The base of the natural logarithms")
```

Then evaluate e. Now try to change e's value with **set** or **setf**.
You shouldn't be able to.

24.8 *(p2)* Modify your `calculator` file so that every occurrence of a quoted operator or a quoted list of operators is replaced by an appropriately named symbolic constant you define near the beginning of the file.

24.9 *(p1)* In your `match` file, define the function

```
(apply-rules tree rule-list)
```

to apply the first rule on the list `RULE-LIST` to `TREE`, the second rule to the result of applying the first, and so on, and return the result of applying the last rule to the results of the second-to-last.

24.10 *(p1)* In your `match` file, define the parameter `*grammar-rules*` to be the following list:

```
(((john ?v ?n) ((n john) ?v ?n))
 ((?n1 loves ?n2) (?n1 (v loves) ?n2))
 ((?n ?v mary) (?n ?v (n mary)))
 ((?n1 (v ?v) (n ?n2)) (?n1 (vp (v ?v) (n ?n2))))
 (((n ?n1) (vp ?v ?n2)) (s (n ?n1) (vp ?v ?n2))))
```

Test `(apply-rules '(John loves Mary) *grammar-rules*)`. You have written a small, admittedly inflexible, parser of a tiny fragment of English.

24.11 *(r)* Create a file named `testvar` in the `test` package. In it, define a variable called `count` with an initial value of 0 and a function called `increment` that, every time it is called, increments `count` by 1. Load this file and test `increment` by calling it a few times; look at the value of `count` after each call. Now reload the `testvar` file. Has `count` been reinitialized? Get out of LISP, back in, and load `testvar` again. What is `count` now? You needn't save `testvar`.

24.12 *(r)* Evaluate

```
(setf x0 1 x1 1 x2 (+ x1 x0)
         x3 (+ x2 x1) x4 (+ x3 x2))
```

Check the value of each `xi`.

24.13 *(r)* Exchange the values of **x1** and **x4** with one call to **setf**.

24.14 *(r)* Exchange the values of **x2** and **x3** with one call to **psetf** and without using a third variable.

CHAPTER 25

SCOPE AND EXTENT

Now that we have entered the world of imperative programming, we must distinguish more carefully the notions of *variables* and *symbols*. Technically, a *variable* is a complex object consisting of a *name*, a *storage location*, and a *value*. In COMMON LISP, *symbols* are used to name variables, just as they are used to name functions. In the past, whenever we spoke of the "value of a symbol," we were just using a shorthand way of saying the "value of the variable the symbol names." As we shall see shortly, just as one symbol can name both a function and a variable, a symbol can simultaneously name several variables.

The *scope* of a variable is the spatiotemporal area of a program in which a given variable has a given name. The *extent* of a variable is the spatiotemporal area of a program in which a given variable has a given storage location.[1] As long as a variable has the same name and storage location, it is easy to change its value; by using `setf`, for example.

What is meant by a LISP program anyway? In standard programming languages—such as Fortran, C, Pascal, Modula-2, and Basic—the notion of a "program" is pretty easy to understand, but in LISP, where one can spend hours in the same LISP run, loading various files and

---

[1] "Storage location" should be taken abstractly. It does not necessarily mean a particular addressable location in the computer's random access memory.

evaluating hundreds of forms, it is easy to lose track of the concept. We should consider one program to consist of everything that is done from the time one enters the COMMON LISP environment until the time one exits that environment. (If I boot my Lisp Machine on a Monday and don't turn it off or reboot it until a week and a half later, I have been running one program for all that week and a half.) Textually, the "code" of that program consists of the entire COMMON LISP implementation, plus every file loaded in the course of the run. The spatial area of a program is the text of the source code, beginning with the COMMON LISP implementation, continuing with everything you type to the LISP listener and including every file you load or that gets loaded automatically. The temporal area of the program is the time from getting into LISP until getting out of it, and everything that happens in between, in the order it happens. For example, if you type in the form (setf x 3), then load some file, and then call some function defined in that file, the text of the file is positioned spatially between the (setf x 3) form and the function call form, and everything evaluated during the loading of the file happened temporally after the setf and before the function call. (The load function explicitly saves and restores the value of *package*, which is why, if you are in one package and load a file that changes the package with in-package, you are still in the original package after the file is loaded.)

COMMON LISP uses *lexical* scope and *dynamic* extent. That is, only the spatial dimension is relevant to issues of scope, and only the temporal dimension is relevant to issues of extent.

Variables are created by COMMON LISP in several ways. One way is by typing a symbol to the LISP listener or by calling one of the assignment functions at the top level. These create *global* variables—variables whose scope and extent spread over the entire program (except for "holes" created by shadowing; see below).

Another way a variable is created is by using a symbol in the lambda list of a defun, defmacro, or lambda form. The scope of such a *local* variable is the entire defun, defmacro, or lambda form (except where it is shadowed). The extent of such a variable is from the time the function or macro is called until the time that it returns. For example, consider the following spatial section of a program:

```
(setq x 3)
```

```
(defun foo (x)
  "Uses a local variable X."
  x)

(defun bar ()
  "Has no local variables."
  x)
```

The global variable **x** occurs in the **setf** form and in the definition of **bar**. A local variable **x** is created by being in the lambda list of the definition of **foo**. This *shadows* the global **x** so that the **x** that occurs in **foo**'s body is the local **x**. Although there are two variables, they are named by the *same* symbol.

If these three forms are evaluated (the order of evaluation doesn't really matter), the value 3 is stored in the storage location of the global **x** (we still say that **x** is *bound* to 3), and the functions **foo** and **bar** are defined. We can then call **bar** and see the value of the global **x**:

```
> (bar)
3
```

If we now call **foo** with an argument, **5** say, the local **x** will be given a storage location, the value **5** will be stored there, and the body will be evaluated—causing the value of the local **x** to be accessed and returned:

```
> (foo 5)
5
```

Now that **foo** has returned, there is no way to access the storage location that was just used by the local **x**. If we call **foo** again, a new storage location will be given to the local variable. One way to see this is by creating *closures.* These are functions whose texts contain nonlocal variables, but that retain the storage locations of those variables with particular values. For example, we can create a series of functions similar to **1+**, but that add different values:

```
> (defun x+function (x)
    "Returns a function that will add X to its argument."
    #'(lambda (n) (+ n x)))
X+FUNCTION
```

Notice that the **n** of the **lambda** form is local to that form (it is in its lambda list), but the **x** there is nonlocal to it, although it is local to the **defun** form. Every call of **x+function** will return a new function:

```
> (setf 2+ (x+function 2))
#<DTP-CLOSURE 13215132>

> (setf 5+ (x+function 5))
#<DTP-CLOSURE 13220200>
```

These two functions are the *values* of the global variables **2+** and **5+**. There are no symbols that name them, so we have to use **funcall** (or **apply**, but **funcall** is easier) to call them:

```
> (funcall 2+ 5)
7
> (funcall 5+ 5)
10
```

Notice that the local variable **x**, whose scope is limited to the **defun** form defining **x+function**, has bifurcated into two extents, one of which is in the closure that is the value of **2+**, the other of which is in the closure that is the value of **5+**, and both these extents are indefinite—they will last as long as the closures last. Neither, however, is the same as that of the global **x**, which remains as we left it:

```
> x
3
```

Exercises

Do the exercises of this chapter in the package **ch25** except where otherwise instructed.

25.1 *(r)* Try for yourself all the interactions of this chapter, noting the different global and local variables.

25.2 *(r)* Enter the definition

```
(defun testset (x)
  (set 'x 5)
  x)
```

Evaluate **x**, then (**testset 7**), and then **x** again. Notice that **set** changed the value of the global **x**, not the local **x**.

25.3 *(r)* Redefine **testset** to be

```
(defun testset (x)
  (setf x 7)
  x)
```

Evaluate **x**, then (**testset 9**), and then **x** again. Notice that **setf** changed the value of the local **x**, not the global **x**.

25.4 *(i)* Define the functions **foo** and **bar** as

```
(defun foo (x)
  "Establishes a binding for X, and calls BAR."
  (bar))
```

```
(defun bar ()
  "Returns the value of the nonlocal X."
  x)
```

Evaluate **x** and then evaluate (**foo 11**). Notice again that the **x** in **bar** is the global **x**, not the local **x** created by **foo**'s lambda list. Older versions of LISP were *dynamically* scoped, so that if you called **bar** directly from the listener, its **x** would be the global **x**, but if **bar** were called from **foo**, as it was here, **bar**'s **x** would be **foo**'s.

25.5 *(i)* Create a file called **test** containing (**setf x 3**) as a top-level form, along with the definitions of **foo** and **bar** as shown in Exercise 25.4. Load the file and test it with the tests from Exercise 25.4.

25.6 *(i)* Compile the file **test**. (Review Chapter 12 if necessary.) Many compilers will warn you that there may be something funny about the **x**s in the definitions of **foo** and **bar**. You can explicitly tell the compiler that you mean to do these strange things by adding *declarations* to the function definitions right after the documentation strings. In this case, we want to declare that we do not intend to use **foo**'s lambda variable **x** in **foo**'s body. We can do this by changing the defun form to

```
(defun foo (x)
  "Establishes a binding for X, and calls BAR."
  (declare (ignore x))
  (bar))
```

We also want to declare that we intend **bar**'s **x** to be nonlocal by changing its definition to

```
(defun bar ()
  "Returns the value of the nonlocal X."
  (declare (special x))
  x)
```

Make these changes to your **test** file, compile it again, and test it again. It should work as before, but this time the compiler shouldn't complain.

25.7 *(i)* Change the declaration in the definition of **foo** in your **test** file to (declare (special x)). Compile and test the file again. This time you should find that the **x** in **bar** is the same as the **x** in **foo**. What you did by declaring **foo**'s **x** to be special was to make it dynamically scoped. Since **bar**'s **x** is also dynamically scoped, they are the same variable in this circumstance. Now call **bar** directly from the listener. Now **bar**'s **x** is dynamically made to be the same as the global **x**. You should use special variables only when extraordinary circumstances demand it.

25.8 *(i)* Edit your **test** file to eliminate the declarations, change all occurrences of **x** to **y**, and change the **setf** form to a **defvar**. Load the file and evaluate **y** and (foo 11). **defvar** *proclaims* its global variable to be special. This is equivalent to declaring the variable to be special in every function that uses the same symbol to name a variable.

CHAPTER 26

SEQUENCES

One way in which I have told less than the whole truth (for good pedagogical reasons) in the discussion of LISP so far concerns the topic of *sequences* of forms. For example, in Chapter 10, I said that the function **defun** takes four arguments—a function name, a list of variables, a documentation string, and a form (and I have since added a declaration), and I said the same about **defmacro**. In fact, that is not true. Actually, the body of a function can be a *sequence* of one or more forms. When the function is called, after binding the variables, the sequence of forms is evaluated one after the other in order. The value of the last form in the sequence is the value returned by the function call. The values of the previous forms in the sequence are ignored. If the sequence consists of just one form, then what I have said before about function evaluation still holds.

So let's consider the general format of **defun**:

```
(defun fn varlist
   doc-string declaration assertions
   form₁ ... formₙ₋₁ formₙ)
```

When *fn* is called, the variables in *varlist* are given new storage locations and are bound to the values of the actual arguments, $form_1$ through $form_n$ are evaluated, and the value of $form_n$ is returned. If

the values of $form_1$ through $form_{n-1}$ are ignored, what good are they?
If we are restricting ourselves to pure, applicative LISP, they are of *no*
good, which is why I have not mentioned this possibility until now.
However, if $form_1$ through $form_{n-1}$ cause side effects, then these side
effects will indeed occur.

The technique of lazy evaluation we looked at in Chapter 19 is very
close to the idea of *generators*. A generator is a closure that returns
another element of some computationally defined set each time it is
called. A generator for the natural numbers can be created by the
function

```
(defun natural-numbers-from (n)
  "Returns a generator function that will generate
   all the natural numbers starting from N."
  (check-type n integer)
  (setf n (1- n))
  #'(lambda ()
      (setf n (1+ n))
      n))
```

The first form in the body decrements n by 1 so that the generator
will start with the original n. The second form evaluates to a closure,
which is returned. That closure also has two forms in its body. The
first increments n; the second returns its new value. The variable n
itself is retained from call to call of the closure, as you have seen before.
Let's try this one out.

```
> (setf natnums (natural-numbers-from 0))
#<DTP-CLOSURE 2376060>

> (funcall natnums)
0
> (funcall natnums)
1
> (funcall natnums)
2
```

Another place where sequences are allowed is in **cond**. In Chapter 14, I said that the form of a **cond** is (cond $(p_1\ e_1)$ ... $(p_n\ e_n)$).
Actually, each e_i can be a sequence of zero or more forms. That is,

each cond "pair" is a list of one or more forms. So let's change terminology and say cond *clause,* instead of cond pair. If the first form of a clause evaluates to NIL, the next clause is considered. If the first form of a clause evaluates to any non-NIL value, the rest of the forms of that clause are evaluated in order, and the value of the last one is returned as the value of the cond. Values of earlier forms in the clause are ignored; they are evaluated for effect only.

Early dialects of LISP did not allow sequences as we have been discussing them. To make up for it, they had a special form called progn. The form of a progn is (progn $form_1$ ... $form_n$). The $form_i$'s are evaluated in order, and the value of the last one is returned as the value of the progn. COMMON LISP retains progn, although the existence of sequences removes most need of it.

In general, a LISP form returns the value of the last form actually evaluated within it, but there are exceptions. For example, prog1 is like progn, but after all the forms are evaluated, the value of the first one is returned. prog2 is also like progn except that the value of the second form is returned.

Exercises

Do the exercises of this chapter in the package ch26 except where otherwise instructed.

26.1 *(r)* Define natural-numbers-from as shown in this chapter, and test the generator it produces.

26.2 *(d)* Create and test a generator for the Fibonacci numbers. (See Exercise 19.7.)

26.3 *(d)* Give x and y the top-level values of nil and origy, respectively, and then evaluate

```
(cond ((null x))
      ((atom y) (setf y (list y)) 'done)
      (y))
```

What was its value? Check the values of x and y. Now change x's value to origx and evaluate the cond form again. What is its value now? What are the values of x and y now? Evaluate the same cond again. What is its value now?

26.4 *(d)* Shadow **progn** and define your own version as a function. [Hint: Use **last** (see page 72).] Test it by evaluating

  (progn (setf x 'a) (setf y 'b) (setf z 'c))

and seeing what values x, y, and z have afterward.

26.5 *(d)* Shadow **prog1** and **prog2**, and define your own versions. Test them with the forms

  (prog1 (setf x 'd) (setf y 'e) (setf z 'f))

and

  (prog2 (setf x 'g) (setf y 'h) (setf z 'i))

Check the values of x, y, and z after evaluating each form.

26.6 *(i)* Using **defvar**, give the variable *stack* the initial value (). Then define three side-effecting functions (**push** e), (**top**), and (**pop**). (**push** e) should **cons** the value of e onto the front of *stack* and return the new value of *stack*. (**top**) should return the **first** element of *stack*. (**pop**) should return the **first** element of *stack* and change *stack* to be its **rest**. Be sure **push** doesn't cause e to be evaluated more than once. The table below should clarify what is wanted.

Form	Value of form	Value of *stack*
		()
(push 23)	(23)	(23)
(push 40)	(40 23)	(40 23)
(top)	40	(40 23)
(pop)	40	(23)
(top)	23	(23)
(pop)	23	()

26.7 *(i)* The body of a function can include **defun** forms, in which case calling the function will result in the definition of other functions. If the embedded **defun**s all have a lambda variable of the outer **defun** as a free, nonlocal variable, then they can each access that variable, but nothing outside that group of functions can access that variable. Use this technique to redo Exercise 26.6. Specifically, define the function (make-stack stack) that establishes a stack with initial value the value of stack and that defines the functions (push e), (top), and (pop) to act on this stack.

26.8 *(p1)* One reason that the parsing rules you used in Exercise 24.10 were so inflexible is that variables can match only a single object. But suppose we had a different class of variables, which could match sequences of zero or more objects. If $x and $y were such variables, the pattern ($x loves $y) would match all the lists (john loves mary), (john loves the girl who lives down the street from him), and (john loves). In each case, x would be paired with the sequence (john), but y would be paired with the sequences, (mary), (the girl who lives down the street from him), and (). Let us call such variables *sequence variables.* Add to your match file the function (svariablep s), that returns True if s is a sequence variable and False if it is not. Consider any symbol whose first character is #\$ to be a sequence variable.

26.9 *(p1)* I assume you have in your match file a recursive function like (match1 pat tree pairs) that does all the work. Add in the appropriate place the cond clause

```
((svariablep (first pat))
 (backtrack-match (first pat)
                  (rest pat) tree '() pairs))
```

and define the function

```
(defun backtrack-match (v pat tree sqce pairs)
  (cond
    ((null pat)
     (cons (list v (append sqce tree)) pairs))
    ((match1 pat tree (cons (list v sqce) pairs)))
    ((null tree) nil)
    (t (backtrack-match v pat (rest tree)
         (append sqce (list (first tree)))
         pairs)))))
```

The call of `backtrack-match` from `match1` tries to match the sequence variable with `()` and the `rest` of the `pat` with the `rest` of the `tree`. `backtrack-match` is a *backtracking* function whose four `cond` clauses do the following:

1. If there is no more pattern, the sequence variable matches the sequence built up so far appended to the rest of the tree.

2. If, assuming the sequence variable matches the sequence built up so far, the rest of the pattern matches the rest of the tree, that match is the match to be returned. Notice the use of a single form in the `cond` clause.

3. Otherwise, if there is no more tree, there is no match.

4. But if there is more tree, given that the current sequence didn't work out, try extending the sequence one more subtree.

`backtrack-match` is called a backtracking function because if the currently proposed sequence doesn't work out in the second `cond` clause, we *backtrack* to this recursive level and try a different sequence. Give `backtrack-match` an appropriate documentation string.

26.10 *(p1)* Trace `backtrack-match` while evaluating
  `(match '($x c) '(a b c))`

26.11 *(p1)* Try:

```
(match '($x loves $y) '(John loves Mary))
(match '($x loves $y)
        '(John loves the girl
                who lives down the street from him))
```
  and
```
(match '($x loves $y) '(John loves))
```

26.12 *(p1)* Redefine the version of `substitute` on your `match` file so that it can use sequence variables.

26.13 *(p1)* Make sure that `(match '($x b $x) '(a b c b a b c))` works and pairs `$x` with the sequence `(a b c)`. If it doesn't, edit your `match` file so that it does.

26.14 *(p1)* Redo Exercise 24.10 with the following set of rules:

```
'((($x John $y) ($x (n John) $y))
  (($x loves $y) ($x (v loves) $y))
  (($x Mary $y) ($x (n Mary) $y))
  (($x (v $y) (n $z)) ($x (vp (v $y) (n $z))))
  (($x (v $y)) ($x (vp (v $y))))
  (((n $x) (vp $y)) (s (n $x) (vp $y))))
```

Also try

```
(apply-rules '(Mary loves John) *grammar-rules*)
```

and

```
(apply-rules '(John loves) *grammar-rules*)
```

Make sure all your modifications to your **match** file are stored for later use.

CHAPTER 27

LOCAL VARIABLES

So far, we have seen variables in several positions. We have seen global variables established by `defparameter`, `defvar`, `setf`, and so on, evaluated at the top level; we have seen local variables established by being listed in a lambda list; and we have seen variables established by a lambda list and then used nonlocally by closures or by one or several defined functions. What we have not yet seen is a way to introduce one or more new local, lexically scoped variables that will be used only within the body of a single function. COMMON LISP does have a way of doing this—the special form `let`.

The format of a `let` form is

$$\text{(let } variables\ declarations\ forms)$$

where *variables* is a list of new local variables whose scope is the `let` form, *declarations*—for example to declare one or more of the new variables to be special—are optional, and *forms* is zero or more forms. When a `let` form is evaluated, the new local variables are established and given initial values of `nil`, the *forms* are evaluated in order, and the value of the last form becomes the value of the `let` form.

As an example of using `let`, let's write a version of *quicksort*. The basic idea of the quicksort algorithm is to choose a number from the list of numbers to be sorted and divide the list into a list of those numbers

less than the chosen number, a list of those equal to the chosen number,
and a list of those greater than the chosen number. Then the first and
third lists are themselves sorted, and the three lists are appended back
together. The standard way of choosing the "chosen" number is to
choose the one in the middle of the list.

```
(defun quicksort (list)
  "Sorts the LIST of numbers, using quicksort."
  (if (< (length list) 2) list
      (let (split less-list equal-list greater-list)
        (setf split
              (nth (truncate (/ (length list) 2)) list))
        (mapcar
          #'(lambda (x)
              (cond
                ((< x split)
                 (setf less-list (cons x less-list)))
                ((= x split)
                 (setf equal-list (cons x equal-list)))
                (t (setf greater-list
                         (cons x greater-list)))))
          list)
        (append (quicksort less-list)
                equal-list
                (quicksort greater-list)))))
```

(**truncate** converts a ratio to an integer by dropping any fractional
amount.)

Instead of appearing by itself, any variable in **let**'s variable list
may appear as (*variable initial-value*); in which case, instead of being
initialized to **nil**, the *variable* is initialized to *initial-value*; all the
initializations are done in parallel, as if by **psetf**. We can use this
facility for our **quicksort**, but also notice that in the above version
(**length list**) is evaluated twice (except when the list is fewer than
two members long). **let** variables are a good way to avoid such extra
evaluation. So a better version of **quicksort** is

```
(defun quicksort (list)
  "Sorts the LIST of numbers, using quicksort."
  (let ((length (length list)))
```

```
(if (< length 2) list
    (let ((split (nth (truncate (/ length 2)) list))
          less-list
          equal-list
          greater-list)
      (mapcar
        #'(lambda (x)
            (cond
              ((< x split)
               (setf less-list (cons x less-list)))
              ((= x split)
               (setf equal-list (cons x equal-list)))
              (t (setf greater-list
                       (cons x greater-list)))))
        list)
      (append (quicksort less-list)
              equal-list
              (quicksort greater-list))))))
```

Notice that the optional initial value feature of let replaces an occurrence of **setf**. As we shall see, almost all uses of **setf** can be replaced by other features of COMMON LISP.

Exercises

Do the exercises of this chapter in the package ch27 except where otherwise instructed.

27.1 *(r)* Make the top-level value of x be (a b c) and the top-level value of y be (d e f). Evaluate

```
(let (x y)
  (setf x '(g h i) y (first x))
  (list x y))
```

Is the **setf** done in sequence or in parallel? Have the top-level values of x and y been changed?

27.2 *(r)* Now evaluate

```
(let ((x '(g h i)) (y (first x)))
  (list x y))
```

Is the assignment in **let** done in sequence or in parallel?

27.3 *(i)* The special form **let*** is exactly like **let**, but it does the initializations in sequence (as **setf** does) instead of in parallel. To see this, evaluate

```
(let* ((x '(g h i)) (y (first x)))
  (list x y))
```

Is the assignment in **let*** done in sequence or in parallel? Have the top-level values of **x** and **y** been changed?

27.4 *(r)* As mentioned in the text, **truncate** converts a ratio to an integer by dropping any fractional amount. Test this by evaluating

```
            (truncate 2)
            (truncate 2.4)
            (truncate 2.6)
            (truncate -2.4)
                 and
            (truncate -2.6)
```

Also test **(/ 5 2)** and **(truncate (/ 5 2))**. Notice that **truncate** returns two values. We have seen this before, on page 169, but will not be able to discuss it in detail.

27.5 *(i)* Other functions to convert from ratios to integers are **round**, **floor**, and **ceiling**. Try all the tests of Exercise 27.4, but with these functions instead of with **truncate**. (For less typing, use **mapcar** in your tests.)

27.6 *(r)* Define **quicksort** as the first version of this chapter, and test it.

27.7 *(r)* Define **quicksort** as the second version of this chapter, and test it.

27.8 *(i)* Recall that `mapcar` produces a list of the results of applying its function argument to each element of its list argument, and notice that this list is being ignored in the body of `quicksort`. `mapc` is a function just like `mapcar`, but it doesn't form an answer list; it is used only for the effect of applying its function. Revise your current version of `quicksort` to use `mapc` instead of `mapcar`.

27.9 *(i)* See what the COMMON LISP macro `push` does by evaluating `(macroexpand '(push 'a x))` and studying the result. Revise your current version of `quicksort` to use `push`. There should be no more occurrences of `setf` in the definition of `quicksort`.

CHAPTER 28

ITERATION

In Chapter 15, we introduced recursion as one method for repeating a computation over and over until some condition is found. Another such method is *iteration.* Although recursion is more in the spirit of LISP, since it is an applicative notion, iteration is the traditional imperative way of repeating computations, and iterative constructs have been included in COMMON LISP for those programmers who prefer them. There are even cases, as we shall see, where iteration is preferable to recursion.

As a good example to begin our discussion of iteration, let's again consider the function **reverse1** of Chapter 17. **reverse1** takes one list as its argument and returns a copy of that list with its top elements reversed. The definition of **reverse1** is

```
(defun reverse1 (l)
  "Returns a copy of the list L
   with the order of members reversed."
  (check-type l list)
  (reverse2 l '()))
```

reverse1 actually does nothing by itself, but calls its help function **reverse2**, a recursive function that takes two lists as arguments and returns the reverse of its first list appended to its second list. The definition of **reverse2** is

```
(defun reverse2 (l1 l2)
  "Returns a list consisting of
   the members of L1 in reverse order
   followed by the members of L2 in original order."
  (check-type l1 list)
  (check-type l2 list)
  (if (null l1) l2
      (reverse2 (rest l1)
                (cons (first l1) l2))))
```

We could express **reverse2** in English as

If l1 is empty, then return l2.
Otherwise,
  return the **reverse2** of (rest l1)
      and (cons (first l1) l2).

This is an appropriate recursive way to think of this operation. An iterative way to think of the operation performed by **reverse2** would be

1. If l1 is empty, then terminate and return l2.

2. Push (first l1) onto l2.

3. Pop (first l1) off l1.

4. Go to Step 1.

The most general iteration construction in COMMON LISP is **loop-return**. **loop** and **return** are two macros that, used together, can form any needed iterative structure. The format for **loop** is

(loop statements)

That is, **loop** takes zero or more *statements*, where a statement is a nonatomic form (a list to be evaluated).[1] **loop** evaluates each *statement* in its body in order, then begins at the beginning again and

---

[1] Atoms are reserved for **go** labels and for keywords of the **loop** facility of the new COMMON LISP standard. I will not discuss **go**, since it has been proved that **go** is not needed, and I will not discuss the new **loop** facility because it is extremely complicated. Everything I do say about **loop**, however, will be true of the new **loop** facility.

evaluates them in order again, and repeats this forever. The way to get out of a `loop` is with `return`. The format for `return` is

(return *form*)

The *form* is evaluated, the innermost `loop` is terminated, and the value of the *form* becomes the value of the `loop`. The *form* is optional; if it is omitted, the returned results will be `nil`. You should notice two things about `loop-return` immediately:

1. `return` will always appear within some conditional form, which will control the number of iterations.

2. `loop` provides no local variables, so it will often appear immediately inside a `let`.

The conditional within which `return` tends to appear will usually be a one-branched conditional: if some condition is True or if some condition is False, `return` (otherwise, don't). COMMON LISP has two such one-branched conditionals, `when` and `unless`:

(when *condition forms*)
(unless *condition forms*)

In both cases, there may be zero or more *forms,* and *condition* is evaluated first. If `when` finds its *condition* to be `nil`, it evaluates to `nil`; otherwise, it evaluates all the *forms,* and the value of the last one becomes the value of the `when`. If `unless` finds its *condition* to be `nil`, it evaluates all the *forms,* and the value of the last one becomes the value of the `unless`; otherwise, its value is the value of the *condition*.

For those used to other imperative languages, the `while` loop

while C do S

may be simulated by

(loop (unless C (return)) S)

and the `until` loop

repeat S until C

may be simulated by

```
(loop S (when C (return)))
```

Before returning to our iterative version of **reverse2**, it will be useful to introduce one more macro, **pop**, which is the opposite of **push**, which you learned about in Exercise 27.9. (pop *list*) is equivalent to (prog1 (first *list*) (setf *list* (rest *list*))). (Also review Exercise 26.6.)

Let's now return to our iterative version of **reverse2**. Using **loop-return**, we can define it as

```
(defun reverse2 (l1 l2)
  "Returns a list consisting of
   the members of L1 in reverse order
   followed by the members of L2 in original order."
  (check-type l1 list)
  (check-type l2 list)
  (loop
    (when (null l1) (return l2))
    (push (pop l1) l2)))
```

Note that this version of **reverse2** does just what the iterative English version does. However, the original **reverse2** was introduced as a help function for only two reasons: we needed an extra variable to hold the reverse of the initial part of the original list, and the recursion had to be done on the two-argument help function rather than on the one-argument main function. This version doesn't use recursion at all, and since we can use **let** to introduce the auxiliary variable, we no longer need a help function.

We will call this iterative reverse function **reverse3**:

```
(defun reverse3 (l)
  "Returns a copy of the list L
   with the order of members reversed."
  (check-type l list)
  (let (l2)
    (loop
      (when (null l) (return l2))
      (push (pop l) l2))))
```

Notice that this **loop** processes every element of the list **l** in order. We have already seen another way to do this, with **mapc**, in Exercise 27.8.

For comparison, let's look at a reverse4 that is like reverse3, but uses mapc:

```
(defun reverse4 (l)
  "Returns a copy of the list L
   with the order of members reversed."
  (check-type l list)
  (let (l2)
    (mapc #'(lambda (e) (push e l2))
          l)
    l2)))
```

This use of mapc is an interesting mix of applicative and imperative styles, but COMMON LISP has a special-purpose iterator specifically for doing things with every element of a list. It is a macro called dolist, and its format is

   (dolist (*variable listform result*) *declarations statements*)

listform must evaluate to a list. The *variable* takes on successive members of this list as its values, and with each one, all the *forms* are evaluated. After the last *form* has been evaluated with *variable* taking as its value the last member of the value of *listform, result* is evaluated, and its value becomes the value of the dolist. *result* is optional; if it is missing, the value of the dolist will be nil. (If a return form is evaluated within the *statements,* it will determine the value of the dolist.) Notice that *variable* is established by the dolist, and its scope is the dolist form, but *listform* and *result* must be defined outside the scope of the dolist. Therefore, it is common for *result* to be a let variable of a let immediately surrounding the dolist. Using dolist, reverse5 is

```
(defun reverse5 (l)
  "Returns a copy of the list L
   with the order of members reversed."
  (check-type l list)
  (let (l2)
    (dolist (e l l2)
      (push e l2))))
```

It is instructive to see how dolist might be defined, since it is a prime example of the use of LISP to enhance the LISP language itself. We will define `dolist` as a macro that expands into a call of `loop`. Because `loop` does not provide a place for declarations, we will ignore the *declarations* of `dolist`. Real COMMON LISP expands `dolist` into a more primitive looping construct than `loop`, which does allow declarations. The basic loop that `dolist` should expand into is:

```
(loop
  (unless listform (return result))
  (setf variable (pop listform))
  statements)
```

However, *variable* should have its scope restricted to the `dolist` expansion form, and we should not side-effect the value of *listform*, so we need to enclose the `loop` in a `let` form:

```
(let (variable (lv listform))
  (loop
    (unless lv (return result))
    (setf variable (pop lv))
    statements))
```

If we assume that *variable, listform, result,* and *statements* are all variables of the macro definition, this `let` form can be constructed using the backquote conventions as:

```
`(let (,variable (lv ,listform))
   (loop
     (unless lv (return ,result))
     (setf ,variable (pop lv))
     ,@statements))
```

Now all we have to do is construct the lambda-list of the `dolist` macro definition. If a call of `dolist` looked like (`dolist` *variable listform result statements*), it would be easy, and the entire definition would look like

```
(defmacro dolist
  (variable listform result &rest statements)
  `(let (,variable (lv ,listform))
```

```
(loop
  (unless lv (return ,result))
  (setf ,variable (pop lv))
  ,@statements)))
```

However, that is not the case, and the reason is that *result* is to be optional. COMMON LISP allows functions and macros to be defined as having optional arguments by placing the keyword &optional before the lambda variables that are to be bound to the optional arguments. If the optional arguments are missing in a particular form, the lambda variables are bound to nil. For example, the function defined as

```
(defun fn (v1 &optional v2 v3)
  "Returns a list of its arguments."
  (list v1 v2 v3))
```

can have one, two, or three arguments, and the effect is shown by:

```
> (fn 'a)
(A NIL NIL)
> (fn 'a 'b)
(A B NIL)
> (fn 'a 'b 'c)
(A B C)
```

If a function is defined with both *&optional* and *&rest* parameters (the *&rest* parameter must come last), extra arguments are bound to the *&optional* parameters preferentially:

```
> (defun fnr (v1 &optional v2 &rest v3)
    "Returns a list of its arguments,
     with all but the first two
     collected into a sublist."
    (list v1 v2 v3))
FNR
> (fnr 'a 'b 'c 'd)
(A B (C D))
```

So, the problem is that we want to be able to leave out a *result* form without the first *statement* being taken as the *result* form. Therefore, the format of a dolist form is (dolist (*variable listform result*) *statements*). So this gives us a definition of dolist like:

```
(defmacro dolist (var-lis-res &rest statements)
  (let ((variable (first var-lis-res))
        (listform (second var-lis-res))
        (result (or (third var-lis-res) nil)))
    '(let (,variable (lv ,listform))
       (loop
         (unless lv (return ,result))
         (setf ,variable (pop lv))
         ,@statements)))))
```

To make this sort of thing easier, COMMON LISP allows an atomic lambda-list parameter to be replaced by an embedded lambda-list in the definition of macros only (*not functions*). The corresponding actual argument must be a list, and the variables in the embedded lambda-list are bound to the elements of that list the same way top-level lambda variables would be bound to top-level arguments. This is called *destructuring*. Here is an example:

```
> (defmacro mcr (v1 (v2 v3) v4)
    "Returns a list of its arguments."
    '(list ',v1 ',v2 ',v3 ',v4))
MCR
> (mcr (a b) (c d) (e f))
((A B) C D (E F))
```

So now we can define dolist as:

```
(defmacro dolist ((variable listform &optional result)
                  &rest statements)
  '(let (,variable (lv ,listform))
     (loop
       (unless lv (return ,result))
       (setf ,variable (pop lv))
       ,@statements)))
```

There is only one remaining problem. The let variable lv was chosen arbitrarily to hold the list being traversed, and the value of result is a form to be evaluated within the let form. What if the value of result happens to contain (or be) lv? Whenever the result form is evaluated, the value of lv will be nil instead of whatever it is outside the dolist form. An example, comparing the above definition of dolist with list:dolist is:

```
> (let ((lv 'foo)) (dolist (e () lv)))
NIL
>(let ((lv 'foo)) (lisp:dolist (e () lv)))
FOO
```

The only way we can be absolutely sure that this cannot happen is to pick a let variable that no one else could possibly use. Fortunately, COMMON LISP has a function, gensym, that takes no arguments and returns made-up symbols guaranteed to be unique—they are not even interned in any package. We can use gensym to create a unique symbol for use in the let form. Our final definition of dolist is:

```
(defmacro dolist ((variable listform &optional result)
                  &body statements)
  "Executes STATEMENTS repeatedly,
   with VARIABLE taking on each of the members
   of the list which is the value of LISTFORM.
   Then the value of RESULT is returned,
   or NIL if RESULT is missing."
  (let ((lv (gensym)))
    `(let (,variable (,lv ,listform))
       (loop
         (unless ,lv (return ,result))
         (setf ,variable (pop ,lv))
         ,@statements))))
```

Notice the substitution of &body for &rest. They are exactly the same, except that using &body tells pretty-printing routines not to indent the *statements* as much as they would otherwise do.

dolist is a prime example of a macro that constructs a program, complete with variables and expressions. It is an example of the ability LISP programmers have to almost completely redefine the look of LISP programs. Few, if any, other programming languages have this capability.

The main point of this chapter was to introduce some of the iterative constructs of COMMON LISP. In particular, you saw three ways of iterating down the members of a list—loop-return, mapc, and dolist. You should use loop-return for general iteration. Use mapc to iterate down lists whenever the function to be mapped is already defined or whenever it is useful enough to deserve a separate definition. Usually, if you need to do something to or with every element of a list and you feel that iteration is preferred to recursion, use `dolist`.

It is usually thought that iteration is faster and takes less space to run than recursion. The reasoning is that since function calls take a relatively long time (for example, to establish lambda variables), iterative loops are faster than recursive loops. Moreover, since recursion requires saving multiple environments, recursive loops require more space than iterative loops (where they can be used). It doesn't always work out that way, however. Since LISP is basically a recursive language, most implementations of COMMON LISP perform recursion very efficiently. In some cases, an interpreted LISP recursive function will even be faster than an interpreted iterative version of the same function, although when the functions are compiled, the reverse may be true. Interpreted recursive functions will generally take more space than the interpreted iterative version, but some compilers can automatically change some occurrences of recursion (those cases known as "tail recursion") into iteration. For example, the recursive version of `reverse2` might be compiled into exactly the same code as the iterative version of `reverse2`. In any case, some recursive functions cannot be expressed iteratively (without simulating recursion), such as the function `depth` of Chapter 18. The best advice is to let the problem determine your approach. Some problems just "feel" recursive, while others "feel" iterative, but to develop this feel requires extensive practice in both styles.

Exercises

Do the exercises of this chapter in the package `ch28` except where otherwise instructed.

28.1 *(d)* Define a recursive function `build-list` that will return a list of the first 100 integers (either ascending or descending). Make the top-level value of `longlist` this list.

28.2 *(r)* Define `reverse1` and the recursive version of `reverse2`. Test them on some short lists, and then test them by evaluating `(reverse1 longlist)`.

28.3 *(r)* Define the iterative functions `reverse3`, `reverse4`, and `reverse5`. Test them on some short lists, and on `longlist`.

28.4 *(i)* COMMON LISP has a function (time *form*) that prints how long it takes to evaluate the *form* and some other statistics. Compare the running times of (reverse1 longlist), (reverse3 longlist), (reverse4 longlist), (reverse5 longlist), and (lisp:reverse longlist).

28.5 *(d)* Give to the top-level variable **reverses** a value of a list of the five reverse functions tested in Exercise 28.4. Perform the test again by typing an appropriate **dolist** form to the LISP listener.

28.6 *(i)* Compile your four reverse functions and **reverse2** by mapping the function **compile** over a list of them.

28.7 *(i)* Evaluate the **dolist** form from Exercise 28.5 again. Compare the times of the compiled reverses with each other and with their own interpreted versions.

28.8 *(d)* If necessary, change **build-list** so that it takes one integer n as an argument and returns a list of the first n integers.

28.9 *(d)* Write an iterative version of **build-list**. Call it **ibuild-list**.

28.10 *(i)* Compare the running times of **build-list** and **ibuild-list** when building lists long enough to show a difference.

28.11 *(i)* Try to find an n such that (build-list n) runs out of space, but (ibuild-list n) doesn't. If you succeed, find the largest n for which you can compare the running times of (build-list n) and (ibuild-list n), and do so. Compile the two functions, and compare them again.

28.12 *(i)* Perform the timing studies for
(reverse1 (ibuild-list n))
(reverse3 (ibuild-list n))
(reverse4 (ibuild-list n))
(reverse5 (ibuild-list n))
and
(reverse (ibuild-list n))

28.13 *(r)* Define the function **fn** as shown in this chapter and test it as shown.

28.14 *(r)* Define the function **fnr** as shown in this chapter and test it as shown.

28.15 *(r)* Define the macro **mcr** as shown in this chapter and test it as shown.

28.16 *(r)* Define **dolist** as:

```
(defmacro dolist ((variable listform
                              &optional result)
                  &rest statements)
  '(let (,variable (lv ,listform))
     (loop
       (unless lv (return ,result))
       (setf ,variable (pop lv))
       ,@statements)))
```

Be sure to shadow **lisp:dolist** first. Check and compare the values of (let ((lv 'foo)) (dolist (e () lv))) and (let ((lv 'foo)) (lisp:dolist (e () lv))).

28.17 *(r)* Evaluate (setf s (gensym)). See if you can fill in the blank in the form (eql s _____) with anything that makes the form True. (Don't waste too much time.)

28.18 *(i)* **gensym** actually can optionally take a single argument—either a positive integer or a string. Try both of these, and in each case, evaluate (**gensym**) with no argument a few times after each call with one argument.

28.19 *(r)* Define **dolist** according to the last version in this chapter, and test it.

28.20 *(d)* Write an iterative version of **member**.

28.21 *(u)* In your **set** file, which you used for Exercise 17.27, define the macro (do (*variable setform result*) *declarations statements*) to act exactly like **dolist**, but iterate over elements of a set rather than over members of a list. Be sure to shadow **lisp:do** in your **set** file. Export **set::do**. (Hint: make **do** forms expand into **dolist** forms.)

28.22 *(d)* In the `ch28` package, define an iterative version of `xprod` (see
Exercise 17.28). Use `set:do`.

CHAPTER 29

INPUT/OUTPUT

In Chapter 25, we discussed the concept of a LISP program, and defined it as all the interaction you do while you are in a run of LISP, all the functions you define, and all the files you load during that run. In this definition, you are a combination programmer and user. Let's now divide this view and consider you separately as programmer for some other user and as user of the program called the COMMON LISP listener.

The only programs you have prepared so far have consisted of a main function and a collection of auxiliary and help functions. To use your program, a user must get into LISP, load the functions, and evaluate form consisting of the name of the main function and the appropriate data as argument forms. The main function will then return the output as the value of the form. This is precisely the attitude of the applicative programmer—a program is a function for transforming input into output.

Many programs that are actually written, however, have a different organization. The typical interactive program prints information out to the user, accepts input data typed by the user, and prints output data to the user. Some of the information typed to the user is in the form of *prompts,* or requests for information, sometimes with directions on what information is desired and how it is to be typed. Notice that

217

the LISP listener itself is such an interactive program. In this chapter, we will see how to simulate the LISP listener. Notice also that these typical programs we are discussing have an iterative, imperative style. That is why I waited until now to discuss them.

If we are to write one of these typical programs, we need two abilities: the ability to input data from the user and the ability to output information to the user. COMMON LISP has many functions to do these jobs in various ways. We will look at just a few.

The basic input function is **read**. Its format is simply (**read**); it is a function of no arguments. It inputs the next S-expression in the input buffer, constructs the LISP object that S-expression represents, and returns that object. **read** also has a side effect, which is to consume that S-expression, so that the next **read** doesn't read it again. On some systems, **read** also causes a prompt character to be issued.

Notice that I said that **read** reads an S-expression. Whether the S-expression is an atom or a list, and no matter over how many lines it extends, **read** always reads and consumes an entire S-expression. By the next S-expression in the input buffer, I mean the next S-expression the user has typed or will type. (On some systems, the user can type ahead—even before the **read** has been executed; on others, the user must wait for a prompt.)

The basic output function comes in four versions:

$$(\text{prin1 } object)$$
$$(\text{princ } object)$$
$$(\text{print } object)$$
$$(\text{pprint } object)$$

where *object* is any LISP object. **prin1** outputs a printed representation of *object*, using escape characters where necessary and putting quote marks around strings. **princ** is like **prin1**, but omits escape characters and quote marks. The output of **prin1** is designed to be read by **read**. The output of **princ** is designed to be read by a human. **print** is like **prin1**, but precedes its output by #\newline and follows it by #\space. **pprint** is like **print** but omits the final #\space. It also prints long lists in an indented, "pretty" format. Each of **prin1**, **princ**, and **print** also returns *object* as its value, besides printing it. **pprint** does not return a value! (This COMMON LISP ability is related to the ability of a function to return multiple values.) A common mistake is forgetting that these functions take only one argument. We will see how to overcome this limitation below. Here are some examples of print and princ:

```
> (print 1024)
1024
1024
> (print 8/12)
2/3
2/3
> (print 0.000575e0)
5.75e-4
5.75e-4
> (print 'f\rank)
|FrANK|
|FrANK|
> (print "Frank")
"Frank"
"Frank"

> (princ 'f\rank)FrANK
|FrANK|
> (princ "Frank")Frank
"Frank"
```

Notice that the first symbol after each form is what was printed by the form; the second is the value of the form. The value is obviously printed by print. By the way, what is printed by princ immediately follows the closing parenthesis because the COMMON LISP I am using doesn't bother to wait for a carriage return after the closing parenthesis of a list-form.

We can now write our LISP listener simulator. Remember, the top-level listener cycles through the operations: reads an S-expression and constructs the object it represents; evaluates the object; and prints a representation of the value. Let's call our LISP simulator lisp.

```
(defun lisp ()
  "Simulates the LISP Listener read-eval-print cycle."
  (print (eval (read)))
  (lisp))
```

It's that simple! **print** is a function, so it gets its argument evaluated. Its argument is a call to **eval**. **eval** is also a function, so it gets its argument evaluated. Its argument is a call to **read**. **read** has no argument. It reads the next S-expression in the input buffer and returns the object it represents. **eval** then gets that object, evaluates it, and returns its value. Then, **print** outputs a representation of that value to the terminal. From the user's point of view, the user has typed in a form, and **lisp** has typed out its value. Finally, the second form in the body of **lisp** is evaluated. This is a recursive call to **lisp** itself, so the cycle continues. The only ways out are to make an error or press the interrupt key. That's one reason this **lisp** function is only a simulator.

One problem with this definition of **lisp** is that it is recursive. As you found out in the last chapter, if a recursive function calls itself enough times, it may eventually run out of space. It just doesn't make sense that the longer you interact with the top-level LISP listener, the more space you take up and the less you have available for useful work. As I said above, an interactive program is essentially an iterative one, and the **lisp** **read-eval-print** loop should also be an iterative loop. In fact, every interactive program is essentially a **read-eval-print** iterative loop. This is precisely what I had in mind at the beginning of Chapter 28, when I said that there are cases where iteration is preferable to recursion. I will leave the iterative LISP simulator for you to write as an exercise.

In our LISP simulator, the fact that **print** takes only one argument didn't bother us, but what if we want to print a long message? For example, we may want to print "Enter a sentence." Notice that (**print Enter a sentence**) is incorrect because it gives **print** three arguments. (It is also incorrect because **print** gets its argument evaluated.) There are three solutions:

1. We may enclose our message in a list:
   (**print '(Enter a sentence)**).

2. We may use the escape character to turn our message into a long atom: (**print 'Enter\ a\ sentence**).

3. We may use a string: (**print "Enter a sentence"**).

The best solution is to use a string.

What if, however, you want to print a message that mixes a canned message with a computed message. For example, after issuing the "Enter a sentence" prompt, we might want to read the sentence and echo out "I heard you say *sentence*", where the actual typed sentence appears instead of *sentence*? Let's assume the sentence is bound to the atom sentence. There are three possibilities:

1. We can print a list:
   (print '(I heard you say ,sentence)).

2. We can write our own print function.

3. We can use COMMON LISP's formatted print function format.

Let's do the last.

The format of format is

   (format *destination control-string arguments*)

destination is either t or nil.[1] If it is t, then format will produce output on the terminal screen and will return nil. If *destination* is nil, format will produce no output and will return what it would have printed as a string. *arguments* is a sequence of zero or more forms whose values are to be printed. *control-string* is a string containing the canned part of the output, plus *directives* that indicate how the *arguments* are to be printed. There are at least 32 different directives; this makes format so complicated that some people refuse to even consider using it. Here I will show only the simplest, most useful directives, and you will probably find yourself using format a lot.

First, there are some directives that don't pertain to the arguments. Rather, they give generally useful directions about how the output should appear. The following table shows what gets printed in each case at the point where the directive appears.

Directive	Output
~%	#\newline
~&	#\newline unless already at the beginning of a line
~~	~
~#\newline	Nothing

---

[1] There are other possibilities, but we will not discuss them.

The last entry requires some explanation. If the *control-string* itself is too long to fit on one line, you may type a ~ and then continue the *control-string* on the next line, even preceding it with some spaces; the #\newline and the succeeding spaces will be ignored.

These are enough directives for some examples:

```
> (format t "~&Enter a sentence:")
Enter a sentence:
NIL
> (format nil "~&Enter a sentence:")
"Enter a sentence:"
> (format t "~&Enter a sentence~%:")
Enter a sentence
:
NIL
> (format t "~&Enter a sentence~~")
Enter a sentence~
NIL
> (format t "~&Enter a sentence
            :")
Enter a sentence

            :
NIL
> (format t "~&Enter a sentence~
            :")
Enter a sentence:
NIL
```

Notice that the NIL printed in every case but one was the value of the format form. The one exception was where the *destination* was nil.

Each of the other format directives directs how an *argument* is to be printed and also "consumes" one argument. The following table shows, for a few of these directives, how its corresponding *argument* is interpreted and printed. (Characters in the directives may appear in upper- or lowercase; it doesn't matter.)

Directive	Argument	How argument is printed
~A	Any object	Without escape characters
~S	Any object	With escape characters
~{*dir*~}	A list	Each member according to *dir*

With `format`, we may evaluate

```
(format t "~&I heard you say ~A." sentence)
```

Our only problem now is how to read the user's sentence. The difficulty is that `read` reads one S-expression, but a sentence is a sequence of words. Again, there are two solutions. We could ask the user to type the sentence enclosed in a set of parentheses; this will be read as a single list. Or we could ask the user to terminate the sentence with some termination symbol. Assuming that the function (`terminatorp symb`) returns True if `symb` is a terminator we have chosen and False otherwise, the function `readasentence` could be defined as follows:

```
(defun readasentence ()
  "Reads a sequence of S-expressions until a terminator is
  encountered.
  Returns a list of the expressions without the
  terminator."
  (let (backwards)
    (loop
      (push (read) backwards)
      (when (terminatorp (first backwards))
        (return (reverse (rest backwards)))))))
```

Exercises

Do the exercises of this chapter in the package `ch29` except where otherwise instructed.

29.1 *(i)* Type `(read)foo` on one line. Is `foo` read and returned?

29.2 *(i)* Type `(read)` on one line and `foo` on the next. Do you have to wait for a prompt?

29.3 *(i)* Try giving `read` an S-expression that extends over more than one line (using carriage returns). Do you have to wait for a prompt on each line?

29.4 *(i)* Can you read more than one S-expression on one line? To find out, evaluate (`progn (list (read) (read))`).

29.5 *(r)* Try for yourself all the interactions shown in the chapter involving calls to `print` and `princ`. Try each object printed there with each of the four printing functions.

29.6 *(d)* Give the variable `list` as its value a list whose members are lists of about 10 members each. Give `list` enough sublists so that `list` cannot fit on one line of your screen. Print `list` with each of the four print functions. Note especially the difference between `print` and `pprint`.

29.7 *(r)* To see more clearly what is printed before and after the argument to the printing functions, evaluate

```
(progn (print 'foo) (print 'bar))
```

and see what appears between the `FOO` and the `BAR`. Remember to differentiate what happened after `FOO` was printed from what happened before the `BAR` was printed. Do this with the other three print functions replacing `print`.

29.8 *(i)* The function `terpri` prints a `#\newline`, and the function `fresh-line` prints a `#\newline` unless it can tell that it is already at the beginning of a new line. Experiment with these two functions.

29.9 *(r)* Try evaluating `(print Enter a sentence)`. You should get an error message.

29.10 *(r)* Evaluate `(print '(Enter a sentence))`. Notice how the output looks.

29.11 *(r)* Evaluate `(print 'Enter\ a\ sentence)`. Replace `print` with a print function that doesn't print the escape bars.

29.12 *(r)* Evaluate `(print "Enter a sentence")`. Replace `print` with a print function that doesn't print the quote marks.

29.13 *(i)* The form `(values)` may be evaluated, but it returns no value. Compare `(pprint 'foo)` with

```
(progn (print 'foo) (values))
```

29.14 *(d)* Devise a form that, when evaluated, just prints a single space. How can you tell whether it really works?

29.15 *(r)* Evaluate (mapc #'print '(Enter a sentence)). Try it with the other three printing functions.

29.16 *(d)* Define a function, prinb, of one argument that prints its argument followed by a space. (It doesn't matter what your prinb returns.) Evaluate (mapc 'prinb '(Enter a sentence)).

29.17 *(r)* Try for yourself all the interactions of this chapter that use format.

29.18 *(r)* Compare the ~A and the ~S directives on arguments for which prin1 and princ would print differently.

29.19 *(r)* Give sentence the top-level value of |Hello|, and type a format form whose effect is to print "I heard you say Hello" on one line, with nothing else on the line before or after it. Don't worry about the value of the form, which may also get printed, as long as it's on another line. Your form must include the variable sentence.

29.20 *(i)* Give sentence the top-level value

          (The moon in June makes me spoon)

and evaluate

          (format t " &I heard you say   A " sentence)

In the ~{*dir*~} directive, the *dir* can actually be any control string (without the quote marks). It can even consume several members of the list-argument. If it doesn't consume all the members of the list-argument the first time, it is used again and again until the list is used up. Revise the format form so that each symbol in sentence is followed by a blank.

29.21 *(i)* Try to end your sentence with a period by adding a period to the control string you used for Exercise 29.20. Chances are you will end up with a space between spoon and the period.

29.22 *(i)* The format directive ~#[*str*$_1$~:;*str*$_2$~] will use the control string *str*$_1$ if there is no argument left or the control string *str*$_2$ if there is any argument left. If this directive is embedded in the ~{*dir*~} directive, the notion of "argument" is replaced by "member" of the list. Using this directive, do Exercise 29.21 again.

29.23 *(r)* Define and test the LISP simulator shown in the text. Is there any difference between the **read** you are using and the one the top-level listener uses?

29.24 *(d)* Redefine the LISP simulator as an iterative function.

29.25 *(d)* Revise your LISP simulator so that it prints a prompt of > followed by a blank space before each "user input."

29.26 *(d)* In the days before COMMON LISP, there were two styles of LISP listener. The one that worked like the COMMON LISP listener was called **eval** LISP, because of its **read-eval-print** loop. The other style was called **evalquote** LISP. It would read two S-expressions at a time. The first had to be the name of a function or a lambda expression. The second had to be a list of the actual arguments being passed to the function. The value of the function applied to the list of arguments was then printed. For example, one set of interactions with **evalquote** LISP might have been

```
> first ((a b c))
A
> cons (a (b c))
(A B C)
```

Edit your LISP simulator so that it is an **evalquote** LISP simulator.

29.27 *(d)* Choose one or more sentence termination symbols, and define (**terminatorp symb**) so that it returns True if **symb** is a terminator and False otherwise.

29.28 *(r)* Define and test **readasentence** as shown in this chapter.

29.29 *(d)* Define an iterative **read-eval-print** loop that prompts the user for a sentence, reads it, and then echoes it preceded by "I heard you say".

29.30 *(i)* If you have not already done this, try to use the period as the terminator symbol for Exercise 29.29. The problem is that if you try to attach it to the last word, it stays attached as part of the symbol, but if you separate it, you will get an error. You can get it to work if you separate it, but precede it with an escape character. However, this is ugly.

29.31 *(d)* Redo Exercise 29.29 recognizing as a terminator symbol any symbol whose last character is a period. Be sure to include this symbol in the sentence you echo.

29.32 *(p1)* In your **match** file, make **apply-rules** an external symbol. Then create a file named **eliza**, in the package **eliza**. Have **eliza** use the **match** package (by including **match** as an argument to **use-package**), so that **apply-rules** will be available in **eliza**. In **eliza**, define the function **eliza** to be an iterative **read-eval-print** loop that reads a sentence and prints the result of transforming it with **apply-rules**. Define a parameter with rules like

```
(($x thinks I am $y) (Do you think you are $y))
```

and

```
((I think I am $x) (How long have you been $x))
```

You have now written a miniature version of the famous ELIZA program, written by Joseph Weizenbaum in the early 1960s.[2] Add additional rules to make an interesting conversation. The idea is for the user to enter statements, and for the program to make responses that just keep the user talking. To make the loading of the **match** file automatic when you load **eliza**, put the form (**provide** '**match**) in your **match** file right before the **in-package** form and

---

[2] J. Weizenbaum, "ELIZA—A computer program for the study of natural language communication between man and machine," *Communications of the ACM 9,* 1 (January 1966), 36–45.

put the form (**require** 'match *path-name*), where *path-name* is the full name of your **match** file, in your **eliza** file right before the **use-package** form.

29.33 *(p2)* In your **calculator** file, define a **read-eval-print** loop that reads an arithmetic expression in normal infix notation and prints its value. Under the control of this **read-eval-print** loop, redo Exercise 4.17. You have now written an interactive desk calculator.

CHAPTER 30

DESTRUCTIVE LIST
MANIPULATION

Throughout this book, so far, I have been warning you against using any destructive list manipulation functions. The time has come to discuss them, but the warning still holds: do not use these functions unless you really understand what you are doing. A mistake can lead to strange errors that are extremely difficult to find.

First, we have to understand how LISP represents lists. Whenever LISP evaluates a call to cons, it gets some computer memory from a place called the *available space list,* or simply *free space.* It configures this memory as a *cons cell.* A cons cell may be thought of as a *record* with two *fields.* The two fields are called the car and the cdr. This comes from terminology of the IBM 704, the machine on which LISP was first implemented. car stood for "Contents of the Address part of Register x," and cdr stood for "Contents of the Decrement part of Register x." car and cdr are actually COMMON LISP functions that, given a cons cell, return the contents of the appropriate field. car is synonymous with first, and cdr is synonymous with rest. We have been using first and rest instead of car and cdr because their meanings are more obvious, but in this chapter, where we are dealing with low-level details, we will use car and cdr.

229

Each field of the cons cell—the car field and the cdr field—contains a *pointer* to the representation of a LISP object. If that object is a list, the pointer will point to another cons cell which represents that list.

We can draw cons cells in a graphical style known as *box notation*. A cons cell looks like a rectangle, divided in two halves. The left half is the car, and the right half is the cdr. If a field holds a pointer to an atom, we will just show a printed representation of that atom in its field. So, the picture of the value of (cons 'car 'cdr) is

This is the box notation for the dotted pair (CAR . CDR).

If a cdr field contains a pointer to nil, we will just show a diagonal line through that field. So, the box notation for the value of (cons 'a nil), which is the dotted pair (A . NIL), and also the list (A), is

However, we will show the box notation of the value of (cons nil nil), which is the dotted pair (NIL . NIL), and the list (NIL), as

If a field contains a pointer to another cons cell, we will show it as an arrow from the field to the cell. So, the box notation for the list (A B C) is

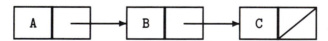

Remember, in dotted pair notation, this is (A . (B . (C . NIL))).

A car might also contain a pointer to a cons cell. The box notation for the list (A (B C) D) is

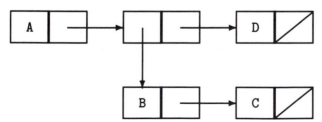

When you define a function, a form is stored in a special place accessible from the function name by the function `symbol-function`. Different implementations of COMMON LISP differ in the precise format of the form stored there, but they all include a list of the forms that constitute the body of the function definition. The simplest such format is a lambda expression. For example, we might want to define the function (hopeful 1), which simply appends (I HOPE) to its argument list. After doing

```
(defun hopeful (l)
  (append l '(i hope)))
```

the value of (symbol-function 'hopeful) might be the lambda expression

```
(lambda (l)
  (append l '(i hope)))
```

In box notation, this lambda expression is

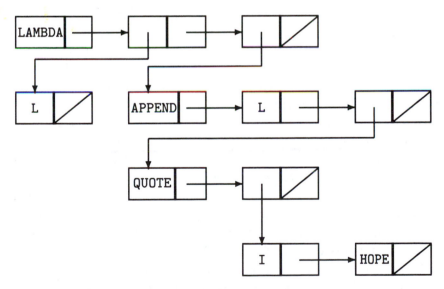

When you give a symbol a value, that value is often stored as a pointer to the object that the symbol is bound to. We can picture the result of (setf x '(a b c)) as

If we now do (setf y (cdr x)) (or, equivalently, (setf y (rest x))), a copy of the actual pointer in the cdr field of the cons cell to which X points is placed in the value cell of Y. This gives:

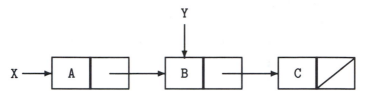

The fussiest equality test in COMMON LISP is eq, which just compares its two arguments, as pointers, for equality. In the above example, (eq y (cdr x)) would return T because Y and the cdr field of X point to the same cons cell. However, (eq y '(b c)) would evaluate to NIL, because two new cons cells would be used to construct the list (B C) in that case.

If this view of LISP lists is now understood, we are ready to talk about destructive list manipulation. The two basic destructive list manipulation functions are (rplaca c o) and (rplacd c o). They stand for RePLACe CAr and RePLACe CDr, respectively. In the case of each of these functions, the value of the first argument must be a cons cell. (rplaca c o) *changes* the car field of c so that it points to o. (rplacd c o) *changes* the cdr field c so that it points to o. Each returns the newly changed cons cell.

Neither rplaca nor rplcad is used much anymore, because they can both be replaced by setf. setf treats its first argument as a *generalized* variable. As long as its first argument form is a form it recognizes as identifying a *place,* setf replaces the value of that place with the value of its second argument. As always, setf returns the value of its second argument. Instead of (rplaca c o), modern COMMON LISPers use (setf (car c) o), and instead of (rplacd c o), modern COMMON LISPers use (setf (cdr c) o).

If X and Y have the values shown in the above diagram, after evaluating (setf (car y) 'd), the situation would look like

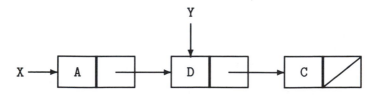

The cons cell Y points to now represents the list (D C). Therefore, the value of Y is now (D C). Y seems to have a new value, although it really doesn't. Y still points to the same cons cell it pointed to before; it is the contents of that cons cell that has changed. Moreover, X has also been changed! It is now (A D C), even though the form (setf (car y) 'd) didn't mention X. That is why destructive list manipulation is so dangerous. By changing one thing, you can change something else that apparently has nothing to do with it.

If we now did (setf (cdr y) '(e f)), the picture would change to

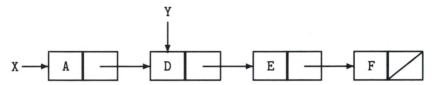

and X would have the value (A D E F).

Earlier we looked at append, and noted that append makes a copy of its first argument, but reuses its second argument. If X were (A B), Y were (C D), and we did (setf z (append x y)), we would get the following situation:

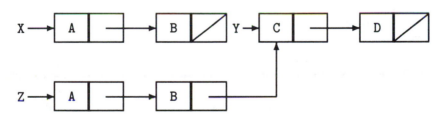

(eq x z) would be NIL, but (eq y (cddr z))[1] would be T. If we now did (setf (car y) 'e), Z would change to (A B E D).

There is also a destructive version of append, which is called nconc. (nconc list1 list2) cdrs down list1 until it finds the last cons cell, then does a rplacd on that cell, changing its cdr to point to list2. Again, if X were (A B), Y were (C D), and we did (setf z (nconc x y)), we would get

---

[1]Compositions of up to four uses of car and cdr are defined as separate functions whose names are found by throwing out intermediate occurrences of c and r, so (cddr z) is the same as (cdr (cdr z)).

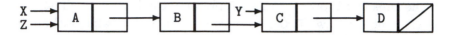

X and Z would now be **eq**, as well as **equal**.

What if X were (A B) and we did (nconc x x)? The picture would be

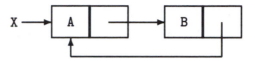

The second cons cell of X would have its **cdr** pointing to the first cons cell of X. This is an infinite list: (A B A B A B ...). The only way to get infinite lists in LISP is with destructive list manipulation.

We could get another kind of infinite list by starting with X as (A B) and doing (setf (cadr x) x). We would then get

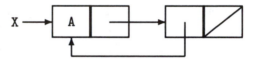

Here X is a sublist of itself: (A (A (A ...))).

The possibility of accidentally making an infinite list is another danger of destructive list manipulation.

Destructive list manipulation is not all bad. There are some good uses for it—if you are careful. One benefit of it is the saving of time and space. If you never use destructive list manipulation, you will use many new cons cells from free space. Most of these will be used for only a short time and then be discarded. We call such discarded cons cells *garbage*. Eventually, all free space will have been used. Then, if we want some more, a special LISP function called the *garbage collector* will automatically be executed, and will look through the computer memory we are using to find and collect the garbage and reconstitute free space. The garbage collector takes a while to operate and slows down our program. (Some implementations of COMMON LISP now spread garbage collection into little pieces done over otherwise idle times, so it's not as noticeable as it used to be.) Nevertheless, automatic garbage collection is one of the major features of LISP. Other languages make the programmers keep track of their own garbage and recycle it themselves. Use of destructive list manipulation, in appropriate places, will generate less garbage and require the garbage collector less often. However, when in doubt, don't use it!

One useful destructive list manipulation function is a mapping function called mapcan. It is like mapcar (see Chapter 21), but nconcs all the results together before returning. Notice that if we nconc the elements of the list ((a b) (c) () (d e)), we get (a b c d e). In particular, empty lists disappear. We can use this for writing a "filter" function that takes a predicate and a list and returns a list containing only those elements of the original list for which the predicate is True. COMMON LISP calls it remove-if-not:

```
(defun remove-if-not (p l)
  "Returns a list of those members of the list L
   for which the predicate function P returns True."
  (check-type p function)
  (check-type l list)
  (mapcan #'(lambda (e) (when (funcall p e) (list e)))
          l))
```

One interesting use of remove-if-not is the quicksort function. Several versions of quicksort were presented in Chapter 27, and you wrote some more versions for the Exercises of that chapter. Compare this version, which uses remove-if-not and nconc, to those in Chapter 27.

```
(defun quicksort (list)
  "Sorts the LIST of numbers, using quicksort."
  (let ((length (length list)))
    (if (< length 2) list
        (let ((split (nth (truncate (/ length 2)) list)))
          (nconc
            (quicksort
              (remove-if-not #'(lambda (n) (< n split))
                             list))
            (remove-if-not #'(lambda (n) (= n split))
                           list)
            (quicksort
              (remove-if-not #'(lambda (n) (> n split))
                             list)))))))
```

Destructive list manipulation is also useful when you are maintaining some large data structure in a global variable and want to change sections without copying large parts unnecessarily.

Exercises

Do the exercises of this chapter in the package ch30 except where otherwise instructed.

30.1 *(r)* Set x to (a b c) and y to (cdr x). What is the value of (eq y (cdr x))? What is the value of (eq y '(b c))?

30.2 *(r)* Do (rplaca y 'd). What is the value of y now? What is the value of x?

30.3 *(r)* Do (rplacd y '(e f)). What is the value of y now? What is the value of x?

30.4 *(r)* Do (setf (car y) 'g). What is the value of y now? What is the value of x?

30.5 *(r)* Do (setf (cdr y) '(h i)). What is the value of y now? What is the value of x?

30.6 *(r)* Set x to (a b), y to (c d), and z to (append x y). What is the value of x now? What is the value of (eq y (cddr z))?

30.7 *(r)* Set x to (a b), y to (c d), and z to (nconc x y). What is the value of x now? What is the value of (eq y (cddr z))? What is the value of (eq x z)?

30.8 *(r)* Make sure you remember your LISP's interrupt key. Then set x to (a b). Then do (nconc x x).

30.9 *(i)* See what the value of the global variable

lisp:*print-circle*

is. If it is not T, set it to be T. When this variable is not NIL, infinite lists will be printed using a technique that shows shared list structure. Type the symbol x to the LISP listener. It should print #1=(A B . #1#). This means that the value of x is a list temporarily called #1#, whose car is A, whose cadr is B, and whose cddr is #1#, itself.

30.10 *(r)* Set x back to (a b). Then do (setf (cadr x) x).

30.11 *(i)* Define hopeful by evaluating the following forms:

```
(setf h '(I hope))
(eval '(defun hopeful (l)
          (append l ',h)))
```

Check that your definition of hopeful agrees with the one in this chapter by doing (symbol-function 'hopeful)
and/or (describe 'hopeful)
and by evaluating (hopeful '(I did that correctly)).
Also check the value of h.

30.12 *(i)* Define (emphatic l) to nconc the list (very much) onto the end of its argument list.

30.13 *(i)* Set the top-level value of s to (I am a good lisper), and then do (setf ss (emphatic (hopeful s))). Look at your definition of hopeful again. What happened? What is the value of h now? This is another danger of destructive list manipulation: function definitions can be changed.

30.14 *(i)* Now evaluate

```
(setf sss
         (emphatic (hopeful '(I know what I am doing))))
```

Make sure you know what happened and why.

30.15 *(i)* Redefine hopeful and emphatic as

```
(defun hopeful (l)
  (append l (list 'I 'hope)))
(defun emphatic (l)
  (nconc l (list 'very 'much)))
```

and do Exercises 30.13 and 30.14 again. You now know the safe way to define functions like these.

30.16 *(i)* COMMON LISP implementations generally allow you to force a garbage collection whenever you want. You may want to do this during interaction with the user, when the time the garbage collector takes won't be noticed, and start a moderately long calculation with as much free space as possible. The function to start an immediate garbage collection may be (gc-immediately). What is it in the implementation you use?
Write it here: _____ and in Appendix B.2.

30.17 *(i)* In many COMMON LISP implementations, you can get the garbage collector to print something to the terminal when it finishes, so you know it has been called. How do you do this in the implementation you use? Write it here: _____ and in Appendix B.2. Do it. Then call the garbage collector to make sure the reporting works.

30.18 Define the following infinitely looping function, whose sole purpose is to consume free space and generate garbage quickly.

```
(defun eat ()
  (let ((n 0) (l '()))
    (loop
      (setf n (1+ n)
            l (append l (list n)))
      (print n))))
```

Call the garbage collector once more, then evaluate (eat), keeping your finger on the interrupt key. Interrupt as soon as the garbage collector is called. How far did the loop get? Now edit eat, changing append to nconc, and try this again. Did you get further?

30.19 *(r)* Define remove-if-not as in this chapter and test it. First shadow lisp:remove-if-not. A good test is (remove-if-not 'numberp '(a 1 s 2 d)).

30.20 *(r)* Define quicksort as in this chapter and test it. Make sure that one of your tests is with a list in which some number appears more than once.

30.21 *(u)* You put the function **bstree:insert** in your **bstree** file for
Exercise 18.14. Now add to that file a destructive version of
bstree:insert, which you should call **bstree:insertd**. When
inserting into the empty or elemental tree, a new tree will have
to be built. Otherwise, inserting a new element into a tree should
require exactly one destructive call to **setf**. For example, to insert **a** into (TREE NIL USEFUL), change the **second** of the tree, so
that the tree is now (TREE A USEFUL), and to insert **search** into
(TREE (A NIL (IS BINARY NIL)) USEFUL), change the **third**
of (IS BINARY NIL) so that the entire tree becomes (TREE (A
NIL (IS BINARY SEARCH)) USEFUL).

30.22 *(u)* Look at the definition of **build-from-list** in your **bstree**
file. Should it use **insert** or **insertd**? Why? If it should use
insertd, change it accordingly.

CHAPTER 31

PROPERTY LISTS

We have seen that every symbol can have several pieces of information associated with it—a name, home package, value, and function. The name, home package, and function of a symbol are associated with it globally; the symbol can have only one of each at any time. The value of a symbol can be associated with it either globally or locally. The functions `symbol-name`, `symbol-package`, and `symbol-function` retrieve the indicated data items from the symbol. Similarly, the function `symbol-value` retrieves the global value of a symbol, if it has one.

An additional item associated globally with every symbol is a data structure called the *property list.* Property lists are one of the unique features of LISP and have been a part of LISP since the beginning. The property list of a symbol may be retrieved by the function `symbol-plist`, but, as we will see below, other functions are generally used to operate on property lists.

Conceptually, a property list is a collection of *properties.* Each property is a pair consisting of an *indicator* and a *value.* Some people call the indicator the "property," and speak of "property-value" lists. Others call the value the "property," and speak of "indicator-property" lists. None of these have a name for the pairs. We will stick with the terms "indicator" and "value" for the elements of the pairs and "property" for the pairs themselves.

The indicators are typically symbols (eq is used for comparison). The values can be any LISP objects. The property list, itself, is a list with an even number of members, the odd members being indicators and the even ones being values.

The main function for dealing with property lists is get. (get *symbol indicator*) returns the value associated with the *indicator* on *symbol*'s property list. A get form also is recognized by setf as indicating a generalized variable, so the way to place a property on some symbol's property list is (setf (get *symbol indicator*) *value*). For example, we might have a data base of people, each represented by the symbol that is his or her first name. If we wanted to store John's age as 24, we could do

```
> (setf (get 'john 'age) 24)
24
```

and we could later retrieve it by

```
> (get 'john 'age)
24
```

What if you try to get a property value and it isn't there? For example, what if we had not yet stored Mary's age and tried (get 'mary 'age)? Let's try it:

```
> (get 'mary 'age)
NIL
```

Again, LISP's overuse of NIL appears (NIL is a symbol, the empty list, and LISP's representation of False). I said that a property value could be any LISP object, but if you try storing NIL as the value of some property, that will be indistinguishable from not having stored any value with that property:

```
> (setf (get 'mary 'phone) nil)
NIL
> (get 'mary 'phone)
NIL
> (get 'john 'phone)
NIL
```

```
> (symbol-plist 'john)
(AGE 24)
> (symbol-plist 'mary)
(PHONE NIL)
```

To remove a property from a symbol's property list, you can evaluate (remprop *symbol indicator*).

```
> (remprop 'john 'age)
(24)
> (symbol-plist 'john)
NIL
```

If a symbol *s* already has a property with the indicator *p* and you do (setf (get *s p*) *v*), the old value won't be modified; it will be discarded, and *v* put in its place. So if you are keeping a list of people's friends under the friends property, you should add Mary as John's new friend by doing

```
(setf (get 'john 'friends)
      (cons 'mary (get 'john 'friends)))}
```

not by (setf (get 'john 'friends) 'mary), because then John will lose his old friends when he takes up with Mary.

Exercises

Do the exercises of this chapter in the package ch31 except where otherwise instructed.

31.1 *(r)* Define x as (defun x (y) (print y) (print y)). Define y as (defun y (x) (x x)). Evaluate (y 'foo). Notice that the function a symbol names is associated with it globally.

31.2 *(r)* Define the function

```
(defun fdef (x)
  (defun yousay (s) (format t "~&You say ~a~%" s))
  (yousay x))
```

Evaluate (yousay 'first-time).
Then, evaluate (fdef 'second-time).
Then, (yousay 'third-time).
Notice that a function you define in one environment is available
in others.

31.3 *(r)* Using `symbol-name`, `symbol-package`, and `symbol-function`
look at the names, home packages, and function definitions of the
symbols you have given function definitions so far in the exercises of this chapter. Also look at the name, home package, and
function definition of the symbol `cons`.

31.4 *(r)* Give x the top-level value of `tlv`, and define the function

```
(defun foo (x)
  (symbol-value 'x))
```

Now evaluate (foo 'bar). Notice that `symbol-value` retrieves
the global value of its argument symbol.

31.5 *(i)* Use `symbol-plist` to look at the property lists of the symbols you examined for Exercise 31.3. Different implementations
of COMMON LISP use property lists to varying extents to store information about symbols. Be careful never to wipe out a symbol's
property list completely in case your COMMON LISP is keeping
valuable information there.

31.6 *(i)* Load your `util` file, and look at the property list of
`util:element`. Some implementations of COMMON LISP put on
the property list of a symbol the path name of the file where that
symbol is given a function definition. In these COMMON LISP's,
(ed *symbol*) will put you into the editor ready to edit *symbol*'s
definition. Try evaluating (ed 'util:element).

31.7 *(r)* Record that John's age is 24 using `john`'s property list.

31.8 *(r)* Retrieve John's age using `get`.

31.9 *(r)* See what you get if you now try to retrieve Mary's age.

31.10 *(r)* Give Mary a phone number of `nil`. Compare (get 'mary
'phone) with (get 'john 'phone). Use `symbol-plist` to compare Mary's and John's property lists.

31.11 *(r)* Use **remprop** to remove Mary's **phone** property. Check her property list again.

31.12 *(d)* Give John the two friends Joe and Sam. Now do (setf (get 'john 'friend) 'mary). Has John lost his old friends?

31.13 *(d)* Give John his two old friends back. Add Mary as a new friend correctly.

31.14 *(i)* Try using **push** to make Betty John's fourth friend.

31.15 *(i)* Make John Harry's only friend. Then add Mary as Harry's second friend. Look closely at Harry's friends to make sure that they are represented as a list of people, rather than as a dotted list. If you have a dotted list, use **remprop**, and then try this exercise again. What should (get 'harry 'friend) be when Harry has one friend?

31.16 *(d)* Define a function (add-friend person friend) so that whenever *a* is *b*'s friend, *b* is also *a*'s friend. Use it to give John, Mary, Jane, and Bill some friends. Now look at a friend list with **get**. Is the property list a globally available structure?

31.17 *(i)* Build a data base of 5 to 10 people. Store the list of people as the value of the indicator **list** under the symbol **people**. Give each person an age, some friends, and an occupation such as **student, teacher, programmer**, and so on. Writing functions as necessary, retrieve some information such as: all people who have an older friend, all people who are the youngest among their friends, all programmers under 15, and all teachers under 30 who have at least one friend who is a student over 40. You may find the function (pushnew *element list*) useful. It pushes *element* onto the *list* unless it already is a **member** of the *list*. You might also find **min** useful. (min $i_1 \ldots i_n$) returns the minimum number among its arguments.

CHAPTER 32

HASH TABLES

In Chapter 31, we discussed the use of property lists to store information about symbols or about the entities the symbols represent (for example, about the people represented by the symbols john, mary, and so on). There are three problems with using property lists: As we saw in the exercises of Chapter 31, property lists may be used by the COMMON LISP environment, and we might unintentionally clobber some of that information. Property lists are global, so their use by one subsystem of functions might interfere with their use by another subsystem of functions (though this problem should be ameliorated by the proper use of packages). Only symbols have property lists; in particular, lists can't have property lists. All these problems may be solved by using *hash tables* instead of property lists.

Hash tables are a type of COMMON LISP object that are used for associating arbitrary pieces of information with each of a set of COMMON LISP objects. The latter objects are called *keys*, and the information associated with a key in a hash table is called a *value*. Together, a key and its associated value are referred to as an *entry* of the hash table. Any number of separate hash tables may be created by a program, each of which may use different keys or may have the same keys associated with different values. For example, a hash table might be used as a private property listlike structure, with symbols as the keys and

247

property listlike lists as the values. Since the values can be any list objects, they can even be hash tables in which indicators are the keys and property listlike values are the values.

The basic theoretical foundation for hash tables is the following idea. Imagine a random access array indexed by integers, and a function (called a *hash function*) that, given any object as argument, produces an integer as value. Further imagine that the hash function has been so designed that no two different objects give the same integer. If we want to store information about some object o in the array, we just apply the hash function h to the object and store the information in the array at position $h(o)$. Later on, if we want to look up the information about object o, we just look in the array at position $h(o)$, and if it's there, we're sure to find it. Hash tables are such arrays. The only problem is that we can't, in general, guarantee that the hash function will produce a different value for each different object without knowing all the objects in advance of designing the hash function. Therefore, the object itself (actually, a pointer to it) is stored in the hash table along with the value. To store or retrieve a value associated with the key k in a hash table, the entry in $h(k)$ is examined to make sure that the key stored there is k. If some other key is stored there, this is called a *collision*, and the entry for k must be stored somewhere else. Sometimes this is done by finding the next available space; sometimes by trying a secondary hash function; and sometimes by storing all colliding entries in a list at the hash table location. In any case, hash tables generally have more space than is needed to store all the entries, in order to reduce collisions, and this use of space is the one negative aspect of using hash tables.

The basic hash function of COMMON LISP is **sxhash**. (**sxhash** *object*) returns a nonnegative fixnum that is guaranteed to be the same for any two LISP objects that are **equal**. Of course, it might also be the same for un-**equal** objects and produce a collision. Since hash tables can have different sizes, it is obvious that the value of **sxhash** is not used directly to index hash tables. This is a second source of collisions.

A hash table is created by evaluating (**make-hash-table**). A new hash table is returned as the value of this form. To use the hash table, you must immediately bind it to some variable; for example,

```
> (setf people (make-hash-table))
#<EQL-HASH-TABLE 1163145>
```

To allow for hash tables of different sizes and with different kinds of keys, the `make-hash-table` function has several optional *keyword* arguments, two of which we will discuss. To adjust the size of the new hash table, you use the `:size` keyword argument to declare the approximate number of entries you expect to store in the hash table. The actual hash table will be bigger than the size you specify, to allow for collisions, but accurate advice will, in general, allow your COMMON LISP system to save space. For example, if you expect to store 15 entries in the hash table, you would create it by evaluating `(make-hash-table :size 15)`. Notice that you provide a keyword argument by listing the keyword and following it by the actual argument. If you later try to store more than 15 entries in your hash table, it's size will be increased automatically; you don't need to worry about it.

As we saw above, storing an entry in a hash table or retrieving one from a hash table often involves comparing the key with a key already stored in the table. You can improve efficiency by using the most fussy equality test necessary. You specify this with the `:test` keyword argument, which must be either `#'eq`, `#'eql`, or `#'equal`.[1] If you don't specify which, `#'eql` will be used. Clearly, if the keys will be symbols, you can use `#'eq`, and if the keys will be lists, you must specify `#'equal`. For example, to create a hash table that will hold about 100 entries keyed by lists, you would evaluate `(make-hash-table :test #'equal :size 100)`. The order of the keyword arguments doesn't matter. Evaluating `(make-hash-table :size 100 :test #'equal)` would do exactly the same thing. For example, to create a hash table for the kind of use we made of property lists in Chapter 31, we might do

```
> (defconstant people
            (make-hash-table :test #'eq :size 15))
PEOPLE
```

To retrieve an entry from a hash table, use

$$(\text{gethash } key \; hash\text{-}table)$$

---

[1] The new COMMON LISP standard will also permit `#'equalp`.

which is a form recognizable as a generalized variable by setf, so it is
also used to store entries.

```
> (setf (gethash 'john people) '(age 24))
(AGE 24)
> (gethash 'john people)
(AGE 24)
T
```

gethash actually returns two values: the entry or nil if none was
found; T or NIL, indicating whether or not an entry was found.

```
> (setf (gethash 'sally people) nil)
NIL
> (gethash 'sally people)
NIL
T
> (gethash 'mary people)
NIL
NIL
```

Notice that people was not quoted. That is because people is a
variable whose value is the hash table that we are using, and the second
argument of gethash must be a hash table.

The function (getf *list indicator*) acts just like (get *symbol indicator*), except that *list* is treated like a property list (it must have an
even number of members, which might be zero). Using this, we can do
things like

```
> (setf (getf (gethash 'mary people) 'phone) "555-1234")
"555-1234"
> (getf (gethash 'mary people) 'phone)
"555-1234"
> (push 'harry (getf (gethash 'john people) 'friends))
(HARRY)
> (push 'mary (getf (gethash 'john people) 'friends))
(MARY HARRY)
> (getf (gethash 'john people) 'friends)
(MARY HARRY)
```

remf is to getf what remprop is to get.

(`hash-table-count` *hash-table*) returns the number of entries in the *hash-table*.

```
> (hash-table-count people)
3
```

To operate on every entry of a hash table, use (`maphash` *function hash-table*), where *function* is a function of two arguments—the key and the value.

```
> (maphash
    #'(lambda (key value)
        (format t
                "~&The key ~a has value ~a.~%"
                key value))
    people)
The key SALLY has value NIL.
The key JOHN has value (FRIENDS (MARY HARRY) AGE 24).
The key MARY has value (PHONE 555-1234).
#<EQ-HASH-TABLE 4607232>
```

There are two functions for removing entries from hash tables.

(remhash key hash-table)

removes the entry for *key*.

(clrhash hash-table)

removes all entries from the *hash-table*.

Many COMMON LISP functions other than `make-hash-table` take keyword arguments. In particular, `member` takes a `:test` keyword argument whose value can be any predicate function of two arguments. (`member` *object list* `:test` *test*) returns the tail of `list` starting with the first member *x* that satisfies (*test object x*), or `NIL` if there is no such member. `member`'s *test* defaults to `eql` if you don't specify another; this is the way we have always used `member` previously. Some example uses of `member` with nondefault tests are

```
> (member 3 '(1 2 5 2 3 8 6) :test #'<)
(5 2 3 8 6)
```

```
> (member "now"
          '("I" "am" "now" "going" "to" "the" "store")
          :test #'string=)
("now" "going" "to" "the" "store")
```

You may define your own functions to have keyword parameters by including **&key** in your lambda list followed by the keyword parameters. (This is to be done after the required parameters, if any, and before the *rest* parameter, if any.) These parameters are not to be in the keyword package; that is just the way the keyword arguments are passed to the function. Keyword arguments that are not supplied default to `nil`. For example,

```
> (defun consem (head &key tail)
    (cons head tail))
CONSEM
> (consem 'a)
(A)
> (consem 'a :tail '(b c))
(A B C)
```

If you want the default keyword argument to be something other than `nil`, you can specify it by enclosing the keyword parameter and the default in a pair of parentheses:

```
> (defun div (&key (numerator 1) (denominator 100.0))
    (/ numerator denominator))
DIV
> (div)
0.01
> (div :numerator 2)
0.02
> (div :denominator 10)
1/10
> (div :numerator 50 :denominator 75.0)
0.6666667
```

Exercises

Do the exercises of this chapter in the package **ch32** except where otherwise instructed.

32.1 *(r)* Try applying the function **sxhash** to various LISP objects. Does it return the same number for two different but **equal** objects? Can you find two **unequal** objects for which it returns the same number? (Mine did for **b** and **"b"**.)

32.2 *(r)* Evaluate (**setf people (make-hash-table)**). What is the type of a hash table? (Use **type-of**.)

32.3 *(i)* Test the function **hash-table-p**, which should return True if and only if its argument is a hash table.

32.4 *(i)* What is the home package of **:size** and **:test**?

32.5 *(i)* What is the value of **:size** and of **:test**? All symbols in the keyword package evaluate to themselves.

32.6 *(r)* Set the value of **people** to be a hash table that will hold about 15 entries, keyed by symbols.

32.7 *(r)* Try for yourself the interactions shown in this chapter dealing with the **people** hash table.

32.8 *(d)* Redo Exercise 31.17, but using a hash table instead of property lists.

32.9 *(d)* Using **member** with a nondefault test, experiment with finding whether a list **equal** to a given list is a member of another list.

32.10 *(r)* Define **consem** as shown in this chapter, and test it.

32.11 *(r)* Define **div** as shown in this chapter, and test it.

32.12 *(u)* Modify the functions in your **bstree** file so that you can have binary search trees of different types of objects. Wherever **eql** is used as the equality test on elements of the tree, replace it by a **:test** keyword parameter that defaults to **eql**, and wherever **string<** is used, replace it by a **:lessp** keyword parameter that defaults to **string<**.

32.13 *(d)* Using **bstree:build-from-list**, **bstree:inorder**, your modified **bstree** functions, and any other help functions you need, define the function **sort-names** to take a list of names and sort them into order. Assume that a name is represented by a list of at least two members, the first of which is the given name, the last of which is the family name, and the intermediate ones are the middle name(s) if the person has them. Use the same ordering principle as does the telephone directory; for example, (Adam Smith) will come after (Ben Adams), but before (Adam B. Smith). You may find the function (butlast *list* &optional *n*) useful. It returns a list exactly like *list* but without its last *n* members. *n* defaults to 1.

Part IV

OBJECT-ORIENTED PROGRAMMING

CHAPTER 33

METHODS

Object-oriented programming is a relatively new style of programming, at least as compared with functional programming and imperative programming. Actually, object-oriented programming differs from the earlier styles in a way that is orthogonal to the difference between them. That is, standard functional programming style (the subject of Part II of this book) and standard imperative programming style (the subject of Part III of this book) have something in common which contrasts with the object-oriented programming style. One can actually do object-oriented programming either in a functional style or in an imperative style. In this part of the book, we will examine object-oriented programming using the mix of functional and imperative programming styles that we have used in Part III.

We have become familiar with the notion that COMMON LISP objects are classified into types. Previously, when we have written a function, we have written it for arguments of particular types. If we wanted to perform the same operation on objects of different types, we had the following choices:

- Write the function in such a way that the difference doesn't matter. For example, **cons** will put any object on the front of a list, regardless of the type of the object.

257

- Write separately named functions for each of the several types. For example, to tell if one object is to be sorted before another, COMMON LISP has < for numbers, `char<` for characters, and `string<` for strings and symbols.

- Write one function, but test the arguments, for example with `typecase`, and use separate code for each different type.

- Write one function, but make the caller provide the appropriate type-dependent routine. For example, COMMON LISP has one `member` function, but the caller must pass the correct type-dependent equality test as a keyword argument.

The commonality among all these techniques, which is the commonality shared by standard functional and imperative styles, is what I will call being *procedure-oriented*. Being procedure-oriented is concentrating on the operation, routine, or procedure to be carried out or on the function to be applied. Types enter procedure-oriented programming mainly as a matter of quality control. When you think of a procedure, it makes sense only for certain types of data. Programming languages allow you to declare the types of the arguments, for example with `check-type`, so that error messages can communicate clearly.

Object-oriented programming involves "inside-out" thinking relative to procedure-oriented programming. Instead of thinking of the procedure, think of the object or of the type of object and think of the sorts of operations that can be performed on that type of object and how those operations are to be carried out, independently of how those same, or similar, operations would be carried out on other types of objects. For example, when thinking about numbers, we might decide that numbers are often compared and implement a < function on numbers. Later, we might be worrying about characters, decide that characters may be compared, and implement a < function for characters. Later, we might implement a < for strings, for symbols, and even for lists. Since these are all the same operation, it makes sense to use the same symbol to name them, but there will be five different definitions, and they will each be grouped with other operations on the same types of objects.

In COMMON LISP, object-oriented programming is provided *via* a package of routines called the *Common Lisp Object System*, or CLOS (pronounced "see-loss" by some and "claus" by others) for short.

CLOS is part of the new, forthcoming COMMON LISP standard, but it is already commonly enough available that we have decided to discuss it in this book. Nevertheless, I will only provide an overview and basic introduction to CLOS. All the details can get very complicated.

The CLOS functions may be in a separate package. In the COMMON LISP I am using, they are all in a package named `clos`, some of them have the package named `ticlos` as their home package, and some, but not all, of them are in the `lisp` package, from where they are inherited into user-defined packages.

In CLOS terminology, a type of data object is called a *class* and an object in a certain class is called an *instance* of that class. Just as the COMMON LISP types are organized into a hierarchy, so are the CLOS classes, and, in fact, many of the predefined COMMON LISP types are also CLOS classes. Unlike normal hierarchies, where each element has exactly one element one level higher than it, a CLOS class may have several immediate "parents." (Such a hierarchy is sometimes called a *tangled hierarchy*.) In particular, COMMON LISP considers `null` to be both a type and a class whose only instance is `nil` and whose immediate superclasses are both the `symbol` class and the `list` class. The tree below shows the hierarchy of CLOS classes that correspond to COMMON LISP types that we have discussed:

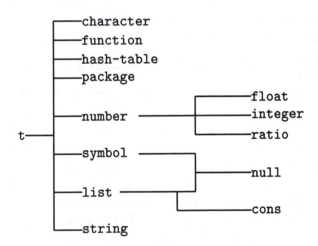

An object-oriented function is called a *generic function*. Generic functions are COMMON LISP objects of type `function` (and so are also instances of the CLOS `function` class). However a generic function only has a name, a lambda-list of parameters, a documentation string, some parts that we won't discuss, and a set of *methods.* A generic function does not have a sequence of forms to be evaluated when it is called. Instead, when a generic function is called, the appropriate, class-specific method is invoked. Which method of a generic function is invoked depends on the classes of the actual arguments. For example, consider applying a generic function to an integer. If the generic function has a method for integers, that method will be invoked. Otherwise, if it has a method for numbers, that method will be invoked. Otherwise, if it has a method for t (the class of all CLOS instances), that method will be invoked. Otherwise, an error will be signaled. In other words, the most specific method, according to the above hierarchy, is the one that will be invoked. That rule is unambiguous except in the case of nil. If a generic function has one method for symbols and another for lists, and we give it nil as its argument, which method will be invoked? CLOS has a rule for linearizing all the superclasses of any class into what is called the *class precedence list.* The method invoked will always be the one for the earliest class on the class precedence list of its argument. The class precedence list for each class in the above tree except for null is found simply by reading up the tree. For example, the class precedence list for integer is (integer number t), and for cons is (cons list t). The class precedence list for null happens to be (null symbol list t). In this book, we will assume that if a generic function has more than one argument, the method identified by considering the class precedence list of every argument will be the same.

Although most of the COMMON LISP types we have discussed in this book are also CLOS classes, none of the functions we have discussed are CLOS generic functions. This means that we cannot take a function we already know about and add new methods to it for classes that it does not already handle. If we want to define any method, we need to define its generic function as well. Defining a method implicitly defines a generic function, but it is a good idea to define the generic method before defining the first method to provide it with a documentation string. The format we will use for defining a generic function is:

```
(clos:defgeneric function-name lambda-list
                  (:documentation doc-string))
```

where *function-name* will be the name of the new generic function, *lambda-list* is like the lambda-list of **defun**, and *doc-string* will be the documentation string of the generic function. **defgeneric** actually has several more optional parts, but we will not discuss them.

For example, let's define the < generic function we talked about at the beginning of this chapter. First of all, < is already the name of a COMMON LISP function, and since that is not a generic function, we must shadow < in order to use it for our own purposes.

```
> (in-package 'ch33)
#<Package CH33 6372362>
> (shadow '<)
T
> (clos:defgeneric < (x y)
    (:documentation
      "Returns True if the first argument sorts
       before the second argument;
       NIL otherwise."))
#<DTP-FUNCTION < 12640044>
> (documentation '< 'function)
"Returns True if the first argument sorts
       before the second argument;
       NIL otherwise."
```

Notice that the value of **defgeneric** is something funny; it is a *generic function object*, and your COMMON LISP will most probably have a different way of printing it than mine does.

To define a method, use the CLOS function **defmethod**, whose format is

    (defmethod   *function-name method-qualifiers method-lambda-list declarations forms*)

method-qualifiers may be omitted; this is what we will do for awhile. The *declarations* and *forms* are what you are used to from the definition of COMMON LISP functions. The *method-lambda-list* is also the same as the lambda-lists you use for defining COMMON LISP functions except that any required parameters may be replaced by the two-member list (*parameter class*), which is the way to say what classes this method is good for. The value returned by **defmethod** is a *method object*.

Now, let's define a < method for numbers.

```
> (defmethod < ((x number) (y number))
    (lisp:< x y))
> (< 3 5)
T
> (< 5 3)
NIL
#<method (TICLOS:METHOD < (NUMBER NUMBER))>
```

We now have a generic method named < and one method for it, which
compares two numbers. Similarly, we can define < methods for the
other classes mentioned above:

```
> (defmethod < ((x character) (y character))
    (char< x y))
#<method (TICLOS:METHOD < (CHARACTER CHARACTER))>
> (< #\a #\e)
T
> (< #\e #\a)
NIL
> (defmethod < ((s1 string) (s2 string))
    (string< s1 s2))
#<method (TICLOS:METHOD < (STRING STRING))>
> (< "store" "straw")
2
> (< "straw" "store")
NIL
> (defmethod < ((s1 symbol) (s2 symbol))
    (string< s1 s2))
#<method (TICLOS:METHOD < (SYMBOL SYMBOL))>
> (< 'frank 'harry)
0
> (< 'harry 'frank)
NIL
```

Notice that the names of the parameters do not have to be the same
for every method of the same generic function, as long as they have
the same number of parameters.

    Now that we have < defined for numbers, characters, strings, and
symbols, let's define it for lists of these types of objects. We'll say
that one list is < another if, at the first member where they differ, the

member of the first is < the member of the second and that a shorter
list is < a longer one whose first members are the same as the members
of the shorter list:

```
> (defmethod < ((l1 list) (l2 list))
    (cond ((null l1) (not (null l2)))
          ((null l2) nil)
          ((equal (first l1) (first l2))
           (< (rest l1) (rest l2)))
          (t (< (first l1) (first l2)))))
#<method (TICLOS:METHOD < (LIST LIST))>
> (< '(1 #\b "c" 'd) '(1 #\b "dog" 'a))
0
> (< '(1 #\b "dog" 'a) '(1 #\b "c" 'd))
NIL
```

Notice the elegance of this! Given that < is the name of a generic
function, we can use < in the definitions of other functions (or in the
definitions of <'s own methods) without worrying about the types of
its arguments; the appropriate method will be called automatically.

Exercises

Do the exercises of this chapter in the package ch33 except where
otherwise instructed.

33.1 *(r)* Shadow lisp:<, and define < as a generic function with a
documentation string, as shown in this chapter.

33.2 *(r)* Define the < methods for numbers, characters, strings, and
symbols as shown in this chapter. Test them.

33.3 *(i)* What happens if you give < arguments of different classes from
the ones you have defined methods for?

33.4 *(i)* What happens if you ask < to compare a string with a symbol?

33.5 *(d)* Define a method for < when both arguments are of the class
t. Use check-type to make sure that each argument is either
a character, number, symbol, or string. Assuming that the arguments are of different classes (Why is this assumption valid?),

make characters sort before numbers, numbers before symbols, and symbols before strings. (HINT: Use `type-of` and `member`.)

33.6 *(r)* Define a < method for comparing two lists as shown in this chapter. Test it.

33.7 *(d)* Redefine the < method you wrote for Exercise 33.5 so that characters, numbers, symbols, and strings all sort before conses.

33.8 *(d)* Test your < on two lists that don't have all corresponding members of the same class.

33.9 *(d)* Test your < on lists with sublists.

33.10 *(d)* Test your < on dotted lists and dotted pairs. Does it work? Should it work? Why?

33.11 *(u)* Redo Exercise 32.12 using the techniques of this chapter. You may use `equal` as the equality test throughout, but make `lessp` a generic function.

CHAPTER 34

CLASSES

In Chapter 33, we learned about CLOS methods and classes. However, the only classes we looked at were those that correspond to COMMON LISP types. Most COMMON LISP implementations implement these classes as *built-in* classes, which are rather restricted. In particular, you cannot define any new subclasses of built-in classes. CLOS's notion of *standard* classes is very flexible and involved. In this chapter, we will look at the basics of standard classes.

Briefly, a CLOS standard class (from now on, I will just say "class") is similar to a Pascal or Modula-2 record, a Cobol or PL/I structure, or what is called a *frame* in artificial intelligence, in that every instance of a class has a number of *slots*, each of which has a *value*. The number of slots, their names, and how they can be used are determined when the class is defined. Classes form a tangled hierarchy and can inherit their slots and how they are named and used from their superclasses. They can also add new slots and techniques that get inherited by their subclasses. An instance of a class has the structure determined by its class and all its superclasses. Besides the structure determined in this way, these classes can be used to define methods of generic functions. The whole thing can get very complicated, so in this chapter, I will just introduce some of the most basic class notions via an example.

The example I will use is a computerized version of a game of solitaire named *Klondike,* usually played with a regular deck of 52 playing cards.[1] One starts the game by dealing twenty-eight cards into seven piles, called *tableau piles,* one to the first pile, two to the second, ..., and seven to the seventh. Actually, this is done crosswise according to the following algorithm:

```
To deal:
    for i from 1 to 7 do
        for j from i to 7 do
            deal a card to tableau pile No. j
```

The cards are dealt facedown. Then, the top card of each pile is turned over, so that seven cards are visible, each hiding a pile of zero to six facedown cards. The remainder of the deck becomes the *stock* and is placed on the table facedown. There are five more piles, each of which is faceup, but begins with no cards in it. Four *foundation* piles are placed above the tableau, and one *waste* pile is placed next to the stock, below the tableau. The program we will develop will print the state of the game before each move; accept a move from the user; if the move is legal, make the move; and display the new game. Right after the deal, the game layout might look like this:

```
-- -- -- --
F1 F2 F3 F4

T1:    AS
T2:    QS
T3:    6H
T4:    4H
T5:    9H
T6:    AC
T7:    2D

   XX      --
STOCK WASTE
```

Empty piles appear as "__", upside-down piles appear as "XX," and a pile whose top card is faceup, appears as an abbreviation of the rank

---

[1]I have taken the description of this game and its rules from A. H. Morehead and G. Mott-Smith, eds., *Hoyles Rules of Games* (New York: New American Library, 1963), pp. 181–182.

and suit of the card. Each pile is labelled. The four foundation piles are labelled F1–F4, the seven tableau piles are labelled T1–T7, and the stock and waste piles are labelled STOCK and WASTE, respectively.

During the course of the game, the following moves are legal:

- You may turn over the top card of the stock and place it faceup on top of the waste pile.

- You may place the top card of the waste pile on top of a tableau pile, but only if it is one lower in rank and the opposite color of the card that currently is on the top. When you do this, overlap the cards so that all faceup cards in the tableau are visible.

- You may move all the faceup cards from one tableau pile onto the top of another tableau pile, but only if the bottommost highest-ranking card of the pile being moved is one lower in rank and the opposite color of the card that currently is on the top of the tableau pile the cards are being moved to.

- If the top card of a tableau pile or the top card of the waste pile is an ace, you may move it to an empty foundation pile.

- If the top card of a tableau pile or the top card of the waste pile is the card of the next-highest rank and of the same suit as the top card of any foundation pile, you may move the card to the top of that foundation pile.

- Whenever all the faceup cards of a tableau pile are removed from that pile, the topmost facedown card of that pile (if there is one) is turned over. This does not count as a move and is not optional.

- When a tableau pile is completely empty, you may put a king there, as soon as you uncover one. This may be from the top of the waste pile, or you may move a faceup king, along with all the faceup cards on top of it, from another tableau pile.

- If you ever get all 52 cards onto the foundation piles, you win.

- If you exhaust the stock, have no legal moves left, and do not have all the cards on the foundation piles, you lose.

To give you a better idea of the program to be written, here are
some moves from a typical game. We start the game by executing
(play), then move a card from one tableau pile to another.

```
> (play)


-- -- -- --
F1 F2 F3 F4

T1:   9D
T2:   JD
T3:   4H
T4:   KH
T5:   2S
T6:   8C
T7:   QS


   XX    --
STOCK WASTE

> move t2 t7


-- -- -- --
F1 F2 F3 F4

T1:   9D
T2:   5C
T3:   4H
T4:   KH
T5:   2S
T6:   8C
T7:   QS JD


   XX    --
STOCK WASTE
```

A few moves later, we get to move a tableau pile of more than one
card onto another.)

```
-- -- -- --
F1 F2 F3 F4

T1:   9D 8C
T2:   5C 4H
T3:   KC
T4:   KH
T5:   2S
T6:   8H
T7:   QS JD

   XX    --
STOCK WASTE
```

> move t7 t4

```
-- -- -- --
F1 F2 F3 F4

T1:   9D 8C
T2:   5C 4H
T3:   KC
T4:   KH QS JD
T5:   2S
T6:   8H
T7:   10H

   XX    --
STOCK WASTE
```

With no more moves among the tableaus, we next turn over a stock card.

> move stock waste

```
-- -- -- --
F1 F2 F3 F4
```

```
T1:   9D 8C
T2:   5C 4H
T3:   KC
T4:   KH QS JD
T5:   2S
T6:   8H
T7:   10H

   XX      JS
STOCK WASTE
```

I allowed the user to type s and w instead of stock and waste, respectively.

```
> move s w


-- -- -- --
F1 F2 F3 F4

T1:   9D 8C
T2:   5C 4H
T3:   KC
T4:   KH QS JD
T5:   2S
T6:   8H
T7:   10H

   XX      7D
STOCK WASTE

> move w t1


-- -- -- --
F1 F2 F3 F4

T1:   9D 8C 7D
T2:   5C 4H
T3:   KC
```

```
T4:   KH QS JD
T5:   2S
T6:   8H
T7:   10H
```

```
   XX    JS
STOCK WASTE
```

Later, a tableau pile becomes empty, and a king is put on it.

```
-- -- -- --
F1 F2 F3 F4
```

```
T1:   9D 8C 7D
T2:   5C 4H 3S
T3:   KC QD
T4:   KH QS JD 10S
T5:   2S
T6:   8H
T7:   10H
```

```
   XX    QH
STOCK WASTE
```

```
> move t1 t4
```

```
-- -- -- --
F1 F2 F3 F4
```

```
T1:   __
T2:   5C 4H 3S
T3:   KC QD
T4:   KH QS JD 10S 9D 8C 7D
T5:   2S
T6:   8H
T7:   10H
```

```
   XX    QH
STOCK WASTE
```

```
> move t4 t1


-- -- -- --
F1 F2 F3 F4

T1:   KH QS JD 10S 9D 8C 7D
T2:   5C 4H 3S
T3:   KC QD
T4:   9H
T5:   2S
T6:   8H
T7:   10H


   XX    QH
STOCK WASTE
```

Still later, an ace finally turns up and gets put on a foundation pile, followed by its 2, and another ace on another foundation pile.

```
-- -- -- --
F1 F2 F3 F4

T1:   KH QS JD 10S 9D 8C 7D 6C 5H
T2:   5C 4H 3S
T3:   KC QD
T4:   9H
T5:   2S
T6:   8H
T7:   10H


   XX    AS
STOCK WASTE


> move w f1


AS -- -- --
F1 F2 F3 F4

T1:   KH QS JD 10S 9D 8C 7D 6C 5H
```

```
T2:   5C 4H 3S
T3:   KC QD
T4:   9H
T5:   2S
T6:   8H
T7:   10H


   XX      10C
STOCK WASTE


> move t5 f1


2S __ __ __
F1 F2 F3 F4


T1:   KH QS JD 10S 9D 8C 7D 6C 5H
T2:   5C 4H 3S
T3:   KC QD
T4:   9H
T5:   AD
T6:   8H
T7:   10H


   XX      10C
STOCK WASTE


> move t5 f2


2S AD __ __
F1 F2 F3 F4


T1:   KH QS JD 10S 9D 8C 7D 6C 5H
T2:   5C 4H 3S
T3:   KC QD
T4:   9H
T5:   QC
T6:   8H
T7:   10H
```

```
   XX      10C
STOCK WASTE
```

Eventually, however, the stock is exhausted, and the game is lost.

```
3S AD 2H __
F1 F2 F3 F4


T1:  KH QS JD 10S 9D 8C 7D 6C 5H 4S 3H 2C
T2:  KD
T3:  __
T4:  9C 8D 7S
T5:  QC JH 10C 9H 8S 7H 6S
T6:  KC QD JC 10H 9S 8H 7C 6H 5C 4H 3C
T7:  4C


   __      5S
STOCK WASTE
```

```
> quit
Sorry, you lose.
```

We will implement this game in the **klondike** package. I will show you some of the implementation in the text. The rest will be left for the exercises. The first thing we will do is define a class of cards. A card has a rank and a suit. It seems reasonable to represent the ranks and the suits by symbols and to have constants that are lists of the ranks and the suits. For example,

```
> (defconstant *ranks*
            '(ace 2 3 4 5 6 7 8 9 10 jack queen king)
   "A list of the 13 ranks in a deck of playing cards.")
*RANKS*
```

I will leave the definition of ***suits*** for you to do.

A class is defined by a call to the **defclass** function, whose format is

```
(defclass class-name ( superclass-names )
  ( slot-specifiers )
  class-options)
```

class-name is any symbol you chose to name the class. *superclass-names* are the names of zero or more superclasses for this class. In this chapter, we will never have more than one superclass per class. *slot-specifiers* specify the slots that instances of this class will have. I will discuss them below. *class-options* are a sequence of options for the class, the only one of which we will use is (:documentation *doc-string*).

A *slot-specifier* may be just a symbol used to name the slot, but more often there are further things to say about the slot, and so the specifier appears as (*slot-name slot-options*). One *slot-option* is *:documentation doc-string*. I will explain the others as I use them in the examples.

We want to define a class of cards whose instances will each have a rank and a suit. No other class is a superclass of the class of cards.

```
> (clos:defclass card ()
    ((rank :initarg :rank :reader rank
           :documentation "The rank of the card")
     (suit :initarg :suit :reader suit
           :documentation "The suit of the card"))
    (:documentation "The class of playing cards"))
#<STANDARD-CLASS CARD>
```

As you can see, the name of this class is `card`, it has no superclasses, its documentation string is `"The class of playing cards"`, and it has two slots named `rank` and `suit`. Each slot has three slot options given: the `:initarg` slot option, the `:reader` slot option, and the `:documentation` slot option. The `:initarg` slot option specifies the keyword argument to be used to initialize the slot when an instance is created. Instances are created with the function `make-instance`, which takes the class name as a required argument, and then a sequence of zero or more `:initarg` keyword arguments. To create the Jack of Clubs, we evaluate

```
> (setf jc (make-instance 'card :rank 'jack :suit 'clubs))
#<CARD 12476644>
```

The printed representation used for a card is not very informative, but the `:reader` slot option specifies a function that can be used to access the slot's value:

```
> (rank jc)
JACK
> (suit jc)
CLUBS
```

Nevertheless, it would be nicer if the printed representation of the
Jack of Clubs were JC. We can get this to happen by specifying appropriate methods for the generic function **print-object**. This is a
function of two arguments—an object and a *stream*. All the output
functions we discussed in Chapter 29 use **print-object**, so specifying **print-object** for a class of objects will affect how its instances
are printed everywhere. A *stream* is what was called a *destination* on
page 221. It can specify what file is to receive the output. However,
we still don't have to worry about it, since we can just pass it along as
the first argument to **format** or as a second, optional argument to the
other output functions. First, let's provide a **print-object** method
for the symbol JACK and specify that it is to appear simply as J.

```
> (defmethod clos:print-object ((obj (eql 'jack)) stream)
    (princ 'J stream))
#<method (TICLOS:METHOD TICLOS:PRINT-OBJECT ((EQL J) T))>
```

Notice that this method-lambda-list has two members. The second is
stream. The first is (obj (eql 'jack)), which says that this method
is applicable whenever the first argument to **print-object** is **eql** to
'jack. Each member of a method-lambda-list must either be a simple
symbol/variable, a list (*symbol class*), or a list (*symbol* (eql *object*)).

Now that this **print-object** method has been defined, the printed
representation COMMON LISP uses for **jack** will always be J.

```
> 'jack
J
> (rank jc)
J
```

Similarly, we can specify that the printed representations of ACE, QUEEN,
and KING will be A, Q, and K, respectively.

Next, we can specify that the symbol CLUBS should be printed as
just C.

```
> (defmethod clos:print-object ((o (eql 'clubs)) stream)
    (princ 'C stream))
#<method (TICLOS:METHOD TICLOS:PRINT-OBJECT ((EQL C) T))>
> (suit jc)
C
```

We can make similar methods for DIAMONDS, HEARTS, and SPADES.

Finally, we can specify that to print a card, just print its rank followed by its suit:

```
> (defmethod clos:print-object ((c card) stream)
    (format stream "~a~a" (rank c) (suit c)))
#<method (TICLOS:METHOD TICLOS:PRINT-OBJECT (CARD T))>
> jc
JC
```

I will assume that we have a constant *deck*, which is a list of the 52 cards in a standard deck. Defining this constant is left as an exercise.

In playing Klondike, the color of a card matters. We could have given each card a color slot, but that would have been redundant, since the color is determined by the suit. Instead, we can define a color function. Since color is only applicable to cards, we could do this by defining a regular COMMON LISP function and using check-type to make sure its argument is a card, but it is more in the spirit of CLOS to use a generic function, whose only method applies to cards. I'll do this, using an option of defgeneric I haven't mentioned yet, in which we can define methods with the generic function:

```
> (clos:defgeneric color (c)
    (:documentation "Returns the color of a card.")
    (:method ((c card))
            (case (suit c)
              ((diamonds hearts) 'red)
              ((clubs spades) 'black))))
#<DTP-FUNCTION COLOR 4300312>
> (color jc)
BLACK
```

This is the first time you've seen COMMON LISP's case function. Look up its definition in the COMMON LISP Manual in Appendix B of this book.

Now that we have defined cards, it is time to work on the Klondike game layout. This consists of thirteen piles: four foundation piles, seven tableau piles, a stock pile, and a waste pile. Since all of these are piles and contain ordered sequences of cards, it is convenient to define a class of piles:

```
> (clos:defclass pile ()
    ((cards :initform '() :accessor cards
           :documentation
           "A list of the cards in the pile"))
    (:documentation "A pile of cards"))
#<STANDARD-CLASS PILE>
```

Here a `pile` has just one slot, named `cards`. That slot is specified with two slot-options we haven't seen before. The `:initform` slot-option provides a form that is evaluated every time a new pile instance is created. The value of the form becomes the value of the slot. Here, the cards of a `pile` are always initialized to be the empty list. The `:accessor` slot-option is like the `:reader` slot-option, except that the `:accessor` function creates a generalized variable that is recognized by `setf`, and so can be used to change the slot's value, as well as to read it. Let's make a pile and put three cards into it.

```
> (setf p (make-instance 'pile))
#<PILE 13222277>
> (cards p)
NIL
> (setf (cards p)
        (list
          jc
          (make-instance 'card :rank 5 :suit 'hearts)))
(JC 5H)
> (push (make-instance 'card :suit 'spades :rank 'ace)
        (cards p))
(AS JC 5H)
> (color (second (cards p)))
BLACK
```

I will leave as exercises the definitions of methods to make the **top** of a pile the first card in its list of cards, the **size** of a pile the length of its list of cards, and **empty** a predicate that is True of a pile when and only when it has no cards in it.

We can divide the thirteen piles of Klondike into five faceup piles (the four foundation piles and the waste pile), one facedown pile (the stock), and seven two-way piles (the tableau piles). This categorization will mainly be so that we can print these different kinds of piles in different ways. For example, the class of faceup piles can be defined as

```
>(clos:defclass face-up-pile (pile)
    ()
    (:documentation "A pile of face-up cards"))
#<STANDARD-CLASS FACE-UP-PILE>
```

Notice that the **face-up-pile** class is declared to be a subclass of the **pile** class and that there is an empty list of slots because a **face-up-pile** has no slots other than the one it has by being a **pile**.

We want to print a **face-up-pile** by printing its **top** card if it has one. We want to print an empty **face-up-pile** as __.

```
> (defmethod clos:print-object ((p face-up-pile) stream)
    (if (cards p)
        (princ (top p) stream)
        (princ '__ stream)))
#<method (TICLOS:METHOD TICLOS:PRINT-OBJECT
                      . (FACE-UP-PILE T))>
```

I'll leave facedown piles for the exercises.

The tableau piles have zero or more faceup cards on top of zero or more facedown cards. We can define them as instances of the **two-way-pile**, which is a subclass of **pile**, but with an extra slot— upcards.

```
> (clos:defclass two-way-pile (pile)
    ((upcards :initform '() :accessor upcards
              :documentation "A second list of cards"))
    (:documentation
      "A pile with some face-up cards
       on top of some face-down cards"))
#<STANDARD-CLASS TWO-WAY-PILE>
```

Since either the facedown part or the faceup part of a **two-way-pile** can be empty independently of the other, we need a predicate to tell whether the faceup part is empty. (We already have **empty** for the facedown part.)

```
> (clos:defgeneric emptyup (p)
    (:documentation
      "Returns T
       if the two-way-pile has no face-up cards")
    (:method ((p two-way-pile))
             (null (upcards p))))
#<DTP-FUNCTION EMPTYUP 4540320>
```

If a **two-way-pile** has any **upcards**, we want to print the pile by printing all the **upcards**, topmost on the right. If the **two-way-pile** has no **upcards**, we would want to print its **cards** as if it were a **face-down-pile**. Therefore the method for printing a **two-way-pile** is

```
> (defmethod clos:print-object ((p two-way-pile) stream)
    (cond ((upcards p) (prin-rev (upcards p) stream))
          ((cards p) (princ 'XX stream))
          (t (princ '__))))
#<method (TICLOS:METHOD TICLOS:PRINT-OBJECT
                        (TWO-WAY-PILE T))>
```

I will leave the function **print-rev** for you to write as an exercise. I will also leave as exercises the method (turnover *pile*), which is used to turn over the top facedown card of a **two-way-pile** when the **upcards** are empty, and a specialized **top** method for **two-way-piles**, which is used to return the first member of **upcards** instead of the first member of **cards**.

Now that we have the notions of **face-up-pile**, **face-down-pile**, and **two-way-pile**, it is time to get more specific to Klondike, and define **foundation-pile**, **tableau-pile**, **stock**, and **waste**. These class definitions are left as exercises.

Finally, we will define the class **layout**. A **layout** will have four **foundation-piles**, seven **tableau-piles**, one **stock**, and one **waste** pile. Since we will want to refer to piles such as the third foundation pile and the fifth tableau pile, it is convenient to use COMMON LISP's

arrays for the set of foundation piles and for the set of tableau piles.
We will not use the full flexibility of COMMON LISP arrays, so our
needs will be satisfied by the following three functions:

- (make-array n) returns an array of n elements, where n is a
  positive integer. Each element can be any COMMON LISP object.

- (aref *array* n) returns the nth element of the array *array*.
  Counting is zero based, so if a2 were created by (make-array
  2), its elements would be accessed by (aref a2 0) and (aref
  a2 1). aref also creates a form recognizable by setf as being a
  generalized variable, so the way to make the first element of a2
  the symbol foo is to evaluate (setf (aref a2 0) 'foo).

- (dotimes (*var n*) *forms*) executes the series of *forms* n times,
  with *var* taking on the values $0, 1, \ldots, n-1$.

The definition of the layout class is

```
> (clos:defclass layout ()
  ((foundations
     :accessor foundations
     :initform (let ((a (make-array 4)))
                 (dotimes (i 4)
                   (setf (aref a i)
                         (make-instance
                           'foundation-pile)))
                 a))
   (tableau
     :accessor tableau
     :initform (let ((a (make-array 7)))
                 (dotimes (i 7)
                   (setf (aref a i)
                         (make-instance 'tableau-pile)))
                 a))
   (stock :accessor stock
          :initform (make-instance 'stock))
   (waste :accessor waste
          :initform (make-instance 'waste)))
   (:documentation "The layout of a Klondike game."))
#<STANDARD-CLASS LAYOUT>
```

Remember that the :initform slot-option is evaluated whenever a new layout is created, so that each new layout will have new, empty piles. I will leave as an exercise defining a print-option for layouts.

Let's now look at the function play:

```
> (defun play ()
    (setf *layout* (make-instance 'layout))
    (shuffle)
    (deal)
    (let (move)
      (loop
        (print *layout*)
        (setf move (read))
        (when (eq move 'quit) (return))
        (moveto (translate (read)) (translate (read)))))
    (if (= 52 (+ (size (aref (foundations *layout*) 0))
                 (size (aref (foundations *layout*) 1))
                 (size (aref (foundations *layout*) 2))
                 (size (aref (foundations *layout*) 3))))
        (princ "You Win!!!")
        (princ "Sorry, you lose."))
    (values))
PLAY
```

This assumes that *layout* has been declared as a global variable. The functions we have left to write are shuffle, deal, moveto, and translate.

A good way to shuffle a deck of cards is to go through the entire deck and exchange each card with a randomly chosen card. This is easy to do using the COMMON LISP function (random n), which returns a random integer between 0 and $n - 1$, inclusively, and using psetf to exchange two values. The definition of shuffle is left as an exercise.

The deal function should first set the stock to be the *deck* and then deal from the stock to the tableau piles as discussed above. This is also an exercise.

The moveto function is an excellent example of a generic function, because, as you can see by reviewing the legal moves outlined above, a move is completely defined by the class of pile the card is being moved from and the class of pile the card is being moved to. These possibilities are outlined below:

- A card may be moved from the `stock` to the `waste` pile.

- A card may be moved from the `waste` pile to a `tableau` pile.

- A card may be moved from the `waste` pile to a `foundation` pile.

- A card may be moved from a `tableau` pile to a `foundation` pile.

- The set of `upcards` may be moved from one `tableau` pile to another `tableau` pile.

Obviously, for each possibility, we will define a `moveto` method.

Some `moveto` methods need to check for the legality of the proposed move before doing it. It is also convenient to define a `legal` generic function, because the legality check subdivides the cases as follows:

- It is legal to put a `card` on a `foundation-pile` only if the `foundation-pile` is empty and the `card` is an ace or if the `card` is the next highest in rank of the same suit as the current top of the `foundation-pile`.

- It is legal to put a `card` on a `tableau-pile` only if the `tableau-pile` is empty and the card is a king or if the card is next lower in rank and the opposite color of the current top card of the `tableau-pile`.

- It is legal to put a list of cards on a `tableau-pile` only if the `tableau-pile` is empty and the last card of the list is a king or if the last card of the list could legally be put onto the `tableau-pile` by itself.

- Any other of the kinds of moves is always legal.

I will define the most complicated of the `moveto` and `legal` methods and leave the rest to you.

```
> (clos:defgeneric moveto (p1 p2)
    (:documentation
      "Moves the appropriate card(s)
       from pile P1 to pile P2."))
#<DTP-FUNCTION MOVETO 13400000>
```

```
> (defmethod moveto ((tp1 tableau-pile)
                     (tp2 tableau-pile))
   (if (legal (upcards tp1) tp2)
       (setf (upcards tp2)
             (append (upcards tp1) (upcards tp2))
             (upcards tp1) '())
       (format t
               "~%It is not legal to put a ~A on a ~A.~%"
               (head tp1) (top tp2))))
#<method (TICLOS:METHOD MOVETO
                        (TABLEAU-PILE TABLEAU-PILE))>
> (clos:defgeneric legal (c p)
   (:documentation
     "Returns T if putting C on P is legal;
      NIL otherwise."))
#<DTP-FUNCTION LEGAL 10640000>
> (defmethod legal ((lc list) (tp tableau-pile))
   (cond ((emptyup tp)
          (and (empty tp)
               (eq (rank (first (last lc))) 'king)))
         (t (legal (first (last lc)) tp))))
#<method (TICLOS:METHOD LEGAL (LIST TABLEAU-PILE))>
```

Finally, whenever the upcards of a tableau pile become empty, the top facedown card is supposed to be turned over. This can happen as a result of either moveto method whose first argument is a tableau-pile. CLOS provides special kinds of methods for such cleanup tasks following other methods. The methods we have seen so far are called *primary* methods. There are also :before methods and :after methods, which are declared just like other methods, but using one of the two *method-qualifiers* :before or :after. When a generic function is called: all applicable :before methods are executed for side effect, most specific first; the most specific primary method is executed, and its value becomes the value of the generic function; all applicable :after methods are executed, least specific first. This might sound confusing, but clears up when it is applied. We will just define one :after method:

```
> (defmethod moveto :after ((tp tableau-pile) (p pile))
```

```
    (when (and (emptyup tp) (not (empty tp)))
      (turnover tp)))
#<method (TICLOS:METHOD MOVETO :AFTER
                        (TABLEAU-PILE PILE))>
```

That pretty much finishes the implementation of the Klondike game. The rest of the details are left to you.

Exercises

Do the exercises of this chapter in a file named **klondike** and in the **klondike** package, except where otherwise instructed.

34.1 *(d)* Implement the computerized Klondike game classes, methods, and so on, shown in this chapter.

34.2 *(d)* Define the constant ***suits*** to be a list of the 4 suits.

34.3 *(d)* Define **print-object** methods to specify that the printed representations of the symbols QUEEN, KING, and ACE will be Q, K, and A respectively.

34.4 *(d)* Define **print-object** methods to specify that the printed representations of the symbols DIAMONDS, HEARTS, and SPADES will be D, H, and S, respectively.

34.5 *(d)* Add to your **klondike** file the form

```
(defconstant *deck* _____
  "A standard deck of 52 cards")
```

where the blank is filled by a form that evaluates to a list of the 52 standard cards—4 suits, each of 13 different ranks.

34.6 *(d)* Define the method **(top p)** to return the first card in the list of **cards** of the pile **p**.

34.7 *(d)* Define the method **(size p)** to return the length of the list of **cards** of the pile **p**.

34.8 *(d)* Define the method **(empty p)** to return True if the pile **p** has no cards in it; False otherwise.

34.9 *(d)* Define the class of facedown piles, and a `print-object` method for them that prints an empty `face-down-pile` as `__`, and a nonempty `face-down-pile` as **XX**.

34.10 *(d)* Define the function (`prin-rev` *list stream*) to print the members of the *list* to the *stream* in reverse order.

34.11 *(d)* Define the method (`turnover` *pile*), so it can be used to turn over the top facedown card of a `two-way-pile` when the `upcards` are empty.

34.12 *(d)* Define a specialized `top` method for `two-way-piles` to return the first member of `upcards`.

34.13 *(d)* Define `foundation-pile` and `waste` to be subclasses of `face-up-pile`, `stock` to be a subclass of `face-down-pile`, and `tableau-pile` to be a subclass of `two-way-pile`.

34.14 *(d)* Define a `print-object` method for the `layout` class, so that they are printed as shown in the sample game in this chapter.

34.15 *(d)* Define `shuffle` as indicated in this chapter. `shuffle` should side effect the global constant `*deck*` by changing the order of its 52 cards.

34.16 *(d)* Define `deal` as indicated in this chapter.

34.17 *(d)* Define (`translate` *symbol*) to return the pile of `*layout*` denoted by the *symbol*. Assume the naming conventions used in the sample play of this chapter.

34.18 *(d)* Finish the implementation of the computerized Klondike game.

34.19 *(d)* It is unfortunate that, looking at the `*layout*`, we cannot tell if a particular `tableau-pile` has any facedown cards in it. Change the `print-object` methods so that the facedown cards of a `tableau-pile` print either as **XX** or `__` just to the left of the `upcards`.

34.20 *(d)* We might have defined a `two-way-pile` as something that consists of two subpiles, a `face-down-pile` and a fanned-face-up-pile. But then, we would want pile not to have any slots, but two subclasses—single-pile and double-pile. face-up-pile and face-down-pile would be subclasses of single-pile, and two-way-pile would be a subclass of double-pile. Write another version of the Klondike game organized this way.

Part V

APPENDICES

APPENDIX A

SOLUTIONS TO SELECTED EXERCISES

Chapter 1 Getting Started

The answers to Exercises 1.1, 1.2, 1.3, 1.6, 1.7, 1.8, 1.9, 1.11, and 1.12 depend on the operating system or COMMON LISP implementation you are using. You must find the answers by consulting your manual, your teacher, a consultant, or a friend. After finding the answers, write them in the book in the spaces provided in the exercises and in Appendix B.2 for later reference.

Chapter 2 Numbers

2.6 Your LISP should interpret 3. as an integer and 3.0 as a floating-point number.

2.13 Also write the answer in Appendix B.2 for later reference.

2.14 Also write the answer in Appendix B.2 for later reference.

Chapter 3 Lists

The exercises of this chapter are intended to make you comfortably familiar with the formats you can use to type lists to the COMMON LISP listener and with the error messages that result from some common mistakes.

Chapter 4 Arithmetic

4.8 > (+)
    0
    > (*)
    1

The other two cause error messages.

Chapter 5 Strings and Characters

5.19 By typing it twice, such as "a\\b".

Chapter 6 Symbols

6.26 By typing an escape symbol before the space, such as

    > 'I\ did\ it
    |I DID IT|

Chapter 7 Packages

7.4 By evaluating (describe 'lisp:pi).

Chapter 8 Basic List Processing

8.7 The first three of the nine forms are:

    (first (first (first *)))
    (first (rest (first (first *))))
    (first (first (rest (first *))))

Chapter 9 The Special form quote

The exercises of this chapter are designed to have you study the equivalence between the quote mark and the quote special form.

Chapter 10 Defining Your Own Functions

10.9 (defun list2 (o1 o2)
        "Returns a list of its two arguments in order."
        (cons o1 (list1 o2)))

10.14 (defun sqr (n)
        "Returns the square of the numeric argument."
        (* n n))

Chapter 11 Defining Functions in Packages

11.4 (defun quad-roots (a b c)
        "Returns a list of the two roots
         of the quadratic equation, ax^2+bx+c."
        (list (/ (+ (- b) (discrim a b c)) (* 2 a))
              (/ (- (- b) (discrim a b c)) (* 2 a))))

Chapter 12 Saving for Another Day

12.2 (defun variablep (s)
        "Returns T if the first character of the symbol S
         is #\?; NIL otherwise."
        (char= (char (symbol-name s) 0) #\?))

Chapter 13 Predicate Functions

13.5 (defun string-or-list-over-5 (o)
        "Returns T if O is
         a string containing more than 5 characters
         or a list containing more than 5 elements;
         NIL otherwise."
        (and (or (stringp o) (listp o))
             (> (length o) 5)))

13.7 (shadow 'lisp:null)

```
(defun null (o)
  "Returns T if O is 'NIL; NIL otherwise."
  (eql o 'nil))
```

13.13 (defun match-element (e1 e2)
```
    "Returns T if E1 and E2 are eql,
     or if either is a variable; NIL otherwise."
    (or (eql e1 e2) (variablep e1) (variablep e2)))
```

Chapter 14 Conditional Expressions

14.7 (defun dont-care (s)
```
    "Returns T if the argument is a question mark;
     NIL otherwise."
    (and (symbolp s) (string= (symbol-name s) "?")))
```

Chapter 15 Recursion

15.13 (defun product (n1 n2)
```
    "Returns the product of two nonnegative integers."
    (assert
      (and (integerp n1) (>= n1 0))
      (n1)
  "N1 must be a nonnegative integer, instead it's ~S."
      n1)
    (assert
      (integerp n2)
      (n2)
      "N2 must  be an integer, instead it's ~S."
      n2)
    (if (zerop n1) 0
        (sum n2 (product (1- n1) n2)))))
```

Chapter 16 Recursion on Lists, Part 1—Analysis

16.6 (defun before (e1 e2 l)
```
    "Returns True if the first element occurs before
```

```
      the second element in the list that is the third
      argument."
(check-type e1 (satisfies util:elementp))
(check-type e2 (satisfies util:elementp))
(check-type l list)
(member e2 (member e1 l)))
```

16.11 (defun equal-lelt (l1 l2)
```
      "Returns T if the corresponding elements
       of L1 and L2 are EQL;  NIL otherwise."
      (check-type l1 list)
      (check-type l2 list)
      (cond ((null l1) (null l2))
            ((null l2) nil)
            ((eql (first l1) (first l2))
             (equal-lelt (rest l1) (rest l2)))
            (t nil)))
```

16.14 (defun assoc (e al)
```
      "Returns the first element of AL,
       all of which must, themselves, be lists,
       whose first element is EQL to the element E."
      (check-type e (satisfies util:elementp))
      (check-type al list)
      (assert
        (or (null al) (listp (first al)))
        (al)
     "All AL's elements should be lists, but AL is ~S."
        al)
      (cond ((null al) nil)
            ((eql (first (first al)) e) (first al))
            (t (assoc e (rest al)))))
```

Chapter 17 Recursion on Lists, Part 2—Synthesis

17.5 (defun firstn (n l)
```
      "Returns a list of
       the first N members of the list L."
      (check-type n integer)
```

```
        (check-type l list)
        (if (zerop n) '()
            (cons (first l) (firstn (1- n) (rest l)))))
```

17.21 `(export '(set makeset union first rest insert))`
```
    ...
    (defun insert (e s)
      "Returns a set just like S,
       but with E added as a new element."
      (check-type s set)
      (if (member e (lisp:rest s)) s
          (cons :set (cons e (lisp:rest s))))))
```

17.27 `(shadow '(set union first rest intersection subsetp`
```
                equal))
    ...
    (export '(set makeset union first rest insert empty
                 intersection complement subsetp equal))
    ...
    (defun equal (s1 s2)
      "Returns T if S1 and S2 contain the same elements;
       NIL otherwise."
      (check-type s1 set)
      (check-type s2 set)
      (unlabelled-equal (lisp:rest s1) (lisp:rest s2)))

    (defun unlabelled-equal (l1 l2)
      "Returns T if S1 and S2 contain the same elements,
       regardless of the order;
       NIL otherwise."
      (and (unlabelled-subsetp l1 l2)
           (unlabelled-subsetp l2 l1)))
```

17.30 `(defun bound-to (v subs)`
```
      "Returns the term that the variable V is bound to
       in the substitution SUBS; NIL if it's unbound."
      (check-type v (satisfies variablep))
      (check-type subs list)
      (second (assoc v subs)))
```

17.34 (defun enclose-expression (expr)
    "EXPR is a list representing an arithmetic
     expression (using only the operators + and -)
     in normal infix notation.
     Returns a list whose one member is EXPR
     transformed into Cambridge Prefix Notation."
    (check-type expr list)
    (cond ((< (length expr) 3) expr)
          (t (combine-expr
                 (second expr) (first expr)
                 (enclose-expression (nthcdr 2 expr)))))))

Chapter 18 Recursion on Trees

18.2 (defun atom-equal (a1 a2)
    "Returns T if A1 and A2 are equal atoms
     of the same type;
     NIL otherwise."
    (typecase a1
      (util:element (eql a1 a2))
      (string (and (stringp a2) (string= a1 a2)))))

    \item[18.18]\index{{\tt inorder}}
    \begin{verbatim}
    (export '(bstree bstreep insert root left right
                      member build-from-list inorder))
    ...
    (defun inorder (bstree)
      "Returns a list of the members of BSTREE
       in sorted order."
      (check-type bstree bstree)
      (cond ((null bstree) '())
            ((atom bstree) (list bstree))
            (t (append
                   (inorder (left bstree))
                   (cons (root bstree)
                         (inorder (right bstree)))))))

18.21 (shadow 'copy-tree)

```
(defun copy-tree (tree)
  "Returns a copy of the tree TREE,
   copying at all levels."
  (typecase tree
    (atom tree)
    (cons (cons (copy-tree (first tree))
                (copy-tree (rest tree)))))))
```

18.26
```
(defun rulep (o)
  "A rule is a list of two trees."
  (and (listp o) (= (length o) 2)))
```

```
(deftype rule ()
  "A rule is a list of two patterns,
   the Left-Hand Side, and the Right-Hand Side."
  '(satisfies rulep))
```

```
(defun lhs (rule)
  "Returns the right-hand side of the RULE."
  (check-type rule rule)
  (first rule))
```

```
(defun rhs (rule)
  "Returns the right-hand side of the RULE."
  (check-type rule rule)
  (second rule))
```

18.28
```
(defun enclose-expression (expr)
  "EXPR is a list representing an arithmetic
   expression (using only the operators + and -)
   in normal infix notation.
   Returns a list whose one member is EXPR
   transformed into Cambridge Prefix Notation."
  (check-type expr list)
  (cond ((< (length expr) 3) expr)
        (t (combine-expr
             (second expr)
             (first expr)
```

```
                    (enclose-expression
                      (enclose-term (nthcdr 2 expr)))))))))

  (defun prefix (expr)
    "Returns the arithmetic expression EXPR
     containing the operators +, -, *, and /.
     transformed into Cambridge Prefix notation."
    (cond ((atom expr) expr)
          ((< (length expr) 3) expr)
          (t (first
                (enclose-expression
                  (enclose-term expr))))))
```

Chapter 19 The Evaluator

19.6 (defun lazy-nth (n list)
```
      "Returns the Nth member of the LIST,
       redeeming promises where necessary."
      (check-type n (and integer (satisfies plusp)))
      (check-type list cons)
      (if (= n 1) (lazy-first list)
          (lazy-nth (1- n) (lazy-rest list)))))
```

19.9 (defun primes-from (n others)
```
      "Returns a list of all prime numbers >= N,
       assuming that OTHERS is a list of all primes < N."
      (check-type n integer)
      (check-type others list)
      (if (relatively-prime n others)
          `(,n :promise primes-from ,(1+ n)
            '(,@others ,n))
          (primes-from (1+ n) others)))
```

19.12 (defun enclose-factor (expr)
```
       "EXPR is a list representing an arithmetic
        expression (using the operators +, -, *, /, and ^)
        in normal infix notation.
        Returns a list like EXPR,
        but with its first factor collected as its first
```

```
    member, and expressed in Cambridge Prefix
    Notation."
(check-type expr list)
(cond ((< (length expr) 3) expr)
      ((member (second expr) '(+ - * /)) expr)
      ((eql (second expr) '^)
       (combine-expr 'expt
                        (first expr)
                        (enclose-factor
                          (prefix-first
                            (nthcdr 2 expr)))))
      (t expr)))
```

19.16
```
(defun discrim (a b c)
  "Returns the square root of the discriminant
   of the equation ax^2 + bx + c."
  (check-type a number)
  (check-type b number)
  (check-type c number)
  (sqrt (compute '(,b * ,b - 4 * ,a * ,c))))
```

```
(defun quad-roots (a b c)
  "Returns a list of the two roots of the equation
   ax^2 + bx + c."
  (check-type a number)
  (check-type b number)
  (check-type c number)
  (list (compute
          '((- ,b + (discrim ,a ,b ,c)) / (2 * ,a)))
        (compute
          '((- ,b - (discrim ,a ,b ,c))
            / (2 * ,a)))))
```

Chapter 20 Functions with Arbitrary Numbers of Arguments

20.5
```
(defun discrim (a b c)
  "Returns the square root of the discriminant
   of the equation ax^2 + bx + c."
```

```
(check-type a number)
(check-type b number)
(check-type c number)
(sqrt (compute b '* b '- 4 '* a '* c)))

(defun quad-roots (a b c)
  "Returns a list of the two roots of the equation
  ax^2 + bx + c."
  (check-type a number)
  (check-type b number)
  (check-type c number)
  (list
    (compute
      `(- ,b + (discrim ,a ,b ,c)) '/ `(2 * ,a))
    (compute
      `(- ,b - (discrim ,a ,b ,c)) '/ `(2 * ,a))))
```

Chapter 21 Mapping Functions

21.5
```
(defun scalar-plus (n vector)
  "Returns a list like VECTOR,
   but with each of its members added to N."
  (check-type n number)
  (check-type vector list)
  (mapcar #'(lambda (x) (+ x n)) vector))
```

21.10
```
(defun discrim (a b c)
  "Returns the square root of the discriminant
   of the equation ax^2 + bx + c."
  (check-type a number)
  (check-type b number)
  (check-type c number)
  (compute `(sqrt (,b * ,b - 4 * ,a * ,c))))
```

Chapter 22 The Applicator

22.9
```
(defun depth (tree)
  "Returns the depth of the argument TREE."
  (if (atom tree) 0
```

```
(1+ (apply #'max (mapcar #'depth tree)))))
```

Chapter 23 Macros

23.9 (shadow 'and)

```
(defmacro and (&rest forms)
  "Return True if every FORM evaluates to True;
   NIL otherwise.
   As soon as one form evaluates to NIL,
   doesn't evaluate the rest."
  (cond ((null forms) t)
        ((null (rest forms)) (first forms))
        (t '(if ,(first forms) (and ,@(rest forms))
               NIL))))
```

Chapter 24 Assignment

24.9 (defun apply-rules (tree rule-list)
```
      "Applies the first rule in RULE-LIST to tree,
       and each successive rule to the results of
       applying the previous list."
      (if (null rule-list) tree
          (apply-rules
            (apply-rule tree (first rule-list))
            (rest rule-list))))
```

24.14 (psetf x2 x3 x3 x2)

Chapter 25 Scope and Extent

25.5 The file test may look like:

```
(setf x 3)

(defun foo (x)
  "Establishes a binding for X, and calls BAR."
  (bar))
```

```
(defun bar ()
  "Returns the value of the non-local X."
  x)
```

Chapter 26 Sequences

26.4 (shadow 'progn)

```
(defun progn (&rest forms)
  "Gets all the FORMs evaluated,
   and returns the value of the last form."
  (first (last forms)))
```

26.6 (shadow '(push pop))

```
(defvar *stack* '() "A global stack")

(defun push (e)
  "Pushes the object E onto *STACK*."
  (setf *stack* (cons e *stack*)))

(defun top ()
  "Returns the top element of *STACK*."
  (first *stack*))

(defun pop ()
  "Pops the top element off *STACK*,
   and returns it."
  (prog1 (first *stack*)
         (setf *stack* (rest *stack*))))
```

26.8 (defun svariablep (s)
```
       "Returns T if S is a sequence variable;
        NIL otherwise."
       (and (symbolp s)
            (char= (char (symbol-name s) 0) #\$)))
```

26.12 (defun boundp (v subs)
```
        "Returns T if variable V is bound to anything
         in the substitution SUBS; NIL otherwise."
```

```
    (check-type v (or (satisfies variablep)
                      (satisfies svariablep)))
    (check-type subs list)
    (assoc v subs))

(defun bound-to (v subs)
  "Returns the term that the variable V is bound to
   in the substitution SUBS; NIL if it's unbound."
  (check-type v (or (satisfies variablep)
                    (satisfies svariablep)))
  (check-type subs list)
  (second (assoc v subs)))

(defun substitute (pat subs)
  "Returns a tree like PAT,
   but with every variable that is bound in
   the substitution SUBS
   replaced by the term it is bound to."
  (check-type subs list)
  (cond ((atom pat)
          (if (and (variablep pat) (boundp pat subs))
              (bound-to pat subs)
              pat))
        ((and (svariablep (first pat))
              (boundp (first pat) subs))
          (append (bound-to (first pat) subs)
                  (substitute (rest pat) subs)))
        (t (cons (substitute (first pat) subs)
                 (substitute (rest pat) subs)))))
```

Chapter 27 Local Variables

```
27.8 (defun quicksort (list)
       "Sorts the LIST of numbers, using quicksort."
       (let ((length (length list)))
         (if (< length 2) list
             (let ((split
                     (nth (truncate (/ length 2)) list))
```

```
                less-list
                equal-list
                greater-list)
           (mapc
             #'(lambda (x)
                 (cond
                   ((< x split)
                    (setf less-list
                          (cons x less-list)))
                   ((= x split)
                    (setf equal-list
                          (cons x equal-list)))
                   (t (setf greater-list
                            (cons x greater-list)))))
             list)
           (append (quicksort less-list)
                   equal-list
                   (quicksort greater-list)))))))
```

Chapter 28 Iteration

28.9
```
(defun ibuild-list (n)
    "Returns a list of the first n integers."
    (let (lst)
      (loop
        (when (zerop n) (return lst))
        (push n lst)
        (setf n (1- n)))))
```

28.21 In the file set:

```
(shadow '(set union first rest intersection
              subsetp equal do))
```

```
(export
  '(set makeset union first rest insert empty
        intersection complement subsetp equal do))
```

```
(defmacro do ((variable setform
```

```
                        &optional (result nil))
                    &body statements)
          "Executes STATEMENTS repeatedly,
           with VARIABLE taking on each of the members
           of the set which is the value of SETFORM.
           Then the value of RESULT is returned,
           or NIL if RESULT is missing."
          '(dolist (,variable (lisp:rest ,setform) ,result)
             ,@statements))
```

Chapter 29 Input/Output

29.14 (princ #\space) will just print one space, but its value will be printed by `print`. That is acceptable, but if you want a form that does nothing but print a space, `(progn (princ #\space) (values))` will do.

To prove it works, evaluate

```
(progn (princ 'x) (princ 'y)
       (princ 'x) (princ #\space) (princ 'y)
       (values))
```

29.20 (format t "~&I heard you say ~{~A ~}" sentence)

29.24 (defun lisp ()
    "Simulates the LISP Listener
     read-eval-print cycle."
    (loop
      (fresh-line)
      (print (eval (read)))
      (terpri)))

29.26 (defun lisp ()
    "Simulates the LISP Listener
     read-eval-print cycle."
    (let (f largs)
     (loop
      (fresh-line)
      (princ "> ")

```
        (setf f (read) largs (read))
        (print (apply f largs))
        (terpri))))
```

29.31 (defun terminatorp (symb)
```
     "Returns T if SYMB is a sentence terminator;
      NIL otherwise."
     (check-type symb symbol)
     (let ((symbstr (symbol-name symb)))
       (char= (char symbstr (1- (length symbstr)))
              #\.)))
```

```
  (defun readasentence ()
    "Reads a sequence of S-expressions until a
     terminator is encountered.
     Returns a list of the expressions without the
     terminator. "
    (let (backwards)
      (loop
        (push (read) backwards)
        (when (terminatorp (first backwards))
          (return (reverse backwards))))))
```

```
  (defun sentence-echoer ()
    "Infinite loop that prompts the user for a
     sentence, and then echoes it."
    (loop
      (format t "~&Enter a sentence: ")
      (format t "~&I heard you say ~{~A~#[~:; ~]~}"
              (readasentence))))
```

Chapter 30 Destructive List Manipulation

30.21 (export '(bstree bstreep insert insertd root left
```
                   right member build-from-list
                   inorder))
```

```
  (defun insertd (elt tree)
    "Returns the binary search tree TREE
```

```
      with the element ELT destructively inserted into
      the proper place."
  (check-type elt util:element)
  (check-type tree bstree)
  (cond
    ((atom tree) (insert-into-atomic-tree elt tree))
    ((eql elt (root tree)) tree)
    ((string< elt (root tree))
     (if (atom (left tree))
         (setf (second tree)
               (insert-into-atomic-tree elt
                                        (left tree)))
         (insertd elt (left tree)))
     tree)
    (t (if (atom (right tree))
           (setf (third tree)
                 (insert-into-atomic-tree
                   elt
                   (right tree)))
           (insertd elt (right tree)))
       tree)))

(defun insert-into-atomic-tree (elt tree)
  "Returns the binary search tree TREE
   with the element ELT inserted in
   the proper place.
   TREE must have at most 1 element in it."
  (check-type elt util:element)
  (check-type tree atom)
  (cond ((null tree) elt )
        ((eql elt tree) tree)
        ((string< elt tree) (list tree elt '()))
        (t (list tree '() elt))))
```

Chapter 31 Property Lists

31.16 (defun add-friend (person friend)
        "Using property lists,

```
    adds PERSON as FRIEND's friend
    and adds FRIEND as PERSON's friend."
  (check-type person symbol)
  (check-type friend symbol)
  (unless (member friend (get person 'friends))
    (push friend (get person 'friends))
    (push person (get friend 'friends))))
```

Chapter 32 Hash Tables

32.8 For example,

```
(defun people-with-older-friends ()
  "Returns a list of all people in the database
  who have an older friend."
  (let (results)
    (maphash
      #'(lambda (person plist)
          (let ((age (getf plist 'age)))
            (dolist (friend (getf plist 'friends))
              (when (> (getf (gethash friend people)
                             'age)
                       age)
                (pushnew person results)))))
      people)
    results))

(defun people-youngest-among-their-friends ()
  "Returns a list of all people in the database
  who are the youngest among their friends."
  (let (results)
    (maphash
      #'(lambda (person plist)
          (when
            (< (getf plist 'age)
               (apply #'min
                      (mapcar
                        #'(lambda (f)
                            (getf (gethash f people)
```

```
                                        'age))
                              (getf plist 'friends)))))
                    (pushnew person results)))
              people)
          results))
```

Chapter 33 Methods

33.5
```
(defmethod < ((x t) (y t))
    (check-type x (or character number symbol string))
    (check-type x (or character number symbol string))
    (member (type-of y)
            (member
              (type-of x)
              '(character number symbol string))))
```

Chapter 34 Classes

34.5
```
(defconstant
    *deck*
    (let ((list '()))
      (dolist (suit *suits*)
        (dolist (rank *ranks*)
          (push
            (make-instance 'card :rank rank :suit suit)
            list)))
      list)
    "A standard deck of 52 cards")
```

34.8
```
(clos:defgeneric empty (p)
    (:documentation
      "Returns T if the pile is empty; NIL otherwise")
    (:method ((p pile))
            (null (cards p))))
```

34.11
```
(clos:defgeneric turnover (p)
    (:documentation
      "Turn over the top face-down card
       in a two-way-pile.")
```

```
      (:method ((p two-way-pile))
              (push (pop (cards p))
                    (upcards p))))
```

34.15
```
(defun shuffle ()
  "Shuffles the *deck*."
  (dotimes (i 52)
    (let ((j (random 52)))
      (psetf (nth i *deck*) (nth j *deck*)
             (nth j *deck*) (nth i *deck*)))))
```

34.17
```
(defun translate (pile)
  "Returns the pile denoted by the symbol PILE."
  (case pile
    ((stock s) (stock *layout*))
    ((waste w) (waste *layout*))
    (f1 (aref (foundations *layout*) 0))
    (f2 (aref (foundations *layout*) 1))
    (f3 (aref (foundations *layout*) 2))
    (f4 (aref (foundations *layout*) 3))
    (t1 (aref (tableau *layout*) 0))
    (t2 (aref (tableau *layout*) 1))
    (t3 (aref (tableau *layout*) 2))
    (t4 (aref (tableau *layout*) 3))
    (t5 (aref (tableau *layout*) 4))
    (t6 (aref (tableau *layout*) 5))
    (t7 (aref (tableau *layout*) 6))
    (t (format t
               "~%I don't understand ~A~
                as the name of a pile.~%"
               pile))))
```

34.19
```
(defmethod clos:print-object ((p two-way-pile)
                              stream)
  (if (cards p)
      (princ '|XX | stream)
      (princ '|__ | stream))
  (when (upcards p) (prin-rev (upcards p) stream)))
```

APPENDIX B

COMMON LISP REFERENCE MANUAL

B.1 Organization

This manual documents all the COMMON LISP functions, macros, and special forms introduced in the text. Although these are enough for the novice to journeyman LISPer, they do not exhaust the features of COMMON LISP. For a complete presentation of the features of standard COMMON LISP, see Guy L. Steele, Jr.'s *COMMON LISP: The Language,* Second Edition (Bedford, MA: Digital Press, 1990).

Appendix B.2 contains a list of the implementation-dependent features mentioned in the text. Since I cannot give the specific details of whatever implementation you are using, you should write them into the book for your later reference. For a complete presentation of the COMMON LISP features specific to the COMMON LISP implementation you are using, see the manual for that implementation.

The rest of this appendix is a list of functions, macros, and special forms. Some of these were introduced several times in the text, first in a simplified form, and later in a more complete form. The manual gives the most complete form possible without showing features that weren't discussed at all in the text. Before finishing the book, you should ignore features you don't understand. After finishing the book,

313

you should be able to use all the features shown. For more advanced features, see Steele's book, cited above.

Appendix B.3 lists macros and special forms that are used to control the flow of execution. Appendix B.4 lists utility functions such as those used for debugging and type checking. Appendix B.5 lists input and output functions. Appendix B.6 lists functions and macros specific to the COMMON LISP Object system. The rest of the appendix is organized alphabetically by the data type of COMMON LISP objects. Within each data type, the functions are listed under the following topics:

Constructors: functions that return objects of the data type from component objects, possibly of other types

Selectors: functions that take objects of the data type as arguments, and return their component objects

Predicates: functions from objects of the data type to {True, False}

Attributes: functions from objects of the data type to objects of some other data type that serve as attributes of the original objects

Operators: functions from objects of the data type to other objects of the data type or functions that perform miscellaneous operations on the objects

Each macro, function, and special form is shown as a typical calling form. Material in `this font` is required exactly as shown. Material in *this font* is to be replaced by actual argument forms. I have tried to choose these terms so that they indicate the proper types of the arguments. If the term is singular, it means that one argument form is required. If the term is plural, it means that a sequence of one or more argument forms is allowed. Material enclosed in square brackets [...] is optional, so a plural term enclosed in square brackets means that zero or more argument forms are allowed. If a list is followed by an asterisk *, it means that the list may be repeated zero or more times. If a sequence of terms is enclosed in brackets {...} and followed by an asterisk, it means that the sequence may be repeated zero or more times. Terms separated by a vertical line | are alternatives. After the form, I show whether it is a `function`, a `macro`, or a `special` form. Functions get their arguments evaluated, macros and special forms control the evaluation of their own argument forms.

B.2   System-Dependent Operations

This information is system dependent, so you should gather it at the appropriate point in reading this book or when doing the appropriate exercise. The exercise is shown in parentheses.

Computer system used: _____

Operating system used: _____

Version of COMMON LISP **used:** _____

How to log on: _____

How to run LISP **(1.1):** _____

How to exit LISP **(1.2):** _____

COMMON LISP **top-level prompt (1.3):** _____

Debugger top-level prompt (1.7): _____

Debugger deeper-level prompt (1.9): _____

To find values of arguments of a broken function (10.3): ____

Interrupt key at top-level listener (1.6): _____

Interrupt key during a computation (15.7): _____

How to go up one debugger level (1.11): _____

How to go up all debugger levels (1.12): _____

To leave the debugger and abort a computation (15.7): ____

To leave the debugger and resume a computation (15.7): __

Backspace character (2.13): _____

Line erase character (2.14): _____

Delete current list sequence (3.6): _____

To start an immediate garbage collection (30.16): _____

Turn on garbage collection reporting (30.17): _____

B.3   Control Functions

B.3.1   Variable Environments

(let ({*symbol* | (*symbol form*)}*)   special form
    [(declare (special *variables*))]
    forms)
Establishes each *symbol* as the name of a variable. The scope
of each of these variables is limited to the let form, unless it is
named in the declaration, in which case that variable has dynamic
scope. If a *form* is given with a *symbol*, the value of the *form*
becomes the initial value of the variable named by the *symbol*.
These *forms* are evaluated in order, but the assignment of their
values to their *variables* is done in parallel. A *variable* without
an initialization *form* is initialized to NIL. *Variables* named in the
declaration that are not established by this let form are special
variables established elsewhere that will be used in the *forms* of
this let. After the establishment and initialization of all the
variables, the *forms* are evaluated in order, and the value of the
last one becomes the value of the let form.

(let* ({*symbol* | (*symbol form*)}*)   special form
    [(declare (special *variables*))]
    forms) Exactly like let except that the assigning of initial values
to the *variables* is done in order so that one variable may be used
in the initialization *form* of a later *variable*.

B.3.2   Assignment

(psetf {*place form*}*)   macro
Just like setf, except evaluates all the *forms* first, then assigns
the values to the corresponding *places* in parallel. Returns NIL.

(psetq {*symbol form*}*)   macro
Just like setq, except evaluates all the *forms* first, then assigns
the values to the corresponding variables in parallel. Returns NIL.

(set *symbol form*)   function
Binds the special (dynamic) variable named *symbol* to the value
of *form*.

(setf {*place form*}*)   macro
> Evaluates the first *form* and stores its value in the generalized
> variable specified by the first *place*, then goes on to the next
> *place form* pair, and so on. Returns the value of the last *form*.

(setq {*symbol form*}*)   special form
> Evaluates the first *form* and stores its value in the variable named
> by the first *symbol* (which is not evaluated), then goes on to the
> next *symbol form* pair, and so on. Returns the value of the last
> *form*.

B.3.3   Sequences

(prog1 *forms*)   macro
> The *forms* are evaluated in order and the value of the first is
> returned.

(prog2 *forms*)   macro
> The *forms* are evaluated in order and the value of the second is
> returned.

(progn [*forms*])   special form
> The *forms* are evaluated in order and the value of the last is
> returned.

B.3.4   Exits

(return [*form*])   macro
> *form* is evaluated and exit is made from the lexically innermost
> dolist, dotimes, or loop form. The value of *form* is returned
> by that form. If *form* is omitted, NIL is returned.

B.3.5   Conditionals

(case *form*   macro
   ((objects1) forms1)

   ...

   ((objectsn) formsn))
> *form* is evaluated. If its value is among the *objectsi,* then the
> *formsi* are evaluated and the value of the last *formsi* is returned
> as the value of the call to case. The *objectsi* are not evaluated. If

the value of *form* is not among any of the *objectsi,* NIL is returned
unless either t or otherwise appears instead of (objectsn), in
which case the *formsn* are evaluated and the value of the last
formsn is returned. If *objectsi* consists of only one object, that
object may appear without the surrounding parentheses as long
as it is not nil, t, otherwise, or a cons. It is an error for one
object to appear among more than one *objectsi.*

(cond (*test1* [*forms1*]) ... (*testn* [*formsn*]))   special form
Evaluates the *testi* in order until one of them, *testj* say, evaluates
to True. Then evaluates *formsj* and returns the value of the last
one. If there are no *formsj,* the value of *testj* is returned. If no
testi evaluates to True, NIL is returned.

(if *test then* [*else*])   special form
If *test* evaluates to True, evaluates and returns the value of *then*;
otherwise, if *else* is present, evaluates and returns the value of
else; otherwise, returns NIL.

(typecase *form* (type1 forms1) ... (typen formsn))   macro
form is evaluated. *formsi* are evaluated for the lowest *i* for which
the value of *form* is of type *typei* and the value of the last *formsi*
is returned as the value of the call to typecase. The *typei* are
not evaluated. If the value of *form* is not any of the *typei,* NIL is
returned unless either t or otherwise appears instead of (typen),
in which case the *formsn* are evaluated and the value of the last
formsn is returned.

(unless *test forms*)   macro
Evaluates *test.* If the value is NIL, evaluates the *forms* in order
and returns the value of the last one. Otherwise, does not evaluate
the *forms* and returns NIL.

(when *test forms*)   macro
Evaluates *test.* If the value is NIL, does not evaluate the *forms*
and returns NIL. Otherwise, evaluates the *forms* in order and
returns the value of the last one.

B.3.6   Iteration

(dolist (*symbol list-form* [*result-form*]) *forms*)   macro
> Evaluates *forms* repeatedly with *symbol* successively bound to the
> members of the value of *list-form* (which must evaluate to a list).
> Then evaluates *result-form,* and returns that value. If *result-form*
> is omitted, dolist returns NIL. Premature exit may be made with
> an explicit return form.

(dotimes (*symbol form resultform*) *forms*)   macro
> Evaluates *forms* repeatedly with *symbol* successively bound to the
> integers zero, 1, and so on, up to, but not including, the value
> of *form,* which should evaluate to an integer. Then *resultform* is
> evaluated and its value is returned. If *form* evaluates to zero or to
> a negative integer, the *forms* are not evaluated at all. Premature
> exit may be made with an explicit return form.

(loop *forms*)   macro
> The *forms* are evaluated in order repeatedly forever. The only
> way to exit a loop is to evaluate a return that is lexically within
> the loop form.

B.3.7   Mapping Functions

(mapc *function lists*)   function
> There must be the same number of *lists* as the number of argu-
> ments *function* takes. *function* is applied to the first member of
> each of the *lists,* the second member, and so on, until the shortest
> list is exhausted. The first of the *lists* is returned.

(mapcan *function lists*)   function
> *function* must return a list, and there must be the same number
> of *lists* as the number of arguments *function* takes. *function* is
> applied to the first member of each of the *lists,* the second mem-
> ber, and so on, until the shortest list is exhausted. The nconc of
> the values is returned.

(mapcar *function lists*)   function
> There must be the same number of *lists* as the number of argu-
> ments *function* takes. *function* is applied to the first member of

each of the *lists,* the second member, and so on, until the shortest
list is exhausted. A list of the values is returned.

B.4   Utility Functions

(assert *assertion* [(*variables1*) [*string variables2*]])   macro
> If the form *assertion* evaluates to True, returns NIL. Otherwise,
> an error is forced and LISP prints an error message and gives
> the user the choice of aborting the computation or replacing the
> current values of the variables listed as *variables1*. If the user
> chooses to replace the current values, the assert form is retried
> with the new values. The error message is formed, in part, by
> applying format to *string* and *variables2*.

(check-type *variable type-specifier*)   macro
> If the *variable* is of the type specified by the *type-specifier*, returns
> NIL. Otherwise, an error is forced and LISP prints an error mes-
> sage and gives the user the choice of aborting the computation
> or replacing the current value of *variable*. If the user chooses the
> latter, the check-type form is retried with the new value.

(deftype *symbol* () *doc-string* '(satisfies *function*))   macro
> Defines *symbol* to be the name of COMMON LISP type consisting
> of all those objects that satisfy the predicate *function,* which must
> be a function of one argument. *doc-string* is retrievable from *sym-*
> *bol* by documentation. The form (satisfies *function*) may be
> replaced by any *type-specifier* that might be used in check-type
> (see above), in which case the type named by *symbol* is the type
> specified by *type-specifier*.

(time *form*)   macro
> Evaluates *form* and prints how long it took to do the evaluation.
> Returns the value of *form.*

(trace [*function-names*])   macro
> Turns on tracing of the specified functions (*function-names* are
> not evaluated.) With no arguments, returns a list of all functions
> being traced.

(untrace [*function-names*])   macro

Turns off tracing of the specified functions (*function-names* are not evaluated.) With no arguments, turns off all tracing.

B.5 Input/Output

(format *stream control-string arguments*)   function

Produces a printed representation of its *arguments,* as specified by the *control-string.* If *stream* is nil, this printed representation is returned as a string. If *stream* is t, the printed representation is printed to the standard output file (usually the terminal). *control-string* is a string of characters that get printed as they appear in the string, intermixed with *format directives.* Some format directives consume arguments and specify how these arguments are printed. Other format directives do not consume arguments, but control the printing in other ways. Nonconsuming directives include

~% Causes a NEWLINE to be printed.

~& Causes a NEWLINE to be printed unless printing is already at the beginning of a new line

~~ Causes the character ~ to be printed.

~#\newline A ~ appearing in the *control-string* right before the end of a line causes the end-of-line and all subsequent blanks to be ignored. It is a way of splitting a long *control-string* over several lines.

Some consuming format directives are

~a or ~A Consumes one argument and prints it without escape characters, as princ would

~s or ~S Consumes one argument and prints it with escape characters, as prin1 would

~{*str*~} Consumes one argument, which must be a list, and prints the members of the list according to the control string *str* as if they were arguments to an embedded call of format. If *str* doesn't consume all the members of the list, it is used again on the next group, and so on.

~#[*str₁*~:;*str₂*~] Uses the control string *str₁* if there is no argument left or the control string *str₂* if there is any argument left. If this directive is embedded in the ~{*str*~} directive, the notion of "argument" is replaced by "member" of the list.

(fresh-line [*stream*])   function

Outputs a NEWLINE to *stream*, which defaults to standard output and returns T, but only if output is not already positioned at the beginning of a new line. In that case, it does nothing and returns NIL.

(pprint *object* [*stream*])   function

Prints a NEWLINE and then prints the *object* using escape characters as appropriate and in a "pretty" indented format. Returns no value. Printing is done into *stream*, which defaults to the standard output.

(prin1 *object* [*stream*])   function

Prints the *object* using escape characters as appropriate. Returns *object*. Printing is done into *stream*, which defaults to the standard output.

(princ *object* [*stream*])   function

Prints the *object* without using escape characters. Returns *object*. Printing is done into *stream*, which defaults to the standard output.

(print *object* [*stream*])   function

Prints the *object* using escape characters as appropriate, preceded by a NEWLINE and followed by a space. Returns *object*. Printing is done into *stream*, which defaults to the standard output.

(read [*stream*])   function

Reads one S-expression from the input *stream*, which defaults to standard input, and returns the object represented by that S-expression.

(terpri [*stream*])   function

Outputs a NEWLINE to *stream*, which defaults to standard output and returns NIL.

B.6   CLOS

The names of these functions and macros may have a special home package (such as clos), and might not be inherited by the user (or common-lisp-user) package automatically.

```
(defclass class-name (superclass-names)                    macro
    ((slot-name [:initarg initarg-name]
        [:initform init-form]
        [:accessor accessor-name]
        [:reader reader-name]
        [:documentation doc-string1])*)
    (:documentation doc-string2))
```
All terms ending in *-name* must be symbols. *class-name* is declared to be the name of a new CLOS class, whose superclasses are those named by *superclass-names*. *doc-string2* is retrievable from *class-name* by the documentation function. Besides the slots this class inherits from its superclasses, each object of this class will have a set of slots each named by a *slot-name*. The slot named by *slot-name* will have each of the following attributes if the corresponding slot option is included in the class definition:

- *initarg-name* will be usable as a keyword parameter in calls of make-instance that create objects of this class. The value of the argument form paired with that keyword will become the initial value of this slot of the object so created. If the keyword is used when the object is created, it will override any *init-form* declared on this slot. *initarg-name* may be any symbol, but it is most convenient if it is a symbol in the keyword package.

- *init-form* will be evaluated each time an object of this class is created, and that value of *init-form* will become the initial value of this slot of that object.

- *accessor-name* will be the name of a method which, given an object of class *class-name* as argument, will return the value of its slot named *slot-name*. In addition, a form whose first member is *accessor-name* will be recognized by setf as a generalized variable, so that a value can be stored in this slot.

- *reader-name* will be the name of a method which, given an object of class *class-name* as argument, will return the value of its slot named *slot-name*.

- *doc-string1* documents the use of this slot. It is to be read in the source code of this definition. It is not retrievable by the documentation function.

(defgeneric *symbol* (*variables1*   macro
                      [&optional *variables2*]
                      [&rest *variable*]
                      [&key *variables3*])
    [(:documentation *doc-string*)]
    [(declare [(ignore *ignored-variables*)]
              [(special *special-variables*)])]
    [(:method *defmethod-material*)]*)

Defines *symbol* to be the name of a generic function with *required* parameters *variables1, optional* parameters *variables2, rest* parameter *variable, keyword* parameters *variables3,* documentation string *doc-string,* and at least the given methods. For the meaning and use of *required, optional, rest,* and *keyword* parameters, see **defun** on page 341. *defmethod-material* consists of all the arguments of **defmethod** except for the name of the generic function. See **defmethod** for an explanation of this material. **defgeneric** returns the generic function object it creates.

(defmethod *symbol* [:before | :after]   macro
    (*variable* | (*variable parameter-specializer*)
           [&optional *variables2*]
           [&rest *variable*]
           [&key *variables3*])
    [(declare [(ignore *ignored-variables*)]
              [(special *special-variables*)])]
    forms)

Defines a method for the generic function named *symbol.* If the generic function already exists, the lambda-list of the method must agree with that of the generic function. If the generic function does not already exist, it is created with the given lambda-list. This method applies to those calls of the generic function whose required actual arguments agree with whatever *parameter-*

specializers are supplied in the lambda-list of this **defmethod**. A *parameter-specializer* is either the name of a CLOS class or a form of the format (**eql** *form*). An actual argument agrees with the former *parameter-specializer* if it is of the given class. An actual argument agrees with the latter *parameter-specializer* if it is **eql** to the value of the given *form*. For the meaning and use of the rest of the material, see **defun** on page 341. **defmethod** returns the method object it creates.

(**make-instance** *symbol* [*initarg-name form*]*)   generic function
Creates an instance of the class named *symbol* and initializes the slot with each *initarg-name* to have as its value the value of the corresponding *form*.

(**print-object** *object stream*)   generic function
Prints the *object* to *stream,* which defaults to standard output. **print-object** is called by all other printing functions, and can call them recursively to specify the printing of different CLOS classes.

B.7   Arrays

B.7.1   Constructors

(**make-array** *n*)   function
Creates and returns an array of *n* elements, indexed from 0 to $n - 1$. Each element can be any COMMON LISP object.

B.7.2   Selectors

(**aref** *array i*)   function
Returns the *i*th element of *array*. *i* must be a nonnegative integer less than the number of elements of *array*. Indexing is zero-based. That is, the first element of *array* is retrieved with (**aref** *array* 0). Forms a generalized variable recognizable by **setf**.

B.8   Boolean Operators

(**and** [*forms*])   macro
Takes an arbitrary number of argument *forms* and evaluates them

one at a time left to right. As soon as one of them evaluates to NIL, returns NIL. If none of them evaluates to NIL, returns the value of the last one.

(not *object*)   function

Returns T if *object* is NIL; NIL otherwise.

(or [*forms*])   macro

Takes an arbitrary number of argument *forms* and evaluates them one at a time left to right. As soon as one of them evaluates to anything other than NIL, returns that value. If all of them evaluate to NIL, returns NIL.

B.9   Character Predicates

(char= *characters*)   function

Returns T if all the characters are the same; NIL otherwise.

B.10   File Operators

(compile-file *filename*)   function

Compiles the file whose name is given by the string *filename* and creates a compiled file with the same path name, but with the standard compiled file extension.

(load *filename*)   function

Reads the file whose name is given by the string *filename* and executes all the top-level forms in it. If *filename* contains an extension, that file will be read. Otherwise, load will either read the file whose name is given by *filename* and whose extension is the standard LISP source extension, or it will read the file whose name is given by *filename* and whose extension is the standard LISP compiled file extension, whichever is more recent.

B.11   Functions

B.11.1   Constructors

(function *fn*)   special form

If *fn* is a symbol, returns the function named by that symbol. If *fn* is a lambda expression, returns the functional closure of that expression. An alternate printed representation of (function *fn*) is #'*fn*.

B.11.2   Operators

(apply *function* [*forms1*] ([*forms2*]))   function
> A list of *forms1* is appended to the list of *forms2,* and the *function* is applied to that list of argument forms. If a symbol is given instead of a *function,* the function the symbol names is used.

(funcall *function* [*forms*])   function
> Applies the *function* to the argument *forms. function* may only be a function; it can't be a macro or a special form.

B.12   Hash Tables

B.12.1   Constructors

(make-hash-table [:test *function*] [:size *integer*])   function
> Creates and returns a hash table big enough to hold approximately *integer* entries, whose keys can be compared for equality with the predicate *function*, which must be one of #'eq, #'eql, or #'equal (or #'equalp, under the new COMMON LISP standard). If *function* is omitted #'eql is used. If *integer* is omitted, some implementation-dependent size is used. The hash table is automatically enlarged if necessary.

B.12.2   Selectors

(gethash *key hash-table*)   function
> Returns the value associated with *key* in the *hash-table*. gethash forms a generalized variable recognized by setf.

B.12.3   Attributes

(hash-table-count *hash-table*)   function
> Returns the number of entries stored in the *hash-table*.

B.12.4   Operators

(clrhash *hash-table*)   function
>   Removes all the entries from *hash-table*. Returns *hash-table*.

(maphash *function hash-table*)   function
>   For each entry in the *hash-table,* the *function* is applied to two
>   arguments: the key and the value. maphash returns NIL.

(remhash *key hash-table*)   function
>   Removes the entry in the *hash-table* keyed by *key.* Returns T if
>   there was such an entry; NIL otherwise.

B.13   Lists and Conses

B.13.1   Constructors

(cons *object list*)   function
>   Returns a list whose first element is *object* and whose other el-
>   ements are the elements of *list* in the same order. Equivalently,
>   cons returns a cons cell whose car field is *object* and whose cdr
>   field is *list*, which may be any type of object.

(copy-list *list*)   function
>   Returns a list that is equal to, but not eq to *list.* Only the
>   top level of cons cells are copied, so if some member of *list* is a
>   sublist, the corresponding member of the new list will be eq to
>   that sublist.

(list [*objects*])   function
>   Returns a list whose members are the *objects* in the given order.

(push *object place*)   macro
>   The *place* form should be a recognizable by setf as a generalized
>   variable. *object* is consed onto the value of *place,* and the resulting
>   object is destructively stored into *place* and returned.

(pushnew *object place* [:test *function*])   macro
>   The *place* form should be a recognizable by setf as a generalized
>   variable containing a list. Unless *object* is already a member of
>   that list, using *function* as the equality function, *object* is consed
>   onto the value of *place,* and the resulting object is destructively

stored into *place* and returned. If *function* is omitted, tt #'eql
is used. If *object* is already a member of the value of *place*, that
value is returned unchanged.

B.13.2   Selectors

(car *cons*)   function
> Returns the contents of the car field of the *cons*. If () is given
> instead of a *cons*, returns (). car is equivalent to first. Forms
> a generalized variable recognizable by setf.

(cdr *cons*)   function
> Returns the contents of the cdr field of the *cons*. If () is given
> instead of a *cons*, returns (). cdr is equivalent to rest. Forms a
> generalized variable recognizable by setf.

(caar *cons*)   function
> Equivalent to (car (car *cons*)). Forms a generalized variable
> recognizable by setf.

(cadr *cons*)   function
> Equivalent to (car (cdr *cons*)). Forms a generalized variable
> recognizable by setf.

(cdar *cons*)   function
> Equivalent to (cdr (car *cons*)). Forms a generalized variable
> recognizable by setf.

(cddr *cons*)   function
> Equivalent to (cdr (cdr *cons*)). Forms a generalized variable
> recognizable by setf.

(first *list*)   function
> Returns the first element of the *list*; NIL if it is empty. Forms a
> generalized variable recognizable by setf.

(second *list*)   function
> Returns the second element of the *list*; NIL if it doesn't have that
> many. Forms a generalized variable recognizable by setf.

(third *list*)   function
> Returns the third element of the *list*; NIL if it doesn't have that
> many. Forms a generalized variable recognizable by setf.

(fourth *list*)   function
> Returns the fourth element of the *list*; NIL if it doesn't have that
> many. Forms a generalized variable recognizable by setf.

(fifth *list*)   function
> Returns the fifth element of the *list*; NIL if it doesn't have that
> many. Forms a generalized variable recognizable by setf.

(sixth *list*)   function
> Returns the sixth element of the *list*; NIL if it doesn't have that
> many. Forms a generalized variable recognizable by setf.

(seventh *list*)   function
> Returns the seventh element of the *list*; NIL if it doesn't have that
> many. Forms a generalized variable recognizable by setf.

(eighth *list*)   function
> Returns the eighth element of the *list*; NIL if it doesn't have that
> many. Forms a generalized variable recognizable by setf.

(ninth *list*)   function
> Returns the ninth element of the *list*; NIL if it doesn't have that
> many. Forms a generalized variable recognizable by setf.

(tenth *list*)   function
> Returns the tenth element of the *list*; NIL if it doesn't have that
> many. Forms a generalized variable recognizable by setf.

(assoc *object alist* [:test *function*])   function
> *alist* must be a list of conses. assoc returns the first element of
> the *alist* whose car is equal to *object* according to the predicate
> *function*. If *function* is absent, #'eql is used.

(butlast *list* [*n*])   function
> Returns a list with all the members of *list* except for the last *n*.
> If *n* is omitted, 1 is used.

(getf *list indicator*)   function
> *list* must have an even number of members. The odd members are
> treated as indicators and the even members as values, making the
> entire *list* look like a property list. getf returns the value paired
> with (coming immediately after) the *indicator* on the *list*. getf

returns NIL if *indicator* is not an *indicator* on *list*. getf forms a generalized variable recognized by setf.

(last *list*)   function

Returns the last cons cell of the *list*. Equivalent to the last non-empty tail of *list* formed by repeatedly applying rest.

(nth *n list*)   function

Returns the *n*th element of the *list*, where *n* is a nonnegative integer; NIL if it doesn't have that many. The first element of *list* is returned by (nth 0 *list*). Forms a generalized variable recognizable by setf.

(nthcdr *n list*)   function

Returns a list with all the members of *list* except for the first *n*.

(pop *place*)   macro

The *place* form should be recognizable by setf as a generalized variable, and its value must be a cons. The car of the cons is returned and *place* is destructively changed to be its cdr.

(rest *list*)   function

Returns the *list* beginning with the second element. Forms a generalized variable recognizable by setf.

B.13.3 Predicates

(member *object list* [:test *function*])   function

If *object* is equal to any member of *list* according to the predicate *function*, returns the tail of *list* beginning at the first such element; otherwise, returns NIL. If *function* is missing, #'eql is used.

(subsetp *list1 list2* [:test *test*])   function

Returns T if every member of *list1* is also a member of *list2* according to the predicate *function*, which defaults to #'eql; otherwise, returns NIL.

B.13.4 Operators

(append [*lists*])   function

Returns a single list that is the concatenation of the argument *lists*.

(intersection *list1* *list2* [:test *function*])   function
> Creates and returns a list containing all the objects that are members of both *list1* and *list2*. Uses *function* as the equality function. If *function* is not specified, uses #'eql.

(nconc [*lists*])   function
> Returns a single list that is the concatenation of all the argument *lists*. Destructively changes all the lists but the last.

(union *list1* *list2* [:test *function*])   function
> Creates and returns a list containing all the objects that are members of either *list1* or *list2*. Uses *function* as the equality function. If *function* is not specified, uses #'eql.

(remf *list indicator*)   macro
> Destructively removes the *indicator*-value pair from the property *list* (see getf on page 330), if one is there and returns some True value. If *indicator* is not an indicator on *list*, remf does nothing and returns NIL.

(reverse *list*)   function
> Returns a list like *list* but with the order of its members in the opposite order.

(rplaca *cons object*)   function
> Destructively changes the car of the *cons* to *object*, and returns the modified *cons*.

(rplacd *cons object*)   function
> Destructively changes the cdr of the *cons* to *object*, and returns the modified *cons*.

B.14   Numbers

B.14.1   Constructors

(random *n*)   function
> Returns a number x of the same type as n, either integer or floating point, such that $0 \leq x < n$.

(**sxhash** *object*)   function
> Returns a nonnegative fixnum which constitutes a hash code for *object*. **sxhash** will produce the same number for two objects that are **equal**.

B.14.2   Predicates

(= [*numbers*])   function
> Returns **T** if the *numbers* are all equal; **NIL** otherwise.

(/= [*numbers*])   function
> Returns **T** if no two *numbers* are equal; **NIL** otherwise.

(< *numbers*)   function
> Returns **T** if each *number* is less than the next; **NIL** otherwise.

(<= *numbers*)   function
> Returns **T** if each *number* is less than or equal to the next; **NIL** otherwise.

(> *numbers*)   function
> Returns **T** if each *number* is greater than the next; **NIL** otherwise.

(>= *numbers*)   function
> Returns **T** if each *number* is greater than or equal to the next; **NIL** otherwise.

(**minusp** *number*)   function
> Returns **T** if *number* is less than zero, **NIL** otherwise.

(**zerop** *number*)   function
> Returns **T** if *number* is zero; **NIL** otherwise.

B.14.3   Operators

(+ [*numbers*])   function
> Returns the sum of the *numbers*.

(- *numbers*)   function
> If given one *number*, returns the negative of it; otherwise, successively subtracts all the rest from the first *number* and returns the result.

(* [*numbers*])   function
> Returns the product of all the *numbers*.

(/ *numbers*)   function
> If given one *number*, returns its reciprocal; otherwise successively divides the first *number* by the rest and returns the result. It is an error for any *number* except the first to be zero.

(1+ *number*)   function
> Equivalent to (+ *number* 1).

(1- *number*)   function
> Equivalent to (- *number* 1).

(ceiling *number*)   function
> Returns the smallest integer greater than or equal to *number*.

(expt *x* *y*)   function
> Returns x^y, where x and y are any numbers.

(floor *number*)   function
> Returns the largest integer less than or equal to *number*.

(max *numbers*)   function
> Returns the maximum of all the *numbers*.

(min *numbers*)   function
> Returns the minimum of all the *numbers*.

(mod *x* *y*)   function
> Returns the integer remainder from dividing x by y.

(round *number*)   function
> Returns the closest integer to *number*. If *number* is halfway between two integers, returns the one divisible by 2.

(sqrt *x*)   function
> Returns $\sqrt{x}$, where x is any number.

(truncate *number*)   function
> Returns the integer part of *number*, discarding the fractional part.

B.15   Objects

Objects include all COMMON LISP objects.

B.15.1   Constructors

(copy-tree *object*)   function
>   If *object* is not a cons, it is returned. Otherwise,

>   (cons (copy-tree (car *object*)) (copy-tree (cdr *object*)))

>   is returned. Circular substructures and other substructure sharing is not preserved.

(values)   function
>   Returns no value.

B.15.2   Predicates

(atom *object*)   function
>   Returns T if the *object* is not a cons; NIL otherwise.

(characterp *object*)   function
>   Returns T if the *object* is a character; NIL otherwise.

(consp *object*)   function
>   Returns T if the *object* is a cons; NIL otherwise.

(eq *object object*)   function
>   Returns T if the two *objects* are identically the same (the same as pointers); NIL otherwise.

(eql *object object*)   function
>   Returns T if the two objects are eq, if they are numbers of the same type and value, or if they are char=; NIL otherwise.

(equal *object object*)   function
>   Returns T if the two objects are structurally the same, and their corresponding components also are (recursively); NIL otherwise. Two arrays are equal only if they are eq, unless they are strings, in which case they are equal if they have the same length and their corresponding characters are char=.

(`equalp` *object object*)   function
> Returns T if the two objects are `equal`, if they are characters or strings and would be `equal` if case were ignored, if they are numbers of the same value ignoring type, or if they are arrays of the same length whose corresponding components are `equalp`; NIL otherwise.

(`floatp` *object*)   function
> Returns T if the `object` is a floating-point number; NIL otherwise.

(`hash-table-p` *object*)   function
> Returns T if the *object* is a hash table; NIL otherwise.

(`integerp` *object*)   function
> Returns T if the object is an integer; NIL otherwise.

(`listp` *object*)   function
> Returns T if the object is a list, including the empty list (); NIL otherwise.

(`numberp` *object*)   function
> Returns T if the object is a number; NIL otherwise.

(`null` *object*)   function
> Returns T if the object is NIL; NIL otherwise.

(`packagep` *object*)   function
> Returns T if the object is a package; NIL otherwise.

(`stringp` *object*)   function
> Returns T if the object is a string; NIL otherwise.

(`symbolp` *object*)   function
> Returns T if the object is a symbol; NIL otherwise.

(`tree-equal` *tree1 tree2* [`:test` *function*])   function
> Returns T if *tree1* and *tree2* are equal according to the predicate *function,* which defaults to `#'eql`, or if they are both conses with `tree-equal car` parts and `tree-equal cdr` parts. Otherwise, returns NIL.

(`typep` *object type*)   function
> Returns T if the *object* is of the given *type;* NIL otherwise.

B.15.3   Attributes

(type-of *object*)   function
>   Returns a symbol that names the type of the object.

B.15.4   Operators

(eval *form*)   function
>   The *form* is evaluated and its value is returned. Notice that there
>   is a double evaluation here: **eval** gets its argument evaluated
>   because it is a function; and **eval** evaluates that result.

(identity *object*)   function
>   Returns *object*.

(macroexpand *form*)   function
>   If *form* is a cons and its **first** member is the name of a macro,
>   the macro *form* is expanded, and this process continues until the
>   result is no longer a macro form. Then this form is returned. If
>   *form* is not a macro form, it is returned unchanged. **macroexpand**
>   returns a second value that is T if the original *form* was a macro
>   form and NIL if it wasn't.

(quote *object*)   special form
>   Returns the *object* unevaluated. LISP reads ' *object* as being the
>   same as (quote *object*).

(subst *new-object old-object tree* [:test *function*])   function
>   Makes and returns a copy of *tree* with every leaf or subtree that
>   is equal to *old-object* according to the predicate *function*, that
>   defaults to #'eql, replaced by *new-object*.

B.16   Packages

B.16.1   Constructors

(defpackage *package-name*   macro
     [(:shadow *symbol-names*)]
     [(:shadowing-import-from *package-name symbol-names*)]*
     [(:use *package-names*)]
     [(:import-from *package-name symbol-names*)]*

    [(:export *symbol-names*)])
    Proposed macro for the new COMMON LISP standard. Creates a
    new package named *package-name* with the indicated relations to
    symbols and other packages.

(find-package *string*)   function
    Returns the package named *string* if it exists; otherwise, returns
    NIL. If a symbol is given instead of *string,* the symbol's name is
    used.

(in-package *string*)   macro
    Changes the current package to the one named *string;* first creates
    the package if it does not already exist. If a symbol is given
    instead of *string,* the symbol's name is used.

(make-package *string*)   function
    Creates a package named *string.* If a package already exists with
    that name, raises an error. If a symbol is given instead of *string,*
    the symbol's name is used.

B.16.2   Selectors

(package-name *package*)   function
    Returns the string that forms the name of the package.

B.16.3   Operators

(provide *module-name*)   function
    Adds the module named *module-name* to the global variable
    modules to indicate that the module has been loaded. *module-
    name* can be a string or a symbol. If it is a symbol, the symbol's
    name is used. This function may be omitted from the new COM-
    MON LISP standard.

(require *module-name* (*pathnames*))   function
    If the module named *module-name* has not already been loaded,
    as indicated by its presence on the global variable *modules*,
    loads the files named *pathnames* in order. If there is only one

pathname, the enclosing parentheses may be omitted. *module-name* can be a string or a symbol. If it is a symbol, the symbol's name is used. This function may be omitted from the new COMMON LISP standard.

(use-package (*packages*))   function

All external symbols in *packages* are made accessible as internal symbols in the current package. *packages* must be packages or package names (if a symbol is given, its name is used). If there is only one *package,* the enclosing parentheses may be omitted. It is an error to try to use the **keyword** package. Returns T.

B.17   Sequences

Sequences include lists, strings, and arrays.

B.17.1   Selectors

(remove-if-not *predicate sequence*)   function

Returns a sequence exactly like *sequence* but containing only those elements that satisfy the *predicate* function.

B.17.2   Attributes

(count *object sequence* [:test *function*])   function

Returns the number of members of the sequence equal to *object* according to the predicate *function.* If *function* is missing, #'eql is used.

(length *sequence*)   function

Returns the number of members of the sequence.

B.17.3   Operators

(substitute *objectn objecto sequence* [:test *function*])   function

Makes and returns a copy of *sequence* with every element that is equal to *objecto* according to the predicate *function,* that defaults to #'eql, replaced by *objectn.*

B.18   Strings

B.18.1   Selectors

(char *string integer*)   function

The *integer* must be a nonnegative integer less than the length of the *string*. Returns the character at position *integer* of the *string*, where the first character of the string is a position 0. Forms a generalized variable recognizable by setf as long as the new value is a character.

B.18.2   Predicates

(string= *string string*)   function

Returns T if the corresponding characters of the two strings are the same (according to char=); NIL otherwise.

(string< *string1 string2*)   function

If *string1* is lexicographically less than *string2*, returns the index of the first place where they differ; otherwise, returns NIL.

B.19   Symbols

B.19.1   Constructors

(defconstant *symbol form doc-string*)   macro

A global variable is created with *symbol* as its name and the value of *form* as its value. *doc-string* is retrievable from *symbol* by documentation. The value of this variable cannot be changed after this initialization.

(defmacro *symbol* (*variables1*   macro

                   [&optional *variables2*]

                   [{&rest | &body} *variable*]

                   [&key *variables3*])

doc-string

[(declare [(ignore *ignored-variables*)]

         [(special *special-variables*)])]

assertions

forms)

Defines *symbol* to be the name of a macro. For the meaning

and use of the arguments, see **defun** below. The only difference between **&body** and **&rest** is that **&body** tells certain printing functions that the remainder of the form should be indented like the body of a function. **defmacro** allows one additional feature in its lambda-list, known as *destructuring*. Wherever a normal lambda-list allows a symbol and does not allow a list, you may put a lambda-list. The actual argument corresponding to that lambda-list is then treated as a list of arguments to be bound to the parameters of the lambda-list.

(**defparameter** *symbol form doc-string*)   macro

A global, special variable is created with *symbol* as its name and the value of *form* as its value. *doc-string* is retrievable from *symbol* by **documentation**.

(**defun** *symbol* (*variables1*   macro

                 [**&optional** *variables2*]
                 [**&rest** *variable*]
                 [**&key** *variables3*])
  doc-string
  [(**declare** [(**ignore** *ignored-variables*)]
       [(**special** *special-variables*)])]
  assertions
  forms)

Defines *symbol* to be the name of a function with *required* parameters *variables1*, *optional* parameters *variables2*, *rest* parameter *variable*, *keyword* parameters *variables3*, documentation string *doc-string*, declarations, assertion forms *assertions*, and body *forms*. The function must be called with at least as many actual argument forms as there are *required* parameters. When the function is called the parameters are bound as follows:

- The *i*th *required* parameter is bound to the value of the *i*th argument form.
- If there are any *optional* parameters, each is handled as follows. If there is a remaining actual argument form, the *optional* parameter is bound to the value of the argument form. Otherwise, it is bound to NIL.
- If there is a *rest* parameter, it is bound to a list of the values of the remaining actual argument forms.

- If there are any *keyword* parameters, they are bound to the arguments that follow the *optional* arguments. There must be an even number of argument forms. The odd argument forms are interpreted as keywords. Each keyword must be a symbol in the **keyword** package with the same name as one of the *keyword* parameters. That *keyword* parameter is bound to the value of the following argument form.

After the parameters are bound, the *assertions* are evaluated for type checking or for other validity checking of the actual arguments. Then the *forms* are evaluated. The value of the function call is the value of the last *form*. *ignored-variables* are parameters that are not used in the body of the function. Declaring them as ignored serves as a reminder that they were not omitted by accident, may prevent a compiler warning message that they have not been used, may cause a compiler message if they are used, and may result in some compiler optimizations. *special-variables* are dynamically scoped variables that either are included in this lambda-list and will be used by other functions or were created elsewhere and will be used in the body of this function.

defun returns *symbol.*

(**defvar** *symbol form doc-string*)   macro
If a global variable with the name *symbol* already is bound to a value, does nothing. Otherwise, a global, special variable is created with *symbol* as its name and the value of *form* as its value. *doc-string* is retrievable from *symbol* by **documentation**.

(**gensym** [*string* | *integer*])   function
Returns a new, uninterned symbol. The symbol's name will consist of a prefix and an integer. If the *string* argument is provided, the prefix will be that string for this call and subsequent calls of **gensym** until changed. If a nonnegative *integer* argument is provided, that will be the integer for this symbol. After each call to **gensym** the integer to be used for future calls is incremented by 1.

B.19.2 Selectors

(get *symbol indicator*)   function
> Returns the value associated with *indicator* on *symbol*'s property list. Returns NIL if *indicator* is not on *symbol*'s property list. get forms a generalized variable recognized by setf.

(symbol-function *symbol*)   function
> Returns the function, macro, or special form named by *symbol*. Produces an error if *symbol* is not the name of a function. Forms a generalized variable recognizable by setf.

(symbol-name *symbol*)   function
> Returns the string that forms the name of the symbol.

(symbol-package *symbol*)   function
> Returns the home package of *symbol*.

(symbol-plist *symbol*)   function
> Returns the property list of *symbol*. Forms a generalized variable recognizable by setf.

(symbol-value *symbol*)   function
> Returns the value of the dynamic (special) variable named by *symbol*. Produces an error if *symbol* has no such value. Forms a generalized variable recognizable by setf.

B.19.3 Predicates

(boundp *symbol*)   function
> Returns T if the dynamically scoped (special or global) variable named by *symbol* is bound to a value; NIL otherwise.

(fboundp *symbol*)   function
> Returns T if *symbol* is the name of a function, macro, or special form. Otherwise, returns NIL.

B.19.4 Attributes

(describe *symbol*)   function
> Prints useful information about the *symbol* including its home package and value.

(documentation *symbol doc-type*)   function
> Returns the documentation string of type *doc-type* for the *symbol;*
> NIL if there is no appropriate documentation. The table below
> shows constructs that can associate a documentation string with
> a symbol, and for each, the proper *doc-type* to use to retrieve that
> documentation string.

Construct	*Doc-type*
defvar	'variable
defparameter	'variable
defconstant	'variable
defun	'function
defmacro	'function
defgeneric	'function
deftype	'type
defclass	'type

B.19.5   Operators

(compile *symbol*)   function
> Compiles the function whose name is *symbol.*

(export '(*symbols*))   function
> Makes *symbols* external symbols in the current package. If there
> is only one *symbol,* it need not be enclosed in a list.

(import '(*symbols*))   function
> Makes *symbols* internal symbols in the current package. If there
> is only one *symbol,* it need not be enclosed in a list.

(remprop *symbol indicator*)   function
> Destructively removes the *indicator*-value pair from *symbol's*
> property list if one is there and returns some True value. If *indi-*
> *cator* is not an indicator on *symbol's* property list, remprop does
> nothing and returns NIL.

(shadow '(*symbols*))   function
> Makes internal symbols in the current package with the same
> names as *symbols.* If there is only one *symbol,* it need not be
> enclosed in a list.

(shadowing-import '(*symbols*))   function
    Imports *symbols*, shadowing any other symbols with the same
names that are already accessible in the package.

INDEX